Black Women Writers Series

Series Editor: Deborah E. McDowell

IOLA LEROY
OR
SHADOWS UPLIFTED

Frances E. W. Harper

With a New Introduction by Hazel V. Carby

Beacon Press Boston

Beacon Press
25 Beacon Street
Boston, Massachusetts 02108

Beacon press books are published under the auspices
of the Unitarian Universalist Association
of Congregations in North America.

The text of this Beacon paperback edition is taken from
the second edition published in Philadelphia
by Garrigues Brothers, 1893.
First published as a Beacon paperback in 1987

Printed in the United States of America

94 93 92 91 90 5 6 7 8

Library of Congress Cataloging-in-Publication Data

Harper, Frances Ellen Watkins, 1825–1911.
Iola Leroy, or, Shadows uplifted.

(Black women writers series)
Reprint. Originally published: Philadelphia, Garrigues Brothers, 1892.
Bibliography: p.
I. Title. II. Title: Shadows uplifted. III. Series.
[PS1799.H716 1987] 813'.3 86-28864
ISBN 0-8070-6317-7

TO MY DAUGHTER

MARY E. HARPER,

THIS BOOK IS LOVINGLY DEDICATED.

CONTENTS

INTRODUCTION BY HAZEL V. CARBY

IOLA LEROY; OR, SHADOWS UPLIFTED was published in 1892 when Frances Ellen Watkins Harper was sixty-seven years old. Traditionally considered the first novel by a black woman, though displaced by Emma Dunham Kelley's *Megda* (1891) and the republication of Harriet Wilson's *Our Nig* (1859), it remains a major work of the "woman's era," the black woman's renaissance of the 1890s, and the culmination of the career of an important black woman intellectual of the nineteenth century.

Frances Harper began her career as a lecturer for antislavery societies in 1854 but temporarily retired from public life when she married Fenton Harper in 1860. When he died four years later, she returned to full-time lecturing, traveling throughout the South speaking to the freed men and women and settling in Philadelphia with her daughter in 1871. During Reconstruction and in the years of disillusion that followed the betrayal and attempted annihilation of a black political presence in the South, Harper's lectures were part of the wider political struggle for black education and black equality before the law. Harper unhesitatingly pursued a career that was not generally considered suitable for a woman, especially one who was black. Indeed, as William Still described in his history of antislavery organization *The Underground Railroad*, because she was so articulate and engaging as a public speaker, audiences concluded that she couldn't possibly be a black woman. Some even speculated that she must be a man, while others reasoned that she was painted to look black.

Frances Watkins published her first collection of poetry and prose, *Forest Leaves* (1845), as a girl and continued to write throughout her life. She incorporated her antislavery verse, published as *Poems on Miscellaneous Subjects* (1854), into her abolitionist lectures; after the war she tried to capture the experiences of the newly emancipated community in *Sketches of Southern Life* (1872). She was a popular poet and her collections were revised, enlarged, and reprinted many times. A long narrative poem *Moses: A Story of the Nile* (1869) was a favorite with her audiences and eventually became the basis of her last published collection, *Idylls of the Bible* (1901). Her verses and articles appeared in antislavery papers: the *Anglo-African Magazine* published her short story "The Two Offers" (1859) and a prose piece, "The Triumph of Freedom—A Dream" (1860). After the war, Harper contributed articles to the magazine of the African Methodist Episcopal Church, the *A.M.E. Church Review*.

Harper was the leading black activist in the Women's Christian Temperance Movement (WCTU), serving as the superintendent for colored work, and was also active in the fight for female suffrage. She struggled against the intense racism of the WCTU, which had segregated chapters, and against the racism she and other black women encountered in the predominantly white suffrage movements. In 1869 Harper, along with Frederick Douglass, took a stand against the leadership of the American Equal Rights Association when Elizabeth Cady Stanton and Susan B. Anthony withdrew their support for black suffrage. Both Anthony and Stanton further compromised the ideals of female equality when they courted white Southern female support at the expense of the interests of black women by agreeing to establish segregated chapters in the South. Though Harper, a committed feminist, did not withdraw her support from white women's organizations, she worked to found black women's organizations. As she declared to the World's Congress of Representative Women, held in Chicago in 1893, the late nineteenth century stood on the "threshold of woman's era," an opportunity for women to gain political and economic power. And for black women the decade saw the emergence of an autonomous black feminist movement; in 1896 Harper was a founding member of the National Association of Colored Women and eventually became its vice-president.

As a political activist, lecturer, and poet, Harper's career has generally been regarded a success, but as a novelist she has received little critical acclaim. Her only novel, *Iola Leroy*, was published in Philadelphia in 1892. And though it enjoyed a measure of success in its day—it went quickly into a second printing in 1893 and a third in 1895—it was not again reprinted until 1971. In 1893 it was noticed by two white journals, the *Nation* and the *Independent*. The *Nation*'s reviewer recommended the book to its readers so that "they may better understand what emancipation is, and what reconstruction should be." A more extensive review in the *Independent* referred to Harper as "one of the most accomplished literary women the colored race has numbered among its members" who had "accumulated a mass of material for a book on the colored people of the South, which is unrivaled in extent and character." Apart from noting its historical interest, the reviewer praised *Iola Leroy* as "a really effective and pathetic delineation of one of the many examples of noble women set free by the War from the horrible wrongs and burdens under which they were suffering." The reviewer also recognized that the political and literary existences of *Iola Leroy* were interdependent, and that the book was effective precisely because it "pleads the cause of a race whose needs were never more pressing . . . and whose destiny is now more closely interwoven with those of the nation than ever." Indeed, historians have continued to find the novel interesting for its representation of life during Reconstruction.

The first significant generation of Afro-American literary critics, those influenced by the Harlem renaissance, were eager to develop an Afro-American aesthetic that was largely a reaction against the politics and moral code of "uplift," which dominated the intellectual and literary production of the 1890s. This new aesthetic separated political intent from literary accomplishment and, consequently, assessed the novel very differently. The mass of historical detail that Harper accumulated during her travels, and that was so highly praised in the nineties, was regarded as unnecessary baggage by Vernon Loggins, who argued that the novel was "so crowded with incidents and with characters that the reader is likely more than once to lose track of what the action is about." Sterling Brown, Arthur Davis, and Ulysses Lee in *The Negro Caravan* (1941) dismissed Harper's politics and condemned her didacticism, judging the novel " 'full of ennobling sentiments'; it is as dull as it is pious. There are repetitions of situations from Brown's *Clotel*, something of a forecast of a sort of literary inbreeding which causes Negro writers to be influenced by other Negroes more than should ordinarily be expected." The emphasis these critics placed on the "literary" quality of the novel was a part of their general effort to delineate the parameters of an Afro-American literary tradition and to establish its canonic texts—a canon from which *Iola Leroy* would be excluded.

This critical aesthetic, which attempted to separate art from ideology, held sway until a "new" black aesthetic emerged in the 1960s. An integral part of the civil rights movement, the aesthetic reasserted the integration of art and politics and recognized the importance of novels "enlisted in the struggle for liberation." Nevertheless, Addison Gayle in the major literary history to come out of the black aesthetic, condemned Harper, not for writing a political novel but for writing a novel with the wrong politics: for standing in an assimilationist tradition rather than a nationalist one.

More recently the black aesthetic has been largely overturned by contemporary academic critics who have based their aesthetic on the premise that art and ideology must remain separate. In reaction against interpretations of the novel as a form of social protest, they have established a canon of those authors who serve to demonstrate an alternative tradition, particularly Jean Toomer, Zora Neale Hurston, and Ralph Ellison. So the major contemporary works of Afro-American literary criticism—Robert Stepto's *From Behind the Veil: A Study of Afro-American Narrative*, Houston Baker's *Blues, Ideology and Afro-American Literature: A Vernacular Theory*, and *Black Literature and Literary Theory*, edited by Henry Louis Gates Jr.—have ignored Harper.

After long neglect, this edition of Harper's novel should occasion a reconsideration and reevaluation of the significance of *Iola Leroy* for American cultural history. That reevaluation will surely come from black feminists who have, to date, posed the greatest challenge to Afro-American scholarship. Enraged at the neglect of black women writers and intellectuals, these feminists have demanded, not the inclusion of a favored few great women, but the rewriting of Afro-American cultural history. Thus, in accord with this demand, Frances Harper should not be inserted into American cultural history merely as an exceptional woman to stand among exceptional men. Rather, to understand the historical significance of *Iola Leroy*, we must consider the wider discourse of black women intellectuals at the turn of the century.

The 1890s was a decade of intense intellectual and political activity for black women. In Chicago in 1893 at the World's Congress of Representative Women, which was part of the Columbian Exposition, six black women—Fannie Barrier Williams, Anna Julia Cooper, Fannie Jackson Coppin, Sarah J. Early, Hallie Quinn Brown, and Frances Harper—accused the international gathering of indifference to the history of black women, whose crucial struggle was to attain sexual autonomy. As black intellectuals and as women, they occupied a contradictory space on the platform: black women had been excluded from the Board of Lady Managers, which organized and controlled the Congress; and black men and women had been excluded from any control over black representation or participation in the Exposition. But these contradictions had to be negotiated in order to assert a public voice in the era of the separation of the races.

Black women had been active organizers within the black community since emancipation, but they also looked toward national suffrage movements to represent their particular concerns as feminists. However, the exclusionary aspects of organizations that were dominated by white women and presumed to represent the interests of "women" forced black women increasingly to form their own club movement. The intellectuals who became the elite of the National Association of Colored Women used the pen as an important strategy in the movement to organize. Ida B. Wells, as a journalist, exposed the relation between political terrorism, economic oppression, and sexual ideologies in her work on lynching, and Anna Julia Cooper attacked the racism of white women's organizations and revealed the links between practices of racism and imperialism in *A Voice from the South* (1892). Victoria Earle Matthews, who wrote popular short stories, gave an address on the importance of the cultural production of race literature to the first national conference of black women in 1895. The political analyses of black women intellectuals were disseminated through their organizations to a wide constituency, and they influenced and were incorporated into fiction that was regarded as a weapon in this movement for social change. In other words, the movement of black women shaped the culture they produced, which in turn shaped the issues around which black women organized.

This context helps to challenge the general sense that Harper's novel is an aberration in an otherwise successful life. Instead we should regard *Iola Leroy* as integral to and a very important part of both the wider context of the black women's movement and of Harper's intellectual project. For Harper, writing a novel could be "of lasting service for the race" in that it would inspire men and women with a deeper sense of justice and humanity." She believed that only black authors could adequately reproduce the condition and concerns of the black community, that "out of the race must come its own thinkers and writers" as it was impossible "for a white man to put himself completely in our place."

Harper regarded *Iola Leroy* as a form of cultural intervention and crafted it with the same political intensity that she gave to her lectures, speeches, and articles. Indeed, in the chapters entitled "Open Questions" and "Friends in Council," Harper reproduced segments of her articles and lectures, including "Colored Women of America" (1878), "Duty to Dependent Races" (1891), and "Women's Political Future," the address to the 1893 World's Congress of Representative Women.

The immediate audience for Harper's novel was black Sunday school students. Harper organized Sunday schools in Philadelphia and worked with local ministers to institute programs for black youth that were designed to curb delinquency, and in 1894 she became a director of the American Association of Education of Colored Youth. Harper's concern for black youth showed a concern for the future of the entire race, for educating the young was educating the future intellectuals and leaders of the community. *Iola Leroy* was a novel written for the edification of black youth: a contribution toward their education in the ethical and moral precepts of intellectual leadership.

But more particularly, Harper directed her voice toward women. The similarities between *Iola Leroy* and William Wells Brown's *Clotel* have often been cited, but perhaps it is even more important to understand the extent of the engagement of *Iola Leroy* with the narrative strategies of the women's fiction that preceded it. Contemporary feminist analysis has detailed the generic features of nineteenth-century white women's fiction. Nina Baym has argued that American white women's fiction between 1820 and 1870 told a single tale with variations: a tale of a young woman, deprived of all support, who has to win her own way in the world. Heroines negotiated their journeys from adolescence to adulthood, and the novels usually concluded with a happy marriage. Baym argues that the initial displacement of the heroine indicated social corruption and her eventual triumph symbolized the reconstruction of a beneficent social order.

This general outline describes the skeletal structure of *Iola Leroy*. Iola is deprived of both material and emotional support when her white father dies and she and her family become slaves. The revelation of her blackness and her relegation to the condition of chattel displaces Iola from her membership within a privileged elite. Her "fall" indicates the depths of social corruption as it is embedded in the institution of slavery. But, unlike the novels Baym surveys, the consequences of change in Iola's condition apply not only to the individual heroine but also to the entire race. The social displacement of a whole people cannot be remedied by the triumph of the individual woman, and the conclusion of Harper's text, though optimistic, does not offer the reader a restored moral order.

Iola Leroy opens during the Civil War when the black population of the Gundover plantation rescue Iola from the clutches of their master and take her to the Union army. However, this is not a novel about slavery: Iola's previous condition and her "fall" into slavery are the prehistory of the text; Harper is more concerned to establish the possibilities of emancipation and Reconstruction. Harper wrote her novel as the Jim Crow laws institutionalized the separation of the races and, although her novel reenacts Reconstruction as a utopia, its failure meant that Harper could not represent a fictional moral order in which equality had actually been achieved.

Iola Leroy works through a plot of inheritance and kinship. Iola is an heiress, the daughter of a rich planter, but her relation to her inheritance and her future is illegitimate since it is based on the concealment of her true identity as a black woman. As a black woman Iola threatens the white patriarchal order and is thus given her rightful maternal inheritance: the condition of slave. As she moves from paternal heiress to paternal orphan, she finds that through her maternal ancestors she is heir to a black family. The search for her true community and her real family structures the course of the novel. The knowledge Iola gains in her journey from adolescence to womanhood legitimates this matriarchal kinship. Thus, Iola does not establish her rightful position in a new social order through a husband, a conventional mechanism for the gaining of a surrogate family, but searches for and finds her maternal family.

Finding a dispersed family, a metaphor for the African diaspora, is an established Afro-American literary convention that Harper uses to represent the discovery of "the people" in the form of Southern "folk." Iola does not share the history of the folk on the Gundover plantation as many of the Northern black intellectuals did not share the history of the newly emancipated that they wanted to represent. Her different history prefigures a future that will be tied to but separate from the future of the folk. The journey to know, or find, the people places Iola in the position of a potential leader, one of the "noble, earnest men, and true women" that Harper considered to be "the greatest need of the race." Iola remains an external observer of the ways of the folk, a position Harper herself occupied when she toured the Southern states and an attitude we find reflected in *Sketches of Southern Life*.

"The folk" are signaled through the use of dialect and, though Harper's construction of this dialect is poor, her representation is a marginal improvement over Brown's portrayal of the folk as buffoons in *Clotel*. The opening chapter set on the Gundover plantation during the Civil War establishes that the slaves exercise a good deal of control over their lives. Their coded language and gay and humorous appearances are disguises for the furtive exchange of news. Slaves share skills of literacy, and those unable to read the written word "read" the attitudes that the white population tries to hide. Whereas Brown painted a picture of jealousy, hypocrisy, and internally reinforced stratification among "the folk," Harper dramatizes a community that meets secretly, possesses an autonomous means of communication, and exercises group resistance to white plantation power. The "folk" are manipulators of skills that become weapons, not least of which is literacy. Literacy, the power of the word, becomes a lesson for Harper's black readership to learn. As one of her folk characters advises, a black person "must not think because a white man says a thing, it must be so, and that a colored man's word is no account 'lonside of his. . . .

if we ever get our freedom, we've got to learn to trust each other and stick together if we would be a people." In Harper's legitimation of the "colored man's word," she was demystifying the ideological power of language and literacy as a force to liberate, not only subordinate.

Didacticism is a dominant characteristic of *Iola Leroy*, and nowhere is Harper's pedagogic intent clearer than in her representation of the importance of black intellectuals to the development of the race as a whole. Harper's representation of a black intellectual elite clearly prefigures the idea of a "Talented Tenth" that W. E. B. Dubois developed in a 1903 essay of that name. In *Iola Leroy* a commitment to uplift is shared by a community of intellectuals who are represented as being responsible for the formulation and articulation of race issues. An important aspect of the novel is that it acts as a forum for and an advocate of the concerns of this intellectual elite. Harper drew directly upon her lectures for material for the intellectual debates figured in the text: subjects that included disfranchisement, mob violence, and the moral progress of the race. These were the issues around which Harper was trying to encourage political agitation; she lived the intellectual activity that she embodied in her fictional world. As an author she regarded her novel as a platform to demonstrate to her readership, as she demonstrated to the audiences who attended her lectures, the need for an educated elite, a "Talented Tenth."

Harper's representation of such an elite has been heavily criticized for idealizing a segment of the black community and for relying upon the figure of the mulatto. For example, Barbara Christian, in *Black Women Novelists: The Development of a Tradition 1892–1976*, has argued that Harper responded to white racist accusations of black degeneracy by representing a black middle class led by mulattos. Christian explains the fictional use of the mulatto, the quadroon, and the octoroon as a direct appeal to a white readership. Iola not only embodies white ideals of beauty but represents a woman of the upper class; thus, Christian's argument continues, white women readers could identify with a heroine who was as white as they and even more wealthy and privileged.

Many critics have explained the frequent occurrence of mulattos in black fiction by concluding that black authors attempted to counter racist images of black people by an appeal to conventions of beauty from dominant white ideologies. But this explanation has two underlying assumptions that need to be questioned: first, that the prime motivation for writing was to counter negative images; and second, that social conventions determine the use of literary conventions. Thus, from a contemporary critical perspective, the dominance of the mulatto figure in Afro-American fiction at the turn of the century appears politically unacceptable, a gesture of acquiescence to a racist social order. But this dismissal misinterprets the historical and narrative function of the figure.

It is no historical accident that the mulatto figure occurs most frequently in Afro-American fiction at a time when the separation of the races was being institutionalized throughout the South. As a mediating device the mulatto had two narrative functions: it enabled an exploration of the social relations between the races, relations that were increasingly proscribed by Jim Crow laws, and it enabled an expression of the sexual relations between the races, since the mulatto was a product not only of proscribed consensual relations but of white sexual domination. In *Iola Leroy* Harper displaces the rigidity of Jim Crow in the South and the formation of ghettos in the North through this narrative figure. Iola, as a heroine, has a maternal and paternal heritage that illustrates the history of the precarious relations between slave masters and their female slaves. The relation between Iola's mother and father is determined not by the parameters of romantic love but by the systemic limitations of a slave society.

The descendants of socially illicit relations have a variety of possible literary existences. One possibility is represented by what happens to Iola's sister Gracie: horrified by the revelation of her blackness, Gracie denies her history and her being and dies. An alternative possibility is "passing," not fully explored in fiction until James Weldon Johnson's *Autobiography of an Ex-Colored Man* (1912). Both Iola and her brother Harry have the narrative opportunity to "pass" and both refuse. Harper's rejection of "passing" as a metaphoric possibility is important. Harry refuses to enter a white unit of the army; and when attached to a black unit, he is immediately placed in a position of leadership. However, as a woman, Iola's decision not to pass is more complicated: her sexual autonomy is immediately threatened. She refuses to accept the protection and control of white male patriarchy, in the form of a marriage proposal by a white doctor, and consequently has to struggle not only as a black person but also as a woman to establish her independence in the face of black male sexism and racist employment practices in the North.

It is significant, however, that Iola does not represent the future intellectual elite. Harper introduces two characters, neither of whom is a mulatto, to embody the possibilities of a "Talented Tenth." Harper emphasizes the blackness of Lucille Delany and the Reverend Carmicle, believing that "every person of unmixed blood who succeeds in any department of literature, art, or science is a living argument for the capability which is in the race." Both Delany and Carmicle are college educated, which Iola is not, and are archetypes of DuBois's exceptional men and women. If Iola condenses the history of the race and, as mulatto, mediates between the races, Delany and Carmicle emerge toward the end of the text as figures of the future. Harper is engaged in far more than establishing positive images of the race. Her characters gain their representativeness from an engagement with history. Each carries an aspect of the history of the black community in his or her individual history, while as a group they represent a historical force: an elite that articulates the possibilities of that black community.

Iola Leroy is both an attempt to create a coherent vision of the relation of intellectuals to "the folk" and an extension of the intellectual world to which Harper belonged. She tried to negotiate the division between mental and manual labor, symbolized as an intellectual versus a folk existence. That division characterized the turn of the century and was embodied in the schism between W. E. B. DuBois and Booker T. Washington.

But as a woman intellectual, Harper employed what she regarded as female virtues and female values to counter the rampant commercial and mechanistic characteristics of the "Gilded Age." While DuBois and

Washington were concerned with what should shape the men of the race, Harper, in her speech to the World's Congress of Representative Women, felt that for women "not the opportunity of discovering new worlds, but that of filling this old world with fairer and higher aims than the greed of gold and the lust of power, is hers. Through weary, wasting years men have destroyed, dashed in pieces, and overthrown, but today we stand on the threshold of woman's era, and woman's work is grandly constructive."

Harper's association of patriarchal power with colonialism, imperialism, racial domination, and a rapidly industrializing state was a shared discourse among black women and shaped the feminist essays of Anna Julia Cooper. For in the work of black women, patriarchal power was white. In the fiction they produced at the turn of the century, this meant that there was no representation of a black patriarchal power. In Pauline Hopkins's *Contending Forces* (1900), the black father is dead before the book opens. Accounts of his struggles in a racist society that attempted to deny him his manhood ennoble his memory, but his absence marks the absence of black patriarchal pressure. Black men exist as brothers and betrothed who do not engage in the patriarchal exchange of women but are present in a utopian framework that accents the possibilities of relationships of equality.

Harper registers this possibility of utopian relations between black men and women in the relation between Iola and the man she intends to marry, Dr. Latimer. But she accomplishes it at the expense of sexuality. Iola and Latimer's relationship is represented as a spiritual rather than a physical union. Sexual attraction is displaced by a joint desire, not for each other, but to uplift the race. This "grand and noble purpose" transcends passion: the words that Latimer whispers to Iola are "more than a tender strain wooing her to love and happiness, they were a clarion call to a life of high and holy worth." The fictional limitations are evident: Harper represses female sexuality to gain an independent heroine. For although Harper could imagine the feminist dream of a "woman's era," she was unable to represent a black heroine who was also a sexual being.

Kate Chopin's open exploration of the sexual contradictions that faced a woman seeking independence, *The Awakening* (1899), has no equivalent in black women's fiction until Nella Larsen's *Quicksand* in 1928. Certainly, black women were in outright rebellion against the dominant sexual ideology that declared them to be immoral, sexually aggressive creatures who were consistently available to sexually service white men. The widespread rape of black women had not ceased with emancipation, and the right to sexual autonomy became a leading issue around which black women organized. But while the writings of Wells analyzed lynching and rape as modes of political oppression utilizing racist sexual ideologies, in novels such as *Contending Forces* and *Iola Leroy*, the impulse to contradict accusations of sexual promiscuity appears to have led to a complete repression of female sexuality.

Yet there is no doubt that *Iola Leroy* is a woman's story. Iola's passage from girlhood to womanhood was an "ordeal of suffering," but she emerges a mature and sober intellectual, an independent and assured feminist. Iola works, not out of financial necessity but because she is convinced that women should work, that "every woman ought to know how to earn her own living" and that "there would be less unhappy marriages if labor were more honored among women." Unlike the dominant conventions of American women's fiction, Harper did not present marriage as the ultimate goal for women. She was more concerned that women be able to provide for their own material prosperity. Iola criticizes the male attitudes that assess the qualities of women with regard to their suitability for wifehood and consider women of ability as "flotsam all adrift until some man had appropriated her." For Harper, each woman's life could be granted purpose and meaning through work and an independent existence. *Iola Leroy* is an integral part of Frances Harper's vision of a "woman's era": an "uprising" of women to establish an alternative moral and social order.

SELECTED BIBLIOGRAPHY

WORKS BY FRANCES E. W. HARPER

Atlanta Offering. Philadelphia: George S. Ferguson, 1895.

"Colored Women of America." *Englishwoman's Review* (January 1878): 10–15.

"Duty to Dependent Races." *National Council of Women of the United States, Transactions*, 86–91. Philadelphia: National Council of Women of the United States, 1891.

Idylls of the Bible. Philadelphia: George S. Ferguson, 1901.

Iola Leroy; or, Shadows Uplifted. Philadelphia: Garrigues Brothers, 1892.

Moses: A Story of the Nile. Philadelphia: Merrihew, 1869.

"National Women's Christian Temperance Union." *A.M.E. Church Review* 5 (1889):242–45.

Poems. Philadelphia: Merrihew & Son, 1871.

Poems on Miscellaneous Subjects. Boston: J. B. Yerrington and Son, 1854.

Sketches of Southern Life. Philadelphia: Ferguson Brothers, 1872.

The Sparrow's Fall and Other Poems. n.p., n.d.

"The Triumph of Freedom—A Dream." *Anglo-African Magazine* (January 1860): 21–22.

"The Two Offers." *Anglo-African Magazine* (September, October 1859): 288–91, 311–13.

"The Woman's Christian Temperance Union and the Colored Woman." *A.M.E. Church Review* 4 (1888): 313–16.

"Woman's Political Future." May Wright Sewall, ed. *World's Congress of Representative Women*. Chicago: Rand McNally, 1894.

Secondary Sources

Baker, Houston A., Jr. *Blues, Ideology, and Afro-American Literature: A Vernacular Theory*. Chicago: University of Chicago Press, 1984.

Baym, Nina. *Woman's Fiction: A Guide to Novels By and About Women in America 1820–1870*. Ithaca, New York: Cornell University Press, 1978.

Bragg, George. "Frances Harper." In *Men of Maryland*. Baltimore, Maryland: Church Advocate Press, 1925.

Brawley, Benjamin Griffith. *Early Negro American Writers*. Chapel Hill: University of North Carolina Press, 1935.

———. *The Negro Genius*. New York: Dodd, Mead, 1937.

———. *The Negro in Literature and Art*. New York: Duffield, 1929.

Brown, Hallie Quinn. *Homespun Heroines and Other Women of Distinction*. Xenia, Ohio: Aldine Publishing, 1926.

Brown, Sterling A., Davis, Arthur P., and Lee, Ulysses. *The Negro Caravan: Writings by American Negroes*. New York: The Dryden Press, 1941.

Brown, William Wells. *Clotel; or, The President's Daughter: A Narrative of Slave Life in the United States*. London: Partridge & Oakey, 1853.

Carby, Hazel V. *Reconstructing Womanhood: The Emergence of the Afro-American Woman Novelist*. New York: Oxford University Press, 1987.

Christian, Barbara. *Black Women Novelists: The Development of a Tradition 1892–1976*. Westport, Connecticut: Greenwood Press, 1980.

Cooper, Anna Julia. *A Voice From the South: By A Black Woman of the South*. Xenia, Ohio: Aldine Publishing House, 1892.

Davis, Elizabeth Lindsay. *Lifting As They Climb: The National Association of Colored Women*. Washington, D.C.: The National Association of Colored Women, 1933.

Clark, Alice. "Frances Ellen Watkins Harper." *Negro History Bulletin* 5 (January 1942):83.

Dearborn, Mary V. *Pocahontas's Daughters: Gender and Ethnicity in American Culture*. New York: Oxford University Press, 1986.

DuBois, W. E. B. "The Talented Tenth." In *The Negro Problem: A Series of Articles by Representative Negroes of Today*. Edited by Booker T. Washington. New York: James Pott, 1903.

Foner, Philip S. *The Voice of Black America: Major Speeches by Negroes in the United States, 1797–1971*. New York: Simon and Schuster, 1972.

Gates, Henry Louis, ed. *Black Literature and Literary Theory*. New York: Methuen, 1984.

Gloster, Hugh M. *Negro Voices in American Fiction*. Chapel Hill: University of North Carolina Press, 1948.

Hanaford, Phebe A. *Daughters of America; or, Women of the Century*. Augusta, Maine: True, 1882.

Hopkins, Pauline. *Contending Forces: A Romance Illustrative of Negro Life North and South*. Boston: Colored Co-operative Publishing, 1900.

James, Edward T., James, Janet Wilson and Boyer, Paul S., eds. *Notable American Women: A Biographical Dictionary, 1607–1950*. Cambridge, Mass.: Harvard University Press, 1971.

Lerner, Gerder. *Black Women in White America*. New York: Random House, 1973.

Loewenberg, Bert James and Bogin, Ruth. *Black Women in Nineteenth Century American Life*. Philadelphia: Pennsylvania State University Press, 1976.

Logan, Rayford and Winston, Michael R. *Dictionary of American Negro Biography*. New York: W. W. Norton, 1982.

McDowell, Deborah E. " 'The Changing Same': Generational Connections and Black Women Novelists." *New Literary History* (Winter 1986).

Scruggs, L. C. *Women of Distinction*. Raleigh, North Carolina: By the Author, 1893.

Stepto, Robert B. *From Behind the Veil: A Study of Afro-American Narrative*. Urbana: University of Illinois Press, 1979.

Sterling, Dorothy, ed. *We Are Your Sisters: Black Women in the Nineteenth Century*. New York: W. W. Norton, 1984.

Still, William. *The Underground Railroad*. Philadelphia: Porter & Coates, 1872.

Wells, Ida B. [Ida B. Wells Barnett]. *On Lynchings: Southern Horrors; A Red Record; Mob Rule in New Orleans*. New York: Arno Press, 1969.

INTRODUCTION.

I CONFESS when I first learned that Mrs. Harper was about to write "a story" on some features of the Anglo-African race, growing out of what was once popularly known as the "peculiar institution," I had my doubts about the matter. Indeed it was far from being easy for me to think that she was as fortunate as she might have been in selecting a subject which would afford her the best opportunity for bringing out a work of merit and lasting worth to the race—such a work as some of her personal friends have long desired to see from her graphic pen. However, after hearing a good portion of the manuscript read, and a general statement with regard to the object in view, I admit frankly that my partial indifference was soon swept away; at least I was willing to wait for further developments.

Being very desirous that one of the race, so long distinguished in the cause of freedom for her intellectual worth as Mrs. Harper has had the honor of being, should not at this late date in life make a blunder which might detract from her own good name, I naturally proposed to await developments before deciding too quickly in favor of giving encouragement to her contemplated effort.

However, I was perfectly aware of the fact that she had much material in her possession for a most interesting book on the subject of the condition of the colored people in the South. I know of no other woman, white or colored, anywhere, who has come so intimately in contact with the colored people in the South as Mrs. Harper. Since emancipation she has labored in every Southern State in the Union, save two, Arkansas and Texas; in the colleges, schools, churches, and the cabins not excepted, she has found a vast field and open doors to teach and speak on the themes of education, temperance, and good home building, industry, morality, and the like, and never lacked for evidences of hearty appreciation and gratitude.

Everywhere help was needed, and her heart being deeply absorbed in the cause she willingly allowed her sympathies to impel her to perform most heroic services.

With her it was no uncommon occurrence, in visiting cities or towns, to speak at two, three, and four meetings a day; sometimes to promiscuous audiences composed of everybody who would care to come.

But the kind of meetings she took greatest interest in were meetings called exclusively for women. In this attitude she could pour out her sympathies to them as she could not do before a mixed audience; and indeed she felt their needs were far more pressing than any other class.

And now I am prepared to most fully indorse her story. I doubt whether she could, if she had tried ever so much, have hit upon a subject so well adapted to reach a large number of her friends and the public with both entertaining and instructive matter as successfully as she has done in this volume.

The grand and ennobling sentiments which have characterized all her utterances in laboring for the elevation of the oppressed will not be found missing in this book.

The previous books from her pen, which have been

so very widely circulated and admired, North and South — "Forest Leaves," "Miscellaneous Poems," "Moses, a Story of the Nile," "Poems," and "Sketches of Southern Life" (five in number)—these, I predict, will be by far eclipsed by this last effort, which will, in all probability, be the crowning effort of her long and valuable services in the cause of humanity.

While, as indicated, Mrs. Harper has done a large amount of work in the South, she has at the same time done much active service in the temperance cause in the North, as thousands of this class can testify.

Before the war she was engaged as a speaker by anti-slavery associations; since then, by appointment of the Women's Christian Temperance Union, she has held the office of "Superintendent of Colored Work" for years. She has also held the office of one of the Directors of the Women's Congress of the United States.

Under the auspices of these influential, earnest, and intelligent associations, she has been seen often on their platforms with the leading lady orators of the nation.

Hence, being widely known not only amongst her own race but likewise by the reformers, laboring for the salvation of the intemperate and others equally unfortunate, there is little room to doubt that the book will be in great demand and will meet with warm congratulations from a goodly number outside of the author's social connections.

Doubtless the thousands of colored Sunday-schools in the South, in casting about for an interesting, moral story-book, full of practical lessons, will not be content to be without "IOLA LEROY, OR SHADOWS UPLIFTED."

WILLIAM STILL.

Frances E. W. Harper

Iola Leroy

CHAPTER I.

MYSTERY OF MARKET SPEECH AND PRAYER-MEETING.

"GOOD mornin', Bob; how's butter dis mornin'?"

"Fresh; just as fresh, as fresh can be."

"Oh, glory!" said the questioner, whom we shall call Thomas Anderson, although he was known among his acquaintances as Marster Anderson's Tom.

His informant regarding the condition of the market was Robert Johnson, who had been separated from his mother in his childhood and reared by his mistress as a favorite slave. She had fondled him as a pet animal, and even taught him to read. Notwithstanding their relation as mistress and slave, they had strong personal likings for each other.

Tom Anderson was the servant of a wealthy planter, who lived in the city of C——, North Carolina. This planter was quite advanced in life, but in his earlier days he had spent much of his time in talking politics in his State and National capitals in winter, and in visiting pleasure resorts and watering places in summer. His plantations were left to the care of overseers who, in their turn, employed negro drivers to aid them in the work of cultivation and discipline. But as the infirmities of age were pressing upon him he had withdrawn from active life, and given the management of his affairs into the hands of his sons. As Robert Johnson and Thomas Anderson passed homeward from the market, having bought provisions for their respective homes, they seemed to be very light-hearted and careless, chatting and joking with each other; but every now and then, after looking furtively around, one would drop into the ears of the other some news of the battle then raging between the North and South which, like two great millstones, were grinding slavery to powder. As they passed along, they were met by another servant, who said in hurried tones, but with a glad accent in his voice:—

"Did you see de fish in de market dis mornin'? Oh, but dey war splendid, jis' as fresh, as fresh kin be."

"That's the ticket," said Robert, as a broad smile overspread his face. "I'll see you later."

"Good mornin', boys," said another servant on his way to market. "How's eggs dis mornin'?"

"Fust rate, fust rate," said Tom Anderson. "Bob's got it down fine."

"I thought so; mighty long faces at de pos'-office dis mornin'; but I'd better move 'long," and with a bright smile lighting up his face he passed on with a quickened tread.

There seemed to be an unusual interest manifested by these men in the state of the produce market, and a unanimous report of its good condition. Surely there was nothing in the primeness of the butter or the freshness of the eggs to change careless looking faces into such expressions of gratification, or to light dull eyes with such gladness. What did it mean?

During the dark days of the Rebellion, when the bondman was turning his eyes to the American flag, and learning to hail it as an ensign of deliverance, some of the shrewder slaves, coming in contact with their masters and overhearing their conversations, invented a phraseology to convey in the most unsuspected manner news to each other from the battle-field. Fragile women and helpless children were left on the plantations while their natural protectors were at the front, and yet these bondmen refrained from violence. Freedom was coming in the wake of the Union army, and while numbers deserted to join their forces, others remained at home, slept in their cabins by night and attended to their work by day; but under this apparently careless exterior there was an undercurrent of thought which escaped the cognizance of their masters. In conveying tidings of the war, if they wished to announce a victory of the Union army, they said the butter was fresh, or that the fish and eggs were in good condition. If defeat befell them, then the butter and other produce were rancid or stale.

Entering his home, Robert set his basket down. In one arm he held a bundle of papers which he had obtained from the train to sell to the boarders, who were all anxious to hear from the seat of battle. He slipped one copy out and, looking cautiously around, said to Linda, the cook, in a low voice:—

"Splendid news in the papers. Secesh routed. Yankees whipped 'em out of their boots. Papers full of it. I tell you the eggs and the butter's mighty fresh this morning."

"Oh, sho, chile," said Linda, "I can't read de newspapers, but ole Missus' face is newspaper nuff for me. I looks at her ebery mornin' wen she comes inter dis kitchen. Ef her face is long an' she walks kine o' droopy den I thinks things is gwine wrong for dem. But ef she comes out yere looking mighty pleased, an' larffin all ober her face, an' steppin' so frisky, den I knows de Secesh is gittin' de bes' ob de Yankees. Robby, honey, does you really b'lieve for good and righty dat dem Yankees is got horns?"

"Of course not."

"Well, I yered so."

"Well, you heard a mighty big whopper."

"Anyhow, Bobby, things goes mighty contrary in dis house. Ole Miss is in de parlor prayin' for de Secesh to gain de day, and we's prayin' in de cabins and kitchens for de Yankees to get de bes' ob it. But wasn't Miss Nancy glad wen dem Yankees run'd away at Bull's Run. It was nuffin but Bull's Run an' run away Yankees. How she did larff and skip 'bout de house. An' den me thinks to myself you'd better not holler till you gits out ob de woods. I specs 'fore dem Yankees gits froo you'll be larffin tother side ob your mouf. While you was gone to market ole Miss com'd out yere, her face looking as long as my arm, tellin' us all 'bout de war and saying dem Yankees whipped our folks all to pieces. And she was 'fraid dey'd all be down yere soon. I thought they couldn't come too soon for we. But I didn't tell her so."

"No, I don't expect you did."

"No, I didn't; ef you buys me for a fool you loses your money shore. She said when dey com'd down yere she wanted all de men to hide, for dey'd kill all de men, but dey wouldn't tech de women."

"It's no such thing. She's put it all wrong. Why them Yankees are our best friends."

"Dat's jis' what I thinks. Ole Miss was jis' tryin to skeer a body. An' when she war done she jis' set down and sniffled an' cried, an' I war so glad I didn't know what to do. But I had to hole in. An' I made out I war orful sorry. An' Jinny said, 'O Miss Nancy, I hope dey won't come yere.' An' she said, 'I'se jis' 'fraid dey will come down yere and gobble up ebery-thing dey can lay dere hands on.' An' she jis' looked as ef her heart war mos' broke, an' den she went inter de house. An' when she war gone, we jis' broke loose. Jake turned somersets, and said he warnt 'fraid ob dem Yankees; he know'd which side his brad was buttered on. Dat Jake is a cuter. When he goes down ter git de letters he cuts up all kines ob shines and capers. An' to look at him skylarking dere while de folks is waitin' for dere letters, an' talkin' bout de war, yer wouldn't think dat boy had a thimbleful of sense. But Jake's listenin' all de time wid his eyes and his mouf wide open, an' ketchin' eberything he kin, an' a heap ob news he gits dat way. As to Jinny, she jis' capered and danced all ober de flore. An' I jis' had to put my han' ober her mouf to keep ole Miss from yere-ing her. Oh, but we did hab a good time. Boy, yer oughter been yere."

"And, Aunt Linda, what did you do?"

"Oh, honey, I war jis' ready to crack my sides larffin, jis' to see what a long face Jinny puts on wen ole Miss is talkin', an' den to see dat face wen missus' back is turned, why it's good as a circus. It's nuff to make a horse larff."

"Why, Aunt Linda, you never saw a circus?"

"No, but I'se hearn tell ob dem, and I thinks dey

mus' be mighty funny. An' I know it's orful funny to see how straight Jinny's face looks wen she's almos' ready to bust, while ole Miss is frettin' and fumin' 'bout dem Yankees an' de war. But, somehow, Robby, I ralely b'lieves dat we cullud folks is mixed up in dis fight. I seed it all in a vision. An' soon as dey fired on dat fort, Uncle Dan'el says to me: 'Linda, we's gwine to git our freedom.' An' I says: 'Wat makes you think so?" An' he says: 'Dey've fired on Fort Sumter, an' de Norf is boun' to whip.'"

"I hope so," said Robert. "I think that we have a heap of friends up there."

"Well, I'm jis' gwine to keep on prayin' an' b'lievin'."

Just then the bell rang, and Robert, answering, found Mrs. Johnson suffering from a severe headache, which he thought was occasioned by her worrying over the late defeat of the Confederates. She sent him on an errand, which he executed with his usual dispatch, and returned to some work which he had to do in the kitchen. Robert was quite a favorite with Aunt Linda, and they often had confidential chats together.

"Bobby," she said, when he returned, "I thinks we ort ter hab a prayer-meetin' putty soon."

"I am in for that. Where will you have it?"

"Lem me see. Las' Sunday we had it in Gibson's woods; Sunday 'fore las', in de old cypress swamp; an' nex' Sunday we'el hab one in McCullough's woods. Las' Sunday we had a good time. I war jis' chock full an' runnin' ober. Aunt Milly's daughter's bin monin all summer, an' she's jis' come throo. We had a powerful time. Eberythin' on dat groun' was jis' alive. I tell yer, dere was a shout in de camp."

"Well, you had better look out, and not shout too much, and pray and sing too loud, because, 'fore you know, the patrollers will be on your track and break up your meetin' in a mighty big hurry, before you can say 'Jack Robinson.'"

"Oh, we looks out for dat. We's got a nice big pot, dat got cracked las' winter, but it will hole a lot o' water, an' we puts it whar we can tell it eberything. We has our own good times. An' I want you to come Sunday night an' tell all 'bout the good eggs, fish, and butter. Mark my words, Bobby, we's all gwine to git free. I seed it all in a vision, as plain as de nose on yer face."

"Well, I hope your vision will come out all right, and that the eggs will keep and the butter be fresh till we have our next meetin'."

"Now, Bob, you sen' word to Uncle Dan'el, Tom Anderson, an' de rest ob dem, to come to McCullough's woods nex' Sunday night. I want to hab a sin-killin' an' debil-dribin' time. But, boy, you'd better git out er yere. Ole Miss'll be down on yer like a scratch cat."

Although the slaves were denied unrestricted travel, and the holding of meetings without the surveillance of a white man, yet they contrived to meet by stealth and hold gatherings where they could mingle their prayers and tears, and lay plans for escaping to the Union army. Outwitting the vigilance of the patrollers and home guards, they established these meetings miles apart, extending into several States.

Sometimes their hope of deliverance was cruelly blighted by hearing of some adventurous soul who, having escaped to the Union army, had been pursued and returned again to bondage. Yet hope survived all these disasters which gathered around the fate of their unfortunate brethren, who were remanded to slavery through the undiscerning folly of those who were strengthening the hands which were dealing their deadliest blows at the heart of the Nation. But slavery had cast such a glamour over the Nation, and so warped the consciences of men, that they failed to read aright the legible transcript of Divine retribution which was written upon the shuddering earth, where the blood of God's poor children had been as water freely spilled.

CHAPTER II.

CONTRABAND OF WAR.

A FEW evenings after this conversation between Robert and Linda, a prayer-meeting was held. Under the cover of night a few dusky figures met by stealth in McCullough's woods.

"Howdy," said Robert, approaching Uncle Daniel, the leader of the prayer-meeting, who had preceded him but a few minutes.

"Thanks and praise; I'se all right. How is you, chile?"

"Oh, I'm all right," said Robert, smiling, and grasping Uncle Daniel's hand.

"What's de news?" exclaimed several, as they turned their faces eagerly towards Robert.

"I hear," said Robert, "that they are done sending the runaways back to their masters."

"Is dat so?" said a half dozen earnest voices. "How did you yere it?"

"I read it in the papers. And Tom told me he heard them talking about it last night, at his house. How did you hear it, Tom? Come, tell us all about it."

Tom Anderson hesitated a moment, and then said:—

"Now, boys, I'll tell you all 'bout it. But you's got to be mighty mum 'bout it. It won't do to let de cat outer de bag."

"Dat's so! But tell us wat you yered. We ain't gwine to say nuffin to nobody."

"Well," said Tom, "las' night ole Mârster had company. Two big ginerals, and dey was hoppin' mad. One ob dem looked like a turkey gobbler, his face war so red. An' he sed one ob dem Yankee ginerals, I thinks dey called him Beas' Butler, sed dat de slaves dat runned away war some big name—I don't know what he called it. But it meant dat all ob we who com'd to de Yankees should be free."

"Contraband of war," said Robert, who enjoyed the distinction of being a good reader, and was pretty well posted about the war. Mrs. Johnson had taught him to read on the same principle she would have taught a pet animal amusing tricks. She had never imagined the time would come when he would use the machinery she had put in his hands to help overthrow the institution to which she was so ardently attached.

"What does it mean? Is it somethin' good for us?"

"I think," said Robert, a little vain of his superior knowledge, "it is the best kind of good. It means if two armies are fighting and the horses of one run away, the other has a right to take them. And it is just the same if a slave runs away from the Secesh to the Union lines. He is called a contraband, just the same as if he were an ox or a horse. They wouldn't send the horses back, and they won't send us back."

"Is dat so?" said Uncle Daniel, a dear old father, with a look of saintly patience on his face. "Well, chillen, what do you mean to do?"

"Go, jis' as soon as we kin git to de army," said Tom Anderson.

"What else did the generals say? And how did you come to hear them, Tom?" asked Robert Johnson.

"Well, yer see, Marster's too ole and feeble to go to de war, but his heart's in it. An' it makes him feel good all ober when dem big ginerals comes an' tells him all 'bout it. Well, I war laying out on de porch fas' asleep an' snorin' dreffull hard. Oh, I war so soun' asleep dat wen Marster wanted some ice-water he had to shake me dreffull hard to wake me up. An' all de time I war wide 'wake as he war."

"What did they say?" asked Robert, who was always on the lookout for news from the battle-field.

"One ob dem said, dem Yankees war talkin' of puttin' guns in our han's and settin' us all free. An' de oder said, 'Oh, sho! ef dey puts guns in dere hands dey'll soon be in our'n; and ef dey sets em free dey wouldn't know how to take keer ob demselves.'"

"Only let 'em try it," chorused a half dozen voices, "an' dey'll soon see who'll git de bes' ob de guns; an' as to taking keer ob ourselves, I specs we kin take keer ob ourselves as well as take keer ob dem."

"Yes," said Tom, "who plants de cotton and raises all de crops?"

> "'They eat the meat and give us the bones,
> Eat the cherries and give us the stones,'

And I'm getting tired of the whole business," said Robert.

"But, Bob," said Uncle Daniel, "you've got a good owner. You don't hab to run away from bad times and wuss a comin'."

"It isn't so good, but it might be better. I ain't got nothing 'gainst my ole Miss, except she sold my mother from me. And a boy ain't nothin' without his mother. I forgive her, but I never forget her, and never expect to. But if she were the best woman on earth I would rather have my freedom than belong to her. Well, boys, here's a chance for us just as soon as the Union army gets in sight. What will you do?"

"I'se a goin," said Tom Anderson, "jis' as soon as dem Linkum soldiers gits in sight."

"An' I'se a gwine wid you, Tom," said another. "I specs my ole Marster'll feel right smart lonesome when I'se gone, but I don't keer 'bout stayin' for company's sake."

"My ole Marster's room's a heap better'n his company," said Tom Anderson, "an' I'se a goner too. Dis yer freedom's too good to be lef' behind, wen you's got a chance to git it. I won't stop to bid ole Marse good bye."

"What do you think," said Robert, turning to Uncle Daniel; "won't you go with us?"

"No, chillen, I don't blame you for gwine; but I'se gwine to stay. Slavery's done got all de marrow out ob dese poor ole bones. Ef freedom comes it won't do me much good; we ole one's will die out, but it will set you youngsters all up."

"But, Uncle Daniel, you're not too old to want your freedom?"

"I knows dat. I lubs de bery name of freedom. I'se been praying and hoping for it dese many years. An' ef I warn't boun', I would go wid you ter-morrer. I won't put a straw in your way. You boys go, and my prayers will go wid you. I can't go, it's no use. I'se gwine to stay on de ole place till Marse Robert comes back, or is brought back."

"But, Uncle Daniel," said Robert, "what's the use of praying for a thing if, when it comes, you won't take it? As much as you have been praying and talking about freedom, I thought that when the chance came you would have been one of the first to take it. Now, do tell us why you won't go with us. Ain't you willing?"

"Why, Robbie, my whole heart is wid you. But when Marse Robert went to de war, he called me into his room and said to me, 'Uncle Dan'el, I'se gwine to de war, an' I want you to look arter my wife an' chillen, an' see dat eberything goes right on de place. An' I promised him I'd do it, an' I mus' be as good as my word. 'Cept de overseer, dere isn't a white man on de plantation, an' I hear he has to report ter-morrer or be treated as a deserter. An' der's nobody here to look arter Miss Mary an' de chillen, but myself, an' to see dat eberything goes right. I promised Marse Robert I would do it, an' I mus' be as good as my word."

"Well, what should you keer?" said Tom Anderson. "Who looked arter you when you war sole from your farder and mudder, an' neber seed dem any more, and wouldn't know dem to-day ef you met dem in your dish?"

"Well, dats neither yere nor dere. Marse Robert couldn't help what his father did. He war an orful mean man. But he's dead now, and gone to see 'bout it. But his wife war the nicest, sweetest lady dat eber I did see. She war no more like him dan chalk's like cheese. She used to visit de cabins, an' listen to de pore women when de overseer used to cruelize dem so bad, an' drive dem to work late and early. An' she used to sen' dem nice things when they war sick, and hab der cabins whitewashed an' lookin' like new pins, an' look arter dere chillen. Sometimes she'd try to git ole Marse to take dere part when de oberseer got too mean. But she might as well a sung hymns to a dead horse. All her putty talk war like porin water on a goose's back. He'd jis' bluff her off, an' tell her she didn't run dat plantation, and not for her to bring him any nigger news. I never thought ole Marster war good to her. I often ketched her crying, an' she'd say she had de headache, but I thought it war de heartache. 'Fore ole Marster died, she got so thin an' peaked I war 'fraid she war gwine to die; but she seed him out. He war killed by a tree fallin' on him, an' ef eber de debil got his own he got him. I seed him in a vision arter he war gone. He war hangin' up in a pit, sayin' 'Oh! oh!' wid no close on. He war allers blusterin', cussin', and swearin' at somebody. Marse Robert ain't a bit like him. He takes right arter his mother. Bad as ole Marster war, I think she jis' lob'd de groun' he walked on. Well, women's mighty curious kind of folks anyhow. I sometimes thinks de wuss you treats dem de better dey likes you."

"Well," said Tom, a little impatiently, "what's yer gwine to do? Is yer gwine wid us, ef yer gits a chance?"

"Now, jes' you hole on till I gits a chance to tell yer why I'se gwine to stay."

"Well, Uncle Daniel, let's hear it," said Robert.

"I was jes' gwine to tell yer when Tom put me out. Ole Marster died when Marse Robert war two years ole, and his pore mother when he war four. When he died, Miss Anna used to keep me 'bout her jes' like I war her shadder. I used to nuss Marse Robert jes' de same as ef I were his own fadder. I used to fix his milk, rock him to sleep, ride him on my back, an' nothin' pleased him better'n fer Uncle Dan'el to ride him piggy-back."

"Well, Uncle Daniel," said Robert, "what has that got to do with your going with us and getting your freedom?"

"Now, jes' wait a bit, and don't frustrate my mine. I seed day arter day Miss Anna war gettin' weaker and thinner, an' she looked so sweet and talked so putty, I thinks to myself, 'you ain't long for dis worl'.' And she said to me one day, 'Uncle Dan'el, when I'se gone, I want you to be good to your Marster Robert.' An' she looked so pale and weak I war almost ready to cry. I couldn't help it. She hed allers bin mighty good to me. An' I beliebs in praisin' de bridge dat carries me ober. She said, 'Uncle Dan'el, I wish you war free. Ef I had my way you shouldn't serve any one when I'm gone; but Mr. Thurston had eberything in his power when he made his will. I war tied hand and foot, and I couldn't help it.' In a little while she war gone—jis' faded away like a flower. I belieb ef dere's a saint in glory, Miss Anna's dere."

"Oh, I don't take much stock in white folks' religion," said Robert, laughing carelessly.

"The way," said Tom Anderson, "dat some of dese folks cut their cards yere, I think dey'll be as sceece in hebben as hen's teeth. I think wen some of dem preachers brings de Bible 'round an' tells us 'bout mindin our marsters and not stealin' dere tings, dat dey preach to please de white folks, an' dey frows coleness ober de meetin'."

"An' I," said Aunt Linda, "neber did belieb in dem Bible preachers. I yered one ob dem sayin' wen he war dyin', it war all dark wid him. An' de way he treated his house-girl, pore thing, I don't wonder dat it war dark wid him."

"O, I guess," said Robert, "that the Bible is all right, but some of these church folks don't get the right hang of it."

"May be dat's so," said Aunt Linda. "But I allers wanted to learn how to read. I once had a book, and tried to make out what war in it, but ebery time my mistus caught me wid a book in my hand, she used to whip my fingers. An' I couldn't see ef it war good for white folks, why it warn't good for cullud folks."

"Well," said Tom Anderson, "I belieb in de good ole-time religion. But arter dese white folks is done fussin' and beatin' de cullud folks, I don't want 'em to come talking religion to me. We used to hab on our place a real Guinea man, an' once he made ole Marse mad, an' he had him whipped. Old Marse war trying to break him in, but dat fellow war spunk to de backbone, an' when he 'gin talkin' to him 'bout savin' his soul an' gittin' to hebbin, he tole him ef he went to hebbin an' foun' he war dare, he wouldn't go in. He wouldn't stay wid any such rascal as he war."

"What became of him?" asked Robert.

"Oh, he died. But he had some quare notions 'bout religion. He thought dat when he died he would go back to his ole country. He allers kep' his ole Guinea name."

"What was it?"

"Potobombra. Do you know what he wanted Marster to do 'fore he died?" continued Anderson.

"No."

"He wanted him to gib him his free papers."

"Did he do it?"

"Ob course he did. As de poor fellow war dying an' he couldn't sell him in de oder world, he jis' wrote him de papers to yumor him. He didn't want to go back to Africa a slave. He thought if he did, his people would look down on him, an' he wanted to go back a free man. He war orful weak when Marster brought him de free papers. He jis' ris up in de bed, clutched dem in his han's, smiled, an' gasped out, 'I'se free at las'; an' fell back on de pillar, an' he war gone. Oh, but he war spunky. De oberseers, arter dey foun' out who he war, gin'rally gabe him a wide birth. I specs his father war some ole Guinea king."

"Well, chillen," said Uncle Daniel, "we's kept up dis meeting long enough. We'd better go home, and not all go one way, cause de patrollers might git us all inter trouble, an' we must try to slip home by hook or crook."

"An' when we meet again, Uncle Daniel can finish his story, an' be ready to go with us," said Robert.

"I wish," said Tom Anderson, "he would go wid us, de wuss kind."

CHAPTER III.

UNCLE DANIEL'S STORY.

THE Union had snapped asunder because it lacked the cohesion of justice, and the Nation was destined to pass through the crucible of disaster and defeat, till she was ready to clasp hands with the negro and march abreast with him to freedom and victory.

The Union army was encamping a few miles from C——, in North Carolina. Robert, being well posted on the condition of affairs, had stealthily contrived to call a meeting in Uncle Daniel's cabin. Uncle Daniel's wife had gone to bed as a sick sister, and they held a prayer-meeting by her bedside. It was a little risky, but as Mr. Thurston did not encourage the visits of the patrollers, and heartily detested having them prying into his cabins, there was not much danger of molestation.

"Well, Uncle Daniel, we want to hear your story, and see if you have made up your mind to go with us," said Robert, after he had been seated a few minutes in Uncle Daniel's cabin.

"No, chillen, I've no objection to finishin' my story, but I ain't made up my mind to leave the place till Marse Robert gits back."

"You were telling us about Marse Robert's mother. How did you get along after she died?"

"Arter she war gone, ole Marster's folks come to look arter things. But eberything war lef' to Marse Robert, an' he wouldn't do widout me. Dat chile war allers at my heels. I couldn't stir widout him, an' when he missed me, he'd fret an' cry so I had ter stay wid him; an' wen he went to school, I had ter carry him in de mornin' and bring him home in de ebenin'. An' I learned him to hunt squirrels, an' rabbits, an' ketch fish, an' set traps for birds. I beliebs he lob'd me better dan any ob his kin' An' he showed me how to read."

"Well," said Tom, "ef he lob'd you so much, why didn't he set you free?"

"Marse Robert tole me, ef he died fust he war gwine ter leave me free—dat I should neber sarve any one else."

"Oh, sho!" said Tom, "promises, like pie crusts, is made to be broken. I don't trust none ob dem. I'se been yere dese fifteen years, an' I'se neber foun' any troof in dem. An' I'se gwine wid dem North men soon's I gits a chance. An' ef you knowed what's good fer you, you'd go, too."

"No, Tom; I can't go. When Marster Robert went to de front, he called me to him an' said: 'Uncle Daniel,' an' he was drefful pale when he said it, 'I are gwine to de war, an' I want yer to take keer of my wife an' chillen, jis' like yer used to take keer of me wen yer called me your little boy.' Well, dat jis' got to me, an' I couldn't help cryin', to save my life."

"I specs," said Tom, "your tear bags must lie mighty close to your eyes. I wouldn't cry ef dem Yankees would make ebery one ob dem go to de front, an' stay dere foreber. Dey'd only be gittin' back what dey's been a doin' to us."

"Marster Robert war nebber bad to me. An' I beliebs in stannin' by dem dat stans by you. Arter Miss Anna died, I had great 'sponsibilities on my shoulders; but

I war orful lonesome, an' thought I'd like to git a wife. But dere warn't a gal on de plantation, an' nowhere's roun', dat filled de bill. So I jis' waited, an' 'tended to Marse Robert till he war ole 'nough to go to college. Wen he went, he allers 'membered me in de letters he used to write his grandma. Wen he war gone, I war lonesomer dan eber. But, one day, I jis' seed de gal dat took de rag off de bush. Gundover had jis' brought her from de up-country. She war putty as a picture!" he exclaimed, looking fondly at his wife, who still bore traces of great beauty. "She had putty hair, putty eyes, putty mouth. She war putty all over; an' she know'd how to put on style."

"O, Daniel," said Aunt Katie, half chidingly, "how you do talk."

"Why, it's true. I 'member when you war de puttiest gal in dese diggins; when nobody could top your cotton."

"I don't," said Aunt Katie.

"Well, I do. Now, let me go on wid my story. De fust time I seed her, I sez to myself, 'Dat's de gal for me, an' I means to hab her ef I kin git her.' So I scraped 'quaintance wid her, and axed her ef she would hab me ef our marsters would let us. I warn't 'fraid 'bout Marse Robert, but I warn't quite shore 'bout Gundover. So when Marse Robert com'd home, I axed him, an' he larf'd an' said, 'All right,' an' dat he would speak to ole Gundover 'bout it.' He didn't relish it bery much, but he didn't like to 'fuse Marse Robert. He wouldn't sell her, for she tended his dairy, an' war mighty handy 'bout de house. He said, I mought marry her an' come to see her wheneber

Marse Robert would gib me a pass. I wanted him to sell her, but he wouldn't hear to it, so I had to put up wid what I could git. Marse Robert war mighty good to me, but ole Gundover's wife war de meanest woman dat I eber did see. She used to go out on de plantation an' boss things like a man. Arter I war married, I had a baby. It war de dearest, cutest little thing you eber did see; but, pore thing, it got sick and died. It died 'bout three o'clock; and in de mornin', Katie, habbin her cows to milk, lef' her dead baby in de cabin. When she com'd back from milkin' her thirty cows, an' went to look for her pore little baby, some one had been to her cabin an' took'd de pore chile away an' put it in de groun'. Pore Katie, she didn't eben hab a chance to kiss her baby 'fore it war buried. Ole Gundover's wife has been dead thirty years, an' she didn't die a day too soon. An' my little baby has gone to glory, an' is wingin' wid the angels an' a lookin' out for us. One ob de las' things ole Gundover's wife did 'fore she died war to order a woman whipped 'cause she com'd to de field a little late when her husband war sick, an' she had stopped to tend him. Dat mornin' she war taken sick wid de fever, an' in a few days she war gone out like de snuff ob a candle. She lef' several sons, an' I specs she would almos' turn ober in her grave ef she know'd she had ten culled granchillen somewhar down in de lower kentry."

"Isn't it funny," said Robert, "how these white folks look down on colored people, an' then mix up with them?"

"Marster war away when Miss 'Liza treated my Katie so mean, an' when I tole him 'bout it, he war tearin' mad, an' went ober an' saw ole Gundover, an' foun' out he war hard up for money, an' he bought Katie and brought her home to lib wid me, and we 's been a libin in clover eber sence. Marster Robert has been mighty good to me. He stood by me in my troubles, an' now his trouble's come, I'm a gwine to stan' by him. I used to think Gundover's wife war jealous ob my Katie. She war so much puttier. Gundover's wife couldn't tech my Katie wid a ten foot pole."

"But, Aunt Katie, you have had your trials," said Robert, now that Daniel had finished his story; "don't you feel bitter towards these people who are fighting to keep you in slavery?"

Aunt Katie turned her face towards the speaker. It was a thoughtful, intelligent face, saintly and calm. A face which expressed the idea of a soul which had been fearfully tempest tossed, but had passed through suffering into peace. Very touching was the look of resignation and hope which overspread her features as she replied, with the simple child-like faith which she had learned in the darkest hour, "The Lord says, we must forgive." And with her that thought, as coming from the lips of Divine Love, was enough to settle the whole question of forgiveness of injuries and love to enemies.

"Well," said Thomas Anderson, turning to Uncle Daniel, "we can't count on yer to go wid us?"

"Boys," said Uncle Daniel, and there was grief in his voice, "I'se mighty glad you hab a chance for your freedom; but, ez I tole yer, I promised Marse Robert I would stay, an' I mus' be as good as my word. Don't you youngsters stay for an ole stager like me. I'm ole an' mos' worn out. Freedom wouldn't do much for me, but I want you all to be as free as the birds; so, you chillen, take your freedom when you kin get it."

"But, Uncle Dan'el, you won't say nothin' 'bout our going, will you?" said the youngest of the company.

Uncle Daniel slowly arose. There was a mournful flash in his eye, a tremor of emotion in his voice, as he said, "Look yere, boys, de boy dat axed dat question war a new comer on dis plantation, but some ob you's bin here all ob your lives; did you eber know ob Uncle Dan'el gittin' any ob you inter trouble?"

"No, no," exclaimed a chorus of voices, "but many's de time you've held off de blows wen de oberseer got too mean, an' cruelized us too much, wen Marse Robert war away. An' wen he got back, you made him settle de oberseer's hash."

"Well, boys," said Uncle Daniel, with an air of mournful dignity, "I'se de same Uncle Dan'el I eber war. Ef any ob you wants to go, I habben't a word to say agin it. I specs dem Yankees be all right, but I knows Marse Robert, an' I don't know dem, an' I ain't a gwine ter throw away dirty water 'til I gits clean."

"Well, Uncle Ben," said Robert, addressing a stalwart man whose towering form and darkly flashing eye told that slavery had failed to put the crouch in his shoulders or general abjectness into his demeanor, "you will go with us, for sure, won't you?"

"Yes," spoke up Tom Anderson, "'cause de trader's done took your wife, an' got her for his'n now."

As Ben Tunnel looked at the speaker, a spasm of agony and anger darkened his face and distorted his features, as if the blood of some strong race were stirring with sudden vigor through his veins. He clutched his hands together, as if he were struggling with an invisible foe, and for a moment he remained silent. Then suddenly raising his head, he exclaimed, "Boys, there's not one of you loves freedom more than I do, but——"

"But what?" said Tom. "Do you think white folks is your bes' friends?"

"I'll think so when I lose my senses."

"Well, now, I don't belieb you're 'fraid, not de way I yeard you talkin' to de oberseer wen he war threatnin' to hit your mudder. He saw you meant business, an' he let her alone. But, what's to hinder you from gwine wid us?"

"My mother," he replied, in a low, firm voice. "That is the only thing that keeps me from going. If it had not been for her, I would have gone long ago. She's all I've got, an' I'm all she's got."

It was touching to see the sorrow on the strong face, to detect the pathos and indignation in his voice, as he said, "I used to love Mirandy as I love my life. I thought the sun rose and set in her. I never saw a handsomer woman than she was. But she fooled me all over the face and eyes, and took up with that hell-hound of a trader, Lukens; an' he gave her a chance to live easy, to wear fine clothes, an' be waited on like a lady. I thought at first I would go crazy, but my poor mammy did all she could to comfort me. She would tell me there were as good fish in the sea as were ever caught out of it. Many a time I've laid my poor head on her lap, when it seemed as if my brain was on fire and my heart was almost ready to burst. But in course of time I got over the worst of it; an' Mirandy is the first an' last woman that ever fooled me. But that dear old mammy of mine, I mean to stick by her as long as there is a piece of her. I can't go over to the army an' leave her behind, for if I did, an' anything should happen, I would never forgive myself."

"But couldn't you take her with you," said Robert, "the soldiers said we could bring our women."

"It isn't that. The Union army is several miles from here, an' my poor mammy is so skeery that, if I were trying to get her away and any of them Secesh would overtake us, an' begin to question us, she would get skeered almost to death, an' break down an' begin to cry, an' then the fat would be in the fire. So, while I love freedom more than a child loves its mother's milk, I've made up my mind to stay on the plantation. I wish, from the bottom of my heart, I could go. But I can't take her along with me, an' I don't want to be free and leave her behind in slavery. I was only five years old when my master and, as I believe, father, sold us both here to this lower country, an' we've been here ever since. It's no use talking, I won't leave her to be run over by everybody."

A few evenings after this interview, the Union soldiers entered the town of C——, and established their headquarters near the home of Thomas Anderson.

Out of the little company, almost every one deserted to the Union army, leaving Uncle Daniel faithful to his trust, and Ben Tunnel hushing his heart's deep aspirations for freedom in a passionate devotion to his timid and affectionate mother.

CHAPTER IV.

ARRIVAL OF THE UNION ARMY.

A FEW evenings before the stampede of Robert and his friends to the army, and as he sat alone in his room reading the latest news from the paper he had secreted, he heard a cautious tread and a low tap at his window. He opened the door quietly and whispered :—

"Anything new, Tom ?"

"Yes."

"What is it ? Come in."

"Well, I'se done bin seen dem Yankees, an' dere ain't a bit of troof in dem stories I'se bin yerin 'bout 'em."

"Where did you see 'em ?"

"Down in de woods whar Marster tole us to hide. Yesterday ole Marse sent for me to come in de settin'-room. An' what do you think? Instead ob makin' me stan' wid my hat in my han' while he went froo a whole rigamarole, he axed me to sit down, an' he tole me he 'spected de Yankees would want us to go inter de army, an' dey would put us in front whar we'd all git killed; an' I tole him I didn't want to go, I didn't want to git all momached up. An' den he said we'd better go down in de woods an' hide. Massa Tom and Frank said we'd better go as quick as eber we could. Dey said dem Yankees would put us in dere wagons and make us haul like we war mules. Marse Tom ain't libin' at de great house jis' now. He's keepin' bachellar's hall."

"Didn't he go to the battle?"

"No; he foun' a pore white man who war hard up for money, an' he got him to go."

"But, Tom, you didn't believe these stories about the Yankees. Tom and Frank can lie as fast as horses can trot. They wanted to scare you, and keep you from going to the Union army."

"I knows dat now, but I didn't 'spect so den."

"Well, when did you see the soldiers? Where are they? And what did they say to you?"

"Dey's right down in Gundover's woods. An' de Gineral's got his headquarters almos' next door to our house."

"That near? Oh, you don't say so!"

"Yes, I do. An', oh, golly, ain't I so glad! I jis' stole yere to told you all 'bout it. Yesterday mornin' I war splittin' some wood to git my breakfas', an' I met one ob dem Yankee sogers. Well, I war so skeered, my heart flew right up in my mouf, but I made my manners to him and said, 'Good mornin', Massa.' He said, 'Good mornin'; but don't call me "massa."' Dat war de fust white man I eber seed dat didn't want ter be called 'massa,' eben ef he war as pore as Job's turkey. Den I begin to feel right sheepish, an' he axed me ef my marster war at home, an' ef he war a Reb. I tole him he hadn't gone to de war, but he war Secesh all froo, inside and outside. He war too ole to go to de war, but dat he war all de time gruntin' an' groanin', an' I 'spected he'd grunt hisself to death."

"What did he say?"

"He said he specs he'll grunt worser dan dat fore dey get froo wid him. Den he axed me ef I would hab some breakfas,' an' I said, 'No, t'ank you, sir.' 'An' I war jis' as hungry as a dorg, but I war 'feared to eat. I war 'feared he war gwine to pizen me."

"Poison you! don't you know the Yankees are our best friends?"

"Well, ef dat's so, I'se mighty glad, cause de woods is full ob dem."

"Now, Tom, I thought you had cut your eye-teeth long enough not to let them Anderson boys fool you. Tom, you must not think because a white man says a thing, it must be so, and that a colored man's word is no account 'longside of his. Tom, if ever we get our freedom, we've got to learn to trust each other and stick together if we would be a people. Somebody else can read the papers as well as Marse Tom and Frank. My ole Miss knows I can read the papers, an' she never tries to scare me with big whoppers 'bout the Yankees. She knows she can't catch ole birds with chaff, so she is just as sweet as a peach to her Bobby. But as soon as I get a chance I will play her a trick the devil never did."

"What's that?"

"I'll leave her. I ain't forgot how she sold my mother from me. Many a night I have cried myself to sleep, thinking about her, and when I get free I mean to hunt her up."

"Well, I ain't tole you all. De gemman said he war 'cruiting for de army; dat Massa Linkum hab set us all free, an' dat he wanted some more sogers to put down dem Secesh; dat we should all hab our freedom, our wages, an' some kind ob money. I couldn't call it like he did."

"Bounty money," said Robert.

"Yes, dat's jis' what he called it, bounty money. An' I said dat I war in for dat, teeth and toe-nails."

Robert Johnson's heart gave a great bound. Was that so? Had that army, with freedom emblazoned on its banners, come at last to offer them deliverance if they would accept it? Was it a bright, beautiful dream, or a blessed reality soon to be grasped by his willing hands? His heart grew buoyant with hope; the lightness of his heart gave elasticity to his step and sent the blood rejoicingly through his veins. Freedom was almost in his grasp, and the future was growing rose-tinted and rainbow-hued. All the ties which bound him to his home were as ropes of sand, now that freedom had come so near.

When the army was afar off, he had appeared to be light-hearted and content with his lot. If asked if he desired his freedom, he would have answered, very naively, that he was eating his white bread and believed in letting well enough alone; he had no intention of jumping from the frying-pan into the fire. But in the depths of his soul the love of freedom was an all-absorbing passion; only danger had taught him caution. He had heard of terrible vengeance being heaped upon the heads of some who had sought their freedom and failed in the attempt. Robert knew that he might abandon hope if he incurred the wrath of men whose overthrow was only a question of time. It would have been madness and folly for him to have attempted an insurrection against slavery, with the words of McClellan ringing in his ears: "If you rise I shall put you down with an iron hand," and with the home guards ready to quench his aspirations for freedom with bayonets and blood. What could a set of unarmed and undisciplined men do against the fearful odds which beset their path?

Robert waited eagerly and hopefully his chance to join the Union army; and was ready and willing to do anything required of him by which he could earn his freedom and prove his manhood. He conducted his plans with the greatest secrecy. A few faithful and trusted friends stood ready to desert with him when the Union army came within hailing distance. When it came, there was a stampede to its ranks of men ready to serve in any capacity, to labor in the tents, fight on the fields, or act as scouts. It was a strange sight to see these black men rallying around the Stars and Stripes, when white men were trampling them under foot and riddling them with bullets.

CHAPTER V.

THE RELEASE OF IOLA LEROY.

"WELL, boys," said Robert to his trusted friends, as they gathered together at a meeting in Gundover's woods, almost under the shadow of the Union army, "how many of you are ready to join the army and fight for your freedom."

"All ob us."

"The soldiers," continued Robert, "are camped right at the edge of the town. The General has his headquarters in the heart of the town, and one of the officers told me yesterday that the President had set us all free, and that as many as wanted to join the army could come along to the camp. So I thought, boys, that I would come and tell you. Now, you can take your bag and baggage, and get out of here as soon as you choose."

"We 'll be ready by daylight," said Tom. "It won't take me long to pack up," looking down at his seedy clothes, with a laugh. "I specs ole Marse'll be real lonesome when I'm gone. An' won't he be hoppin' mad when he finds I'm a goner? I specs he'll hate it like pizen."

"O, well," said Robert, "the best of friends must part. Don't let it grieve you."

"I'se gwine to take my wife an' chillen," said one of the company.

"I'se got nobody but myself," said Tom; "but dere's a mighty putty young gal dere at Marse Tom's. I wish I could git her away. Dey tells me dey's been sellin' her all ober de kentry; but dat she's a reg'lar spitfire; dey can't lead nor dribe her."

"Do you think she would go with us?" said Robert.

"I think she's jis' dying to go. Dey say dey can't do nuffin wid her. Marse Tom's got his match dis time, and I'se glad ob it. I jis' glories in her spunk."

"How did she come there?"

"Oh, Marse bought her ob de trader to keep house for him. But ef you seed dem putty white han's ob hern you'd never tink she kept her own house, let 'lone anybody else's."

"Do you think you can get her away?"

"I don't know; 'cause Marse Tom keeps her mighty close. My! but she's putty. Beautiful long hair comes way down her back; putty blue eyes, an' jis' ez white ez anybody's in dis place. I'd jis' wish you could see her yoresef. I heerd Marse Tom talkin' 'bout her las' night to his brudder; tellin' him she war mighty airish, but he meant to break her in."

An angry curse rose to the lips of Robert, but he repressed it and muttered to himself, "Graceless scamp, he ought to have his neck stretched." Then turning to Tom, said:—

"Get her, if you possibly can, but you must be mighty mum about it."

"Trus' me for dat," said Tom.

Tom was very anxious to get word to the beautiful but intractable girl who was held in durance vile by her reckless and selfish master, who had tried in vain to drag her down to his own low level of sin and shame. But all Tom's efforts were in vain. Finally he applied to the Commander of the post, who immediately gave orders for her release. The next day Tom had the satisfaction of knowing that Iola Leroy had been taken as a trembling dove from the gory vulture's nest and given a place of security. She was taken immediately to the General's headquarters. The General was much impressed by her modest demeanor, and surprised to see the refinement and beauty she possessed. Could it be possible that this young and beautiful girl had been a chattel, with no power to protect herself from the highest insults that lawless brutality could inflict upon innocent and defenseless womanhood? Could he ever again glory in his American citizenship, when any white man, no matter how coarse, cruel, or brutal, could buy or sell her for the basest purposes? Was it not true that the cause of a hapless people had become entangled with the lightnings of heaven, and dragged down retribution upon the land?

The field hospital was needing gentle, womanly ministrations, and Iola Leroy, released from the hands of her tormentors, was given a place as nurse; a position to which she adapted herself with a deep sense of relief. Tom was doubly gratified at the success of his endeavors, which had resulted in the rescue of the beautiful young girl and the discomfiture of his young master who, in the words of Tom, "was mad enough to bite his head off" (a rather difficult physical feat).

Iola, freed from her master's clutches, applied herself readily to her appointed tasks. The beautiful, girlish face was full of tender earnestness. The fresh, young voice was strangely sympathetic, as if some great sorrow had bound her heart in loving compassion to every sufferer who needed her gentle ministrations.

Tom Anderson was a man of herculean strength and remarkable courage. But, on account of physical defects, instead of enlisting as a soldier, he was forced to remain a servant, although he felt as if every nerve in his right arm was tingling to strike a blow for freedom. He was well versed in the lay of the country, having often driven his master's cotton to market when he was a field hand. After he became a coachman, he had become acquainted with the different roads and localities of the country. Besides, he had often accompanied his young masters on their hunting and fishing expeditions. Although he could not fight in the army, he proved an invaluable helper. When tents were to be pitched, none were more ready to help than he. When burdens were to be borne, none were more willing to bend beneath them than Thomas Anderson. When the battle-field was to be searched for the wounded and dying, no hand was more tender in its ministrations of kindness than his. As a general factotum in the army, he was ever ready and willing to serve anywhere and at any time, and to gather information from every possible source which could be of any service to the Union army. As a Pagan might worship a distant star and wish to call it his own, so he loved Iola. And he never thought he could do too much for the soldiers who had rescued her and were bringing deliverance to his race.

"What do you think of Miss Iola?" Robert asked him one day, as they were talking together.

"I jis' think dat she's splendid. Las' week I had

to take some of our pore boys to de hospital, an' she war dere, lookin' sweet an' putty ez an angel, a nussin' dem pore boys, an' ez good to one ez de oder. It looks to me ez ef dey ralely lob'd her shadder. She sits by 'em so patient, an' writes 'em sech nice letters to der frens, an' yit she looks so heart-broke an' pitiful, it jis' gits to me, an' makes me mos' ready to cry. I'm so glad dat Marse Tom had to gib her up. He war too mean to eat good victuals."

"He ought," said Robert, "to be made to live on herrings' heads and cold potatoes. It makes my blood boil just to think that he was going to have that lovely looking young girl whipped for his devilment. He ought to be ashamed to hold up his head among respectable people."

"I tell you, Bob, de debil will neber git his own till he gits him. When I seed how he war treating her I neber rested till I got her away. He buyed her, he said, for his housekeeper; as many gals as dere war on de plantation, why didn't he git one ob dem to keep house, an' not dat nice lookin' young lady? Her han's look ez ef she neber did a day's work in her life. One day when he com'd down to breakfas,' he chucked her under de chin, an' tried to put his arm roun' her waist. But she jis' frew it off like a chunk ob fire. She looked like a snake had bit her. Her eyes fairly spit fire. Her face got red ez blood, an' den she turned so pale I thought she war gwine to faint, but she didn't, an' I yered her say, 'I'll die fust.' I war mad 'nough to stan' on my head. I could hab tore'd him all to pieces wen he said he'd hab her whipped."

"Did he do it?"

"I don't know. But he's mean 'nough to do enythin'. Why, dey say she war sole seben times in six weeks, 'cause she's so putty, but dat she war game to de las'."

"Well, Tom," said Robert, "getting that girl away was one of the best things you ever did in your life."

"I think so, too. Not dat I specs enytin' ob it. I don't spose she would think ob an ugly chap like me; but it does me good to know dat Marse Tom ain't got her."

CHAPTER VI.

ROBERT JOHNSON'S PROMOTION AND RELIGION.

Robert Johnson, being able to meet the army requirements, was enlisted as a substitute to help fill out the quota of a Northern regiment. With his intelligence, courage, and prompt obedience, he rose from the ranks and became lieutenant of a colored company. He was daring, without being rash; prompt, but not thoughtless; firm, without being harsh. Kind and devoted to the company he drilled, he soon won the respect of his superior officers and the love of his comrades.

"Johnson," said a young officer, Captain Sybil, of Maine, who had become attached to Robert, "what is the use of your saying you're a colored man, when you are as white as I am, and as brave a man as there is among us. Why not quit this company, and take your place in the army just the same as a white man? I know your chances for promotion would be better."

"Captain, you may doubt my word, but to-day I would rather be a lieutenant in my company than a captain in yours."

"I don't understand you."

"Well, Captain, when a man's been colored all his life it comes a little hard for him to get white all at once. Were I to try it, I would feel like a cat in a strange garret. Captain, I think my place is where I am most needed. You do not need me in your ranks, and my company does. They are excellent fighters, but they need a leader. To silence a battery, to capture a flag, to take a fortification, they will rush into the jaws of death."

"Yes, I have often wondered at their bravery."

"Captain, these battles put them on their mettle. They have been so long taught that they are nothing and nobody, that they seem glad to prove they are something and somebody."

"But, Johnson, you do not look like them, you do not talk like them. It is a burning shame to have held such a man as you in slavery."

"I don't think it was any worse to have held me in slavery than the blackest man in the South."

"You are right, Johnson. The color of a man's skin has nothing to do with the possession of his rights."

"Now, there is Tom Anderson," said Robert," he is just as black as black can be. He has been bought and sold like a beast, and yet there is not a braver man in all the company. I know him well. He is a noble-hearted fellow. True as steel. I love him like a brother. And I believe Tom would risk his life for me any day. He don't know anything about his father or mother. He was sold from them before he could remember. He can read a little. He used to take lessons from a white gardener in Virginia. He would go between the hours of 9 P. M. and 4 A. M. He got a book of his own, tore it up, greased the pages, and hid them in his hat. Then if his master had ever knocked his hat off he would have thought them greasy papers, and not that Tom was carrying his library on his head. I had another friend who lived near us. When he was nineteen years old he did not know how many letters there were in the A B C's. One night, when his work was done, his boss came into his cabin and saw him with a book in his hand. He threatened to give him five hundred lashes if he caught him again with a book, and said he hadn't work enough to do. He was getting out logs, and his task was ten logs a day. His employer threatened to increase it to twelve. He said it just harassed him; it set him on fire. He thought there must be something good in that book if the white man didn't want him to learn. One day he had an errand in the kitchen, and he heard one of the colored girls going over the A B C's. Here was the key to the forbidden knowledge. She had heard the white children saying them, and picked them up by heart, but did not know them by sight. He was not content with that, but sold his cap for a book and wore a cloth on his head instead. He got the sounds of the letters by heart, then cut off the bark of a tree, carved the letters on the smooth inside, and learned them. He wanted to learn how to write. He had charge of a warehouse where he had a chance to see the size and form of letters. He made the beach of the river his copybook, and thus he learned to write. Tom never got very far with his learning, but I used to get the papers and tell him all I knew about the war."

"How did you get the papers?"

"I used to have very good privileges for a slave. All of our owners were not alike. Some of them were quite clever, and others were worse than git out. I used to get the morning papers to sell to the boarders and others, and when I got them I would contrive to hide a paper, and let some of the fellow-servants know how things were going on. And our owners thought we cared nothing about what was going on."

"How was that? I thought you were not allowed to hold meetings unless a white man were present."

"That was so. But we contrived to hold secret meetings in spite of their caution. We knew whom we could trust. My ole Miss wasn't mean like some of them. She never wanted the patrollers around prowling in our cabins, and poking their noses into our business. Her husband was an awful drunkard. He ran through every cent he could lay his hands on, and she was forced to do something to keep the wolf from the door, so she set up a boarding-house. But she didn't take in Tom, Dick, and Harry. Nobody but the big bugs stopped with her. She taught me to read and write, and to cast up accounts. It was so handy for her to have some one who could figure up her accounts, and read or write a note, if she were from home and wanted the like done. She once told her cousin how I could write and figure up. And what do you think her cousin said?"

"'Pleased,' I suppose, 'to hear it.'"

"Not a bit of it. She said, if I belonged to her, she would cut off my thumbs; her husband said, 'Oh, then he couldn't pick cotton.' As to my poor thumbs, it did not seem to be taken into account what it would cost me to lose them. My ole Miss used to have a lot of books. She would let me read any one of them except a novel. She wanted to take care of my soul, but she wasn't taking care of her own."

"Wasn't she religious?"

"She went for it. I suppose she was as good as most of them. She said her prayers and went to church, but I don't know that that made her any better. I never did take much stock in white folks' religion."

"Why, Robert, I'm afraid you are something of an infidel."

"No, Captain, I believe in the real, genuine religion. I ain't got much myself, but I respect them that have. We had on our place a dear, old saint, named Aunt Kizzy. She was a happy soul. She had seen hard times, but was what I call a living epistle. I've heard her tell how her only child had been sold from her, when the man who bought herself did not want to buy her child. Poor little fellow! he was only two years old. I asked her one day how she felt when her child was taken away. 'I felt,' she said, 'as if I was going to my grave. But I knew if I couldn't get justice here, I could get it in another world.'"

"That was faith," said Captain Sybil, as if speaking to himself, "a patient waiting for death to redress the wrongs of life."

"Many a time," continued Robert, "have I heard her humming to herself in the kitchen and saying, 'I has my trials, ups and downs, but it won't allers be so. I specs one day to wing and wing wid de angels, Hallelujah! Den I specs to hear a voice sayin', "Poor ole Kizzy, she's done de bes' she kin. Go down, Gabriel, an' tote her in." Den I specs to put on my golden slippers, my long white robe, an' my starry crown, an' walk dem golden streets, Hallelujah!' I've known that dear, old soul to travel going on two miles, after her work was done, to have some one read to her. Her favorite chapter began with, 'Let not your heart be troubled, ye believe in God, believe also in Me.'"

"I have been deeply impressed," said Captain Sybil, "with the child-like faith of some of these people. I do not mean to say that they are consistent Christians, but I do think that this faith has in a measure underlain the life of the race. It has been a golden thread woven amid the sombre tissues of their lives. A ray of light shimmering amid the gloom of their condition. And what would they have been without it?"

"I don't know. But I know what she was with it. And I believe if there are any saints in glory, Aunt Kizzy is one of them."

"She is dead, then?"

"Yes, went all right, singing and rejoicing until the the last, 'Troubles over, troubles over, and den my troubles will be over. We'll walk de golden streets all 'roun' in de New Jerusalem.' Now, Captain, that's the kind of religion that I want. Not that kind which could ride to church on Sundays, and talk so solemn with the minister about heaven and good things, then come home and light down on the servants like a thousand of bricks. I have no use for it. I don't believe in it. I never did and I never will. If any man wants to save my soul he ain't got to beat my body. That ain't the kind of religion I'm looking for. I ain't got a bit of use for it. Now, Captain, ain't I right?"

"Well, yes, Robert, I think you are more than half right. You ought to know my dear, old mother who lives in Maine. We have had colored company at our house, and I never saw her show the least difference between her colored and white guests. She is a Quaker preacher, and don't believe in war, but when the rest of the young men went to the front, I wanted to go also. So I thought it all over, and there seemed to be no way out of slavery except through the war. I had been taught to hate war and detest slavery. Now the time had come when I could not help the war, but I could strike a blow for freedom. So I told my mother I was going to the front, that I expected to be killed, but I went to free the slave. It went hard with her. But I thought that I ought to come, and I believe my mother's prayers are following me."

"Captain," said Robert, rising, "I am glad that I have heard your story. I think that some of these Northern soldiers do two things—hate slavery and hate niggers."

"I am afraid that is so with some of them. They would rather be whipped by Rebels than conquer with negroes. Oh, I heard a soldier," said Captain Sybil, "say, when the colored men were being enlisted, that he would break his sword and resign. But he didn't do either. After Colonel Shaw led his charge at Fort Wagner, and died in the conflict, he got bravely over his prejudices. The conduct of the colored troops there and elsewhere has done much to turn public opinion in their favor. I suppose any white soldier would rather have his black substitute receive the bullets than himself."

CHAPTER VII.

TOM ANDERSON'S DEATH.

"WHERE is Tom?" asked Captain Sybil; "I have not seen him for several hours."

"He's gone down the sound with some of the soldiers," replied Robert. "They wanted Tom to row them."

"I am afraid those boys will get into trouble, and the Rebs will pick them off," responded Sybil.

"O, I hope not," answered Robert.

"I hope not, too; but those boys are too venturesome."

"Tom knows the lay of the land better than any of us," said Robert. "He is the most wide-awake and gamiest man I know. I reckon when the war is over Tom will be a preacher. Did you ever hear him pray?"

"No; is he good at that?"

"First-rate," continued Robert. "It would do you good to hear him. He don't allow any cursing and swearing when he's around. And what he says is law and gospel with the boys. But he's *so* good-natured; and they *can't* get mad at him."

"Yes, Robert, there is not a man in our regiment I would sooner trust than Tom. Last night, when he brought in that wounded scout, he couldn't have been more tender if he had been a woman. How gratefully the poor fellow looked in Tom's face as he laid him down so carefully and staunched the blood which had been spurting out of him. Tom seemed to know it was an artery which had been cut, and he did just the right thing to stop the bleeding. He knew there wasn't a moment to be lost. He wasn't going to wait for the doctor. I have often heard that colored people are ungrateful, but I don't think Tom's worst enemy would say that about him."

"Captain," said Robert, with a tone of bitterness in his voice, "what had we to be grateful for? For ages of poverty, ignorance, and slavery? I think if anybody should be grateful, it is the people who have enslaved us and lived off our labor for generations. Captain, I used to know a poor old woman who couldn't bear to hear any one play on the piano."

"Is that so? Why, I always heard that colored people were a musical race."

"So we are; but that poor woman's daughter was sold, and her mistress took the money to buy a piano. Her mother could never bear to hear a sound from it."

"Poor woman!" exclaimed Captain Sybil, sympathetically; "I suppose it seemed as if the wail of her daughter was blending with the tones of the instrument. I think, Robert, there is a great deal more in the colored people than we give them credit for. Did you know Captain Sellers?"

"The officer who escaped from prison and got back to our lines?" asked Robert.

"Yes. Well, he had quite an experience in trying to escape. He came to an aged couple, who hid him in their cabin and shared their humble food with him. They gave him some corn-bread, bacon, and coffee which he thought was made of scorched bran. But he said that he never ate a meal that he relished more than the one he took with them. Just before he went they knelt down and prayed with him. It seemed as if his very hair stood on his head, their prayer was so solemn. As he was going away the man took some shingles and nailed them on his shoes to throw the bloodhounds off his track. I don't think he will ever cease to feel kindly towards colored people. I do wonder what has become of the boys? What can keep them so long?"

Just as Captain Sybil and Robert were wondering at the delay of Tom and the soldiers they heard the measured tread of men who were slowly bearing a burden. They were carrying Tom Anderson to the hospital, fearfully wounded, and nigh to death. His face was distorted, and the blood was streaming from his wounds. His respiration was faint, his pulse hurried, as if life were trembling on its frailest cords.

Robert and Captain Sybil hastened at once towards the wounded man. On Robert's face was a look of intense anguish, as he bent pityingly over his friend.

"O, this is dreadful! How did it happen?" cried Robert.

Captain Sybil, pressing anxiously forward, repeated Robert's question.

"Captain," said one of the young soldiers, advancing and saluting his superior officer, "we were all in the boat when it struck against a mud bank, and there was not strength enough among us to shove her back into the water. Just then the Rebels opened fire upon us. For awhile we lay down in the boat, but still they kept firing. Tom took in the whole situation, and said:

'Some one must die to get us out of this. I mought's well be him as any. You are soldiers and can fight. If they kill me, it is nuthin'.' So Tom leaped out to shove the boat into the water. Just then the Rebel bullets began to rain around him. He received seven or eight of them, and I'm afraid there is no hope for him."

"O, Tom, I wish you hadn't gone. O, Tom! Tom!" cried Robert, in tones of agony.

A gleam of grateful recognition passed over the drawn features of Tom, as the wail of his friend fell on his ear. He attempted to speak, but the words died upon his lips, and he became unconscious.

"Well," said Captain Sybil, "put him in one of the best wards. Give him into Miss Leroy's care. If good nursing can win him back to life, he shall not want for any care or pains that she can bestow. Send immediately for Dr. Gresham."

Robert followed his friend into the hospital, tenderly and carefully helped to lay him down, and remained awhile, gazing in silent grief upon the sufferer. Then he turned to go, leaving him in the hands of Iola, but hoping against hope that his wounds would not be fatal.

With tender devotion Iola watched her faithful friend. He recognized her when restored to consciousness, and her presence was as balm to his wounds. He smiled faintly, took her hand in his, stroked it tenderly, looked wistfully into her face, and said, "Miss Iola, I ain't long fer dis! I'se 'most home!"

"Oh, no," said Iola, "I hope that you will soon get over this trouble, and live many long and happy days."

"No, Miss Iola, it's all ober wid me. I'se gwine to glory; gwine to glory; gwine to ring dem charmin' bells. Tell all de boys to meet me in heben; dat dey mus' 'list in de hebenly war."

"O, Mr. Tom," said Iola, tenderly, "do not talk of leaving me. You are the best friend I have had since I was torn from my mother. I should be so lonely without you."

"Dere's a frien' dat sticks closer dan a brudder. He will be wid yer in de sixt' trial, an' in de sebbent' he'll not fo'sake yer."

"Yes," answered Iola, "I know that. He is all our dependence. But I can't help grieving when I see you suffering so. But, dear friend, be quiet, and try to go to sleep."

"I'll do enythin' fer yer, Miss Iola."

Tom closed his eyes and lay quiet. Tenderly and anxiously Iola watched over him as the hours waned away. The doctor came, shook his head gravely, and, turning to Iola, said, "There is no hope, but do what you can to alleviate his sufferings."

As Iola gazed upon the kind but homely features of Tom, she saw his eyes open and an unexpressed desire upon his face.

Tenderly and sadly bending over him, with tears in her dark, luminous eyes, she said, "Is there anything I can do for you?"

"Yes," said Tom, with laboring breath; "let me hole yore han', an' sing 'Ober Jordan inter glory' an' 'We'll anchor bye and bye.'"

Iola laid her hand gently in the rough palm of the dying man, and, with a tremulous voice, sang the parting hymns.

Tenderly she wiped the death damps from his dusky

brow, and imprinted upon it a farewell kiss. Gratitude and affection lit up the dying eye, which seemed to be gazing into the eternities. Just then Robert entered the room, and, seating himself quietly by Tom's bedside, read the death signs in his face.

"Good-bye, Robert," said Tom, "meet me in de kingdom." Suddenly a look of recognition and rapture lit up his face, and he murmured, "Angels, bright angels, all's well, all's well!"

Slowly his hand released its pressure, a peaceful calm overspread his countenance, and without a sigh or murmur Thomas Anderson, Iola's faithful and devoted friend, passed away, leaving the world so much poorer for her than it was before. Just then Dr. Gresham, the hospital physician, came to the bedside, felt for the pulse which would never throb again, and sat down in silence by the cot.

"What do you think, Doctor," said Iola, "has he fainted?"

"No," said the doctor, "poor fellow! he is dead."

Iola bowed her head in silent sorrow, and then relieved the anguish of her heart by a flood of tears. Robert rose, and sorrowfully left the room.

Iola, with tearful eyes and aching heart, clasped the cold hands over the still breast, closed the waxen lid over the eye which had once beamed with kindness or flashed with courage, and then went back, after the burial, to her daily round of duties, feeling the sad missing of something from her life.

CHAPTER VIII.

THE MYSTIFIED DOCTOR.

"COLONEL," said Dr. Gresham to Col. Robinson, the commander of the post, "I am perfectly mystified by Miss Leroy."

"What is the matter with her?" asked Col. Robinson. "Is she not faithful to her duties and obedient to your directions?"

"Faithful is not the word to express her tireless energy and devotion to her work," responded Dr. Gresham. "She must have been a born nurse to put such enthusiasm into her work."

"Why, Doctor, what is the matter with you? You talk like a lover."

A faint flush rose to the cheek of Dr. Gresham as he smiled, and said, "Oh! come now, Colonel, can't a man praise a woman without being in love with her?"

"Of course he can," said Col. Robinson; "but I know where such admiration is apt to lead. I've been there myself. But, Doctor, had you not better defer your love-making till you're out of the woods?"

"I assure you, Colonel, I am not thinking of love or courtship. That is the business of the drawing-room, and not of the camp. But she did mystify me last night."

"How so?" asked Col. Robinson.

"When Tom was dying," responded the doctor, "I saw that beautiful and refined young lady bend over and kiss him. When she found that he was dead, she just cried as if her heart was breaking. Well, that was a new thing to me. I can eat with colored people, walk, talk, and fight with them, but kissing them is something I don't hanker after."

"And yet you saw Miss Leroy do it?"

"Yes; and that puzzles me. She is one of the most refined and lady-like women I ever saw. I hear she is a refugee, but she does not look like the other refugees who have come to our camp. Her accent is slightly Southern, but her manner is Northern. She is self-respecting without being supercilious; quiet, without being dull. Her voice is low and sweet, yet at times there are tones of such passionate tenderness in it that you would think some great sorrow has darkened and overshadowed her life. Without being the least gloomy, her face at times is pervaded by an air of inexpressible sadness. I sometimes watch her when she is not aware that I am looking at her, and it seems as if a whole volume was depicted on her countenance. When she smiles, there is a longing in her eyes which is never satisfied. I cannot understand how a Southern lady, whose education and manners stamp her as a woman of fine culture and good breeding, could consent to occupy the position she so faithfully holds. It is a mystery I cannot solve. Can you?"

"I think I can," answered Col. Robinson.

"Will you tell me?" queried the doctor.

"Yes, on one condition."

"What is it?"

"Everlasting silence."

"I promise," said the doctor. "The secret between us shall be as deep as the sea."

"She has not requested secrecy, but at present, for her sake, I do not wish the secret revealed. Miss Leroy was a slave."

"Oh, no," said Dr. Gresham, starting to his feet, "it can't be so! A woman as white as she a slave?"

"Yes, it is so," continued the colonel. "In these States the child follows the condition of its mother. This beautiful and accomplished girl was held by one of the worst Rebels in town. Tom told me of it and I issued orders for her release."

"Well, well! Is that so?" said Dr. Gresham, thoughtfully stroking his beard. "Wonders will never cease. Why, I was just beginning to think seriously of her."

"What's to hinder your continuing to think?" asked Col. Robinson.

"What you tell me changes the whole complexion of affairs," replied the doctor.

"If that be so I am glad I told you before you got head over heels in love."

"Yes," said Dr. Gresham, absently.

Dr. Gresham was a member of a wealthy and aristocratic family, proud of its lineage, which it could trace through generations of good blood to its ancestral isle. He had become deeply interested in Iola before he had heard her story, but after it had been revealed to him he tried to banish her from his mind; but his constant observation of her only increased his interest and admiration. The deep pathos of her story, the tenderness of her ministrations, bestowed alike on black and white, and the sad loneliness of her condition, awakened within him a desire to defend and protect her all through her future life. The fierce clashing of war had not taken all the romance out of his nature. In Iola he saw realized his ideal of the woman whom he was willing to marry. A woman, tender, strong, and courageous, and rescued only by the strong arm of his Government from a fate worse than death. She was young in years, but old in sorrow; one whom a sad destiny had changed from a light-hearted girl to a heroic woman. As he observed her, he detected an undertone of sorrow in her most cheerful words, and observed a quick flushing and sudden paling of her cheek, as if she were living over scenes that were thrilling her soul with indignation or chilling her heart with horror. As nurse and physician, Iola and Dr. Gresham were constantly thrown together. His friends sent him magazines and books, which he gladly shared with her. The hospital was a sad place. Mangled forms, stricken down in the flush of their prime and energy; pale young corpses, sacrificed on the altar of slavery, constantly drained on her sympathies. Dr. Gresham was glad to have some reading matter which might divert her mind from the memories of her mournful past, and also furnish them both with interesting themes of conversation in their moments of relaxation from the harrowing scenes through which they were constantly passing. Without any effort or consciousness on her part, his friendship ripened into love. To him her presence was a pleasure, her absence a privation; and her loneliness drew deeply upon his sympathy. He would have merited his own self-contempt if, by word or deed, he had done anything to take advantage of her situation. All the manhood and chivalry of his nature rose in her behalf, and, after carefully revolving the matter, he resolved to win her for his bride, bury her secret in his Northern home, and hide from his aristocratic relations all knowledge of her mournful past. One day he said to Iola:—

"This hospital life is telling on you. Your strength is failing, and although you possess a wonderful amount of physical endurance, you must not forget that saints have bodies and dwell in tabernacles of clay, just the same as we common mortals."

"Compliments aside," she said, smiling; "what are you driving at, Doctor?"

"I mean," he replied, "that you are running down, and if you do not quit and take some rest you will be our patient instead of our nurse. You'd better take a furlough, go North, and return after the first frost."

"Doctor, if that is your only remedy," replied Iola, "I am afraid that I am destined to die at my post. I have no special friends in the North, and no home but this in the South. I am homeless and alone."

There was something so sad, almost despairing in her tones, in the drooping of her head, and the quivering of her lip, that they stirred Dr. Gresham's heart with sudden pity, and, drawing nearer to her, he said, "Miss Leroy, you need not be all alone. Let me claim the privilege of making your life bright and happy. Iola, I have loved you ever since I have seen your devotion to our poor, sick boys. How faithfully you, a young and gracious girl, have stood at your post and performed your duties. And now I ask, will you not permit me to clasp hands with you for life? I do not ask for a hasty reply. Give yourself time to think over what I have proposed."

CHAPTER IX.

EUGENE LEROY AND ALFRED LORRAINE.

NEARLY twenty years before the war, two young men, of French and Spanish descent, sat conversing on a large verandah which surrounded an ancient home on the Mississippi River. It was French in its style of architecture, large and rambling, with no hint of modern improvements.

The owner of the house was the only heir of a Creole planter. He had come into possession of an inheritance consisting of vast baronial estates, bank stock, and a large number of slaves. Eugene Leroy, being deprived of his parents, was left, at an early age, to the care of a distant relative, who had sent him to school and college, and who occasionally invited him to spend his vacations at his home. But Eugene generally declined his invitations, as he preferred spending his vacations at the watering places in the North, with their fashionable and not always innocent gayeties. Young, vivacious, impulsive, and undisciplined, without the restraining influence of a mother's love or the guidance of a father's hand, Leroy found himself, when his college days were over, in the dangerous position of a young man with vast possessions, abundant leisure, unsettled principles, and uncontrolled desires. He had no other object than to extract from life its most seductive draughts of ease and pleasure. His companion, who sat opposite him on the verandah, quietly smoking a cigar, was a remote cousin, a few years older than himself, the warmth of whose Southern temperament had been modified by an infusion of Northern blood.

Eugene was careless, liberal, and impatient of details, while his companion and cousin, Alfred Lorraine, was selfish, eager, keen, and alert; also hard, cold, methodical, and ever ready to grasp the main chance. Yet, notwithstanding the difference between them, they had formed a warm friendship for each other.

"Alfred," said Eugene, "I am going to be married."

Lorraine opened his eyes with sudden wonder, and exclaimed: "Well, that's the latest thing out! Who is the fortunate lady who has bound you with her silken fetters? Is it one of those beautiful Creole girls who were visiting Augustine's plantation last winter? I watched you during our visit there and thought that you could not be proof against their attractions. Which is your choice? It would puzzle me to judge between the two. They had splendid eyes, dark, luminous, and languishing; lovely complexions and magnificent hair. Both were delightful in their manners, refined and cultured, with an air of vivacity mingled with their repose of manner which was perfectly charming. As the law only allows us one, which is your choice? Miss Annette has more force than her sister, and if I could afford the luxury of a wife she would be my choice."

"Ah, Alf," said Eugene, "I see that you are a practical business man. In marrying you want a wife to assist you as an efficient plantation mistress. One who would tolerate no waste in the kitchen and no disorder in the parlor."

"Exactly so," responded Lorraine; "I am too poor

to marry a mere parlor ornament. You can afford to do it; I cannot."

"Nonsense, if I were as poor as a church mouse I would marry the woman I love."

"Very fine sentiments," said Lorraine, "and were I as rich as you I would indulge in them also. You know, when my father died I had great expectations. We had always lived in good style, and I never thought for a moment he was not a rich man, but when his estate was settled I found it was greatly involved, and I was forced to face an uncertain future, with scarcely a dollar to call my own. Land, negroes, cattle, and horses all went under the hammer. The only thing I retained was the education I received at the North; that was my father's best investment, and all my stock in trade. With that only as an outfit, it would be madness for me to think of marrying one of those lovely girls. They remind me of beautiful canary birds, charming and pretty, but not fitted for the wear and tear of plantation life. Well, which is your choice?"

"Neither," replied Eugene.

"Then, is it that magnificent looking widow from New Orleans, whom we met before you had that terrible spell of sickness and to whom you appeared so devoted?"

"Not at all. I have not heard from her since that summer. She was fascinating and handsome, but fearfully high strung."

"Were you afraid of her?"

"No; but I valued my happiness too much to trust it in her hands."

"Sour grapes!" said Lorraine.

"No! but I think that slavery and the lack of outside interests are beginning to tell on the lives of our women. They lean too much on their slaves, have too much irresponsible power in their hands, are narrowed and compressed by the routine of plantation life and the lack of intellectual stimulus."

"Yes, Eugene, when I see what other women are doing in the fields of literature and art, I cannot help thinking an amount of brain power has been held in check among us. Yet I cannot abide those Northern women, with their suffrage views and abolition cant. They just shock me."

"But your mother was a Northern woman," said Eugene.

"Yes; but she got bravely over her Northern ideas. As I remember her, she was just as much a Southerner as if she had been to the manor born. She came here as a school-teacher, but soon after she came she married my father. He was easy and indulgent with his servants, and held them with a very loose rein. But my mother was firm and energetic. She made the niggers move around. No shirking nor dawdling with her. When my father died, she took matters in hand, but she only outlived him a few months. If she had lived I believe that she would have retrieved our fortune. I know that she had more executive ability than my father. He was very squeamish about selling his servants, but she would have put every one of them in her pocket before permitting them to eat her out of house and home. But whom *are* you going to marry?"

"A young lady who graduates from a Northern seminary next week," responded Eugene.

"I think you are very selfish," said Lorraine. "You might have invited a fellow to go with you to be your best man."

"The wedding is to be strictly private. The lady whom I am to marry has negro blood in her veins."

"The devil she has!" exclaimed Lorraine, starting to his feet, and looking incredulously on the face of Leroy. "Are you in earnest? Surely you must be jesting."

"I am certainly in earnest," answered Eugene Leroy. "I mean every word I say."

"Oh, it can't be possible! Are you mad?" exclaimed Lorraine.

"Never was saner in my life."

"What under heaven could have possessed you to do such a foolish thing? Where did she come from."

"Right here, on this plantation. But I have educated and manumitted her, and I intend marrying her."

"Why, Eugene, it is impossible that you can have an idea of marrying one of your slaves. Why, man, she is your property, to have and to hold to all intents and purposes. Are you not satisfied with the power and possession the law gives you?"

"No. Although the law makes her helpless in my hands, to me her defenselessness is her best defense."

"Eugene, we have known each other all of our lives, and, although I have always regarded you as eccentric, I never saw you so completely off your balance before. The idea of you, with your proud family name, your vast wealth in land and negroes, intending to marry one of them, is a mystery I cannot solve. Do explain to me why you are going to take this extremely strange and foolish step."

"You never saw Marie?"

"No; and I don't want to."

"She is very beautiful. In the North no one would suspect that she has one drop of negro blood in her veins, but here, where I am known, to marry her is to lose caste. I could live with her, and not incur much if any social opprobrium. Society would wink at the transgression, even if after she had become the mother of my children I should cast her off and send her and them to the auction block."

"Men," replied Lorraine, "would merely shrug their shoulders; women would say you had been sowing your wild oats. Your money, like charity, would cover a multitude of faults."

"But if I make her my lawful wife and recognize her children as my legitimate heirs, I subject myself to social ostracism and a senseless persecution. We Americans boast of freedom, and yet here is a woman whom I love as I never loved any other human being, but both law and public opinion debar me from following the inclination of my heart. She is beautiful, faithful, and pure, and yet all that society will tolerate is what I would scorn to do."

"But has not society the right to guard the purity of its blood by the rigid exclusion of an alien race?"

"Excluding it! How?" asked Eugene.

"By debarring it from social intercourse."

"Perhaps it has," continued Eugene, "but should not society have a greater ban for those who, by consorting with an alien race, rob their offspring of a right to their names and to an inheritance in their property, and who fix their social status among an enslaved and outcast race? Don't eye me so curiously; I am not losing my senses."

"I think you have done that already," said Lorraine. "Don't you know that if she is as fair as a lily, beautiful as a houri, and chaste as ice, that still she is a negro?"

"Oh, come now; she isn't much of a negro."

"It doesn't matter, however. One drop of negro blood in her veins curses all the rest."

"I know it," said Eugene, sadly, "but I have weighed the consequences, and am prepared to take them."

"Well, Eugene, your course is *so* singular! I do wish that you would tell me why you take this unprecedented step?"

Eugene laid aside his cigar, looked thoughtfully at Lorraine, and said, "Well, Alfred, as we are kinsmen and life-long friends, I will not resent your asking my reason for doing that which seems to you the climax of absurdity, and if you will have the patience to listen I will tell you."

"Proceed, I am all attention."

"My father died," said Eugene, "as you know, when I was too young to know his loss or feel his care and, being an only child, I was petted and spoiled. I grew up to be wayward, self-indulgent, proud, and imperious. I went from home and made many friends both at college and in foreign lands. I was well supplied with money and, never having been forced to earn it, was ignorant of its value and careless of its use. My lavish expenditures and liberal benefactions attracted to me a number of parasites, and men older than myself led me into the paths of vice, and taught me how to gather the flowers of sin which blossom around the borders of hell. In a word, I left my home unwarned and unarmed against the seductions of vice. I returned an initiated devotee to debasing pleasures. Years of my life were passed in foreign lands; years in which my soul slumbered and seemed pervaded with a moral paralysis; years, the memory of which fills my soul with sorrow and shame. I went to the capitals of the old world to see life, but in seeing life I became acquainted with death, the death of true manliness and self-respect. You look astonished; but I tell you, Alf, there is many a poor clod-hopper, on whom are the dust and grime of unremitting toil, who feels more self-respect and true manliness than many of us with our family prestige, social position, and proud ancestral halls. After I had lived abroad for years, I returned a broken-down young man, prematurely old, my constitution a perfect wreck. A life of folly and dissipation was telling fearfully upon me. My friends shrank from me in dismay. I was sick nigh unto death, and had it not been for Marie's care I am certain that I should have died. She followed me down to the borders of the grave, and won me back to life and health. I was slow in recovering and, during the time, I had ample space for reflection, and the past unrolled itself before me. I resolved, over the wreck and ruin of my past life, to build a better and brighter future. Marie had a voice of remarkable sweetness, although it lacked culture. Often when I was nervous and restless I would have her sing some of those weird and plaintive melodies which she had learned from the plantation negroes. Sometimes I encouraged her to talk, and I was surprised at the native vigor of her intellect. By degrees I became acquainted with her history. She was all alone in the world. She had no recollection of her father, but remembered being torn from her mother while clinging to her dress. The trader who bought her mother did not wish to buy her. She remembered having a brother, with whom she used to play, but she had been separated from him also, and since then had lost all trace of them. After she was sold from her mother she became the property of an excellent old lady, who seems to have been very careful to imbue her mind with good principles; a woman who loved purity, not only for her own daughters, but also for the defenseless girls in her home. I believe it was the lady's intention to have freed Marie at her death, but she died suddenly, and, the estate being involved, she was sold with it and fell into the hands of my agent. I became deeply interested in her when I heard her story, and began to pity her."

"And I suppose love sprang from pity."

"I not only pitied her, but I learned to respect her. I had met with beautiful women in the halls of wealth and fashion, both at home and abroad, but there was something in her different from all my experience of womanhood."

"I should think so," said Lorraine, with a sneer; "but I should like to know what it was."

"It was something such as I have seen in old cathedrals, lighting up the beauty of a saintly face. A light which the poet tells was never seen on land or sea. I thought of this beautiful and defenseless girl adrift in the power of a reckless man, who, with all the advantages of wealth and education, had trailed his manhood in the dust, and she, with simple, childlike faith in the Unseen, seemed to be so good and pure that she commanded my respect and won my heart. In her presence every base and unholy passion died, subdued by the supremacy of her virtue."

"Why, Eugene, what has come over you? Talking of the virtue of these quadroon girls! You have lived so long in the North and abroad, that you seem to have lost the cue of our Southern life. Don't you know that these beautiful girls have been the curse of our homes? You have no idea of the hearts which are wrung by their presence."

"But, Alfred, suppose it is so. Are they to blame for it? What can any woman do when she is placed in the hands of an irresponsible master; when she knows that resistance is vain? Yes, Alfred, I agree with you, these women are the bane of our Southern civilization; but they are the victims and we are the criminals."

"I think from the airs that some of them put on when they get a chance, that they are very willing victims."

"So much the worse for our institution. If it is cruel to debase a hapless victim, it is an increase of cruelty to make her contented with her degradation. Let me tell you, Alf, you cannot wrong or degrade a woman without wronging or degrading yourself."

"What is the matter with you, Eugene? Are you thinking of taking priest's orders?"

"No, Alf," said Eugene, rising and rapidly pacing the floor, "you may defend the system as much as you please, but you cannot deny that the circumstances it creates, and the temptations it affords, are sapping our strength and undermining our character."

"That may be true," said Lorraine, somewhat irritably, "but you had better be careful how you air your Northern notions in public."

"Why so?"

"Because public opinion is too sensitive to tolerate any such discussions."

"And is not that a proof that we are at fault with respect to our institutions?"

"I don't know. I only know we are living in the midst of a magazine of powder, and it is not safe to enter it with a lighted candle."

"Let me proceed with my story," continued Eugene. "During the long months in which I was convalescing, I was left almost entirely to the companionship of Marie. In my library I found a Bible, which I began to read from curiosity, but my curiosity deepened into interest when I saw the rapt expression on Marie's face. I saw in it a loving response to sentiments to which I was a stranger. In the meantime my conscience was awakened, and I scorned to take advantage of her defenselessness. I felt that I owed my life to her faithful care, and I resolved to take her North, manumit, educate, and marry her. I sent her to a Northern academy, but as soon as some of the pupils found that she was colored, objections were raised, and the principal was compelled to dismiss her. During my search for a school I heard of one where three girls of mixed blood were pursuing their studies, every one of whom would have been ignominiously dismissed had their connection with the negro race been known. But I determined to run no risks. I found a school where her connection with the negro race would be no bar to her advancement. She graduates next week, and I intend to marry her before I return home. She was faithful when others were faithless, stood by me when others deserted me to die in loneliness and neglect, and now I am about to reward her care with all the love and devotion it is in my power to bestow. That is why I am about to marry my faithful and devoted nurse, who snatched me from the jaws of death. Now that I have told you my story, what say you?"

"Madness and folly inconceivable!" exclaimed Lorraine.

"What to you is madness and folly is perfect sanity with me. After all, Alf, is there not an amount of unreason in our prejudices?"

"That may be true; but I wasn't reasoned into it, and I do not expect to be reasoned out of it."

"Will you accompany me North?"

"No; except to put you in an insane asylum. You are the greatest crank out," said Lorraine, thoroughly disgusted.

"No, thank you; I'm all right. I expect to start North to-morrow. You had better come and go."

"I would rather follow you to your grave," replied Lorraine, hotly, while an expression of ineffable scorn passed over his cold, proud face.

CHAPTER X.

SHADOWS IN THE HOME.

On the next morning after this conversation Leroy left for the North, to attend the commencement and witness the graduation of his ward. Arriving in Ohio, he immediately repaired to the academy and inquired for the principal. He was shown into the reception-room, and in a few moments the principal entered.

"Good morning," said Leroy, rising and advancing towards him; "how is my ward this morning?"

"She is well, and has been expecting you. I am glad you came in time for the commencement. She stands among the foremost in her class."

"I am glad to hear it. Will you send her this?" said Leroy, handing the principal a card. The principal took the card and immediately left the room.

Very soon Leroy heard a light step, and looking up he saw a radiantly beautiful woman approaching him.

"Good morning, Marie," he said, greeting her cordially, and gazing upon her with unfeigned admiration. "You are looking very handsome this morning."

"Do you think so?" she asked, smiling and blushing. "I am glad you are not disappointed; that you do not feel your money has been spent in vain."

"Oh, no, what I have spent on your education has been the best investment I ever made."

"I hope," said Marie, "you may always find it so. But Mas——"

"Hush!" said Leroy, laying his hand playfully on her lips; "you are free. I don't want the dialect of slavery to linger on your lips. You must not call me that name again."

"Why not?"

"Because I have a nearer and dearer one by which I wish to be called."

Leroy drew her nearer, and whispered in her ear a single word. She started, trembled with emotion, grew pale, and blushed painfully. An awkward silence ensued, when Leroy, pressing her hand, exclaimed: "This is the hand that plucked me from the grave, and I am going to retain it as mine; mine to guard with my care until death us do part."

Leroy looked earnestly into her eyes, which fell beneath his ardent gaze. With admirable self-control, while a great joy was thrilling her heart, she bowed her beautiful head and softly repeated, "Until death us do part."

Leroy knew Southern society too well to expect it to condone his offense against its social customs, or give the least recognition to his wife, however cultured, refined, and charming she might be, if it were known that she had the least infusion of negro blood in her veins. But he was brave enough to face the consequences of his alliance, and marry the woman who was the choice of his heart, and on whom his affections were centred.

After Leroy had left the room, Marie sat awhile thinking of the wonderful change that had come over her. Instead of being a lonely slave girl, with the fatal dower of beauty, liable to be bought and sold, exchanged, and bartered, she was to be the wife of a wealthy planter;

a man in whose honor she could confide, and on whose love she could lean.

Very interesting and pleasant were the commencement exercises in which Marie bore an important part. To enlist sympathy for her enslaved race, and appear to advantage before Leroy, had aroused all of her energies. The stimulus of hope, the manly love which was environing her life, brightened her eye and lit up the wonderful beauty of her countenance. During her stay in the North she had constantly been brought in contact with anti-slavery people. She was not aware that there was so much kindness among the white people of the country until she had tested it in the North. From the anti-slavery people in private life she had learned some of the noblest lessons of freedom and justice, and had become imbued with their sentiments. Her theme was "American Civilization, its Lights and Shadows."

Graphically she portrayed the lights, faithfully she showed the shadows of our American civilization. Earnestly and feelingly she spoke of the blind Sampson in our land, who might yet shake the pillars of our great Commonwealth. Leroy listened attentively. At times a shadow of annoyance would overspread his face, but it was soon lost in the admiration her earnestness and zeal inspired. Like Esther pleading for the lives of her people in the Oriental courts of a despotic king, she stood before the audience, pleading for those whose lips were sealed, but whose condition appealed to the mercy and justice of the Nation. Strong men wiped the moisture from their eyes, and women's hearts throbbed in unison with the strong, brave words that were uttered in behalf of freedom for all and chains for none. Generous applause was freely bestowed, and beautiful bouquets were showered upon her. When it was known that she was to be the wife of her guardian, warm congratulations were given, and earnest hopes expressed for the welfare of the lonely girl, who, nearly all her life, had been deprived of a parent's love and care. On the eve of starting South Leroy procured a license, and united his destiny with the young lady whose devotion in the darkest hour had won his love and gratitude.

In a few days Marie returned as mistress to the plantation from which she had gone as a slave. But as unholy alliances were common in those days between masters and slaves, no one took especial notice that Marie shared Leroy's life as mistress of his home, and that the family silver and jewelry were in her possession. But Leroy, happy in his choice, attended to the interests of his plantation, and found companionship in his books and in the society of his wife. A few male companions visited him occasionally, admired the magnificent beauty of his wife, shook their heads, and spoke of him as being very eccentric, but thought his marriage the great mistake of his life. But none of his female friends ever entered his doors, when it became known that Marie held the position of mistress of his mansion, and presided at his table. But she, sheltered in the warm clasp of loving arms, found her life like a joyous dream.

Into that quiet and beautiful home three children were born, unconscious of the doom suspended over their heads.

"Oh, how glad I am," Marie would often say, "that these children are free." I could never understand how a cultured white man could have his own children enslaved. I can understand how savages, fighting with each other, could doom their vanquished foes to slavery, but it has always been a puzzle to me how a civilized man could drag his own children, bone of his bone, flesh of his flesh, down to the position of social outcasts, abject slaves, and political pariahs."

"But, Marie," said Eugene, "all men do not treat their illegitimate children in the manner you describe. The last time I was in New Orleans I met Henri Augustine at the depot, with two beautiful young girls. At first I thought that they were his own children, they resembled him so closely. But afterwards I noticed that they addressed him as 'Mister.' Before we parted he told me that his wife had taken such a dislike to their mother that she could not bear to see them on the place. At last, weary of her dissatisfaction, he had promised to bring them to New Orleans and sell them. Instead, he was going to Ohio to give them their freedom, and make provision for their future."

"What a wrong!" said Marie.

"Who was wronged?" said Leroy, in astonishment.

"Every one in the whole transaction," answered Marie. "Your friend wronged himself by sinning against his own soul. He wronged his wife by arousing her hatred and jealousy through his unfaithfulness. He wronged those children by giving them the *status* of slaves and outcasts. He wronged their mother by imposing upon her the burdens and cares of maternity without the rights and privileges of a wife. He made her crown of motherhood a circlet of shame. Under other circumstances she might have been an honored wife and happy mother.

And I do think such men wrong their own legitimate children by transmitting to them a weakened moral fibre."

"Oh, Marie, you have such an uncomfortable way of putting things. You make me feel that we have done those things which we ought not to have done, and have left undone those things which we ought to have done."

"If it annoys you," said Marie, "I will stop talking."

"Oh, no, go on," said Leroy, carelessly; and then he continued more thoughtfully, "I know a number of men who have sent such children North, and manumitted, educated, and left them valuable legacies. We are all liable to err, and, having done wrong, all we can do is to make reparation."

"My dear husband, this is a wrong where reparation is impossible. Neither wealth nor education can repair the wrong of a dishonored birth. There are a number of slaves in this section who are servants to their own brothers and sisters; whose fathers have robbed them not simply of liberty but of the right of being well born. Do you think these things will last forever?"

"I suppose not. There are some prophets of evil who tell us that the Union is going to dissolve. But I know it would puzzle their brains to tell where the crack will begin. I reckon we'll continue to jog along as usual. 'Cotton fights, and cotton conquers for American slavery.'"

Even while Leroy dreamed of safety the earthquake was cradling its fire; the ground was growing hollow beneath his tread; but his ear was too dull to catch the sound; his vision too blurred to read the signs of the times.

"Marie," said Leroy, taking up the thread of the discourse, "slavery is a sword that cuts both ways. If it wrongs the negro, it also curses the white man. But we are in it, and what can we do?"

"Get out of it as quickly as possible."

"That is easier said than done. I would willingly free every slave on my plantation if I could do so without expatriating them. Some of them have wives and children on other plantations, and to free them is to separate them from their kith and kin. To let them remain here as a free people is out of the question. My hands are tied by law and custom."

"Who tied them?" asked Marie.

"A public opinion, whose meshes I cannot break. If the negro is the thrall of his master, we are just as much the thralls of public opinion."

"Why do you not battle against public opinion, if you think it is wrong?"

"Because I have neither the courage of a martyr, nor the faith of a saint; and so I drift along, trying to make the condition of our slaves as comfortable as I possibly can. I believe there are slaves on this plantation whom the most flattering offers of freedom would not entice away."

"I do not think," said Marie, "that some of you planters understand your own slaves. Lying is said to be the vice of slaves. The more intelligent of them have so learned to veil their feelings that you do not see the undercurrent of discontent beneath their apparent good humor and jollity. The more discontented they are, the more I respect them. To me a contented slave is an abject creature. I hope that I shall see the day when there will not be a slave in the land. I hate the whole thing from the bottom of my heart."

"Marie, your Northern education has unfitted you for Southern life. You are free, yourself, and so are our children. Why not let well enough alone?"

"Because I love liberty, not only for myself but for every human being. Think how dear these children are to me; and then for the thought to be forever haunting me, that if you were dead they could be turned out of doors and divided among your relatives. I sometimes lie awake at night thinking of how there might be a screw loose somewhere, and, after all, the children and I might be reduced to slavery."

"Marie, what in the world is the matter with you? Have you had a presentiment of my death, or, as Uncle Jack says, 'hab you seed it in a vision?'"

"No, but I have had such sad forebodings that they almost set me wild. One night I dreamt that you were dead; that the lawyers entered the house, seized our property, and remanded us to slavery. I never can be satisfied in the South with such a possibility hanging over my head."

"Marie, dear, you are growing nervous. Your imagination is too active. You are left too much alone on this plantation. I hope that for your own and the children's sake I will be enabled to arrange our affairs so as to find a home for you where you will not be doomed to the social isolation and ostracism that surround you here."

"I don't mind the isolation for myself, but the children. You have enjoined silence on me with respect to their connection with the negro race, but I do not think we can conceal it from them very long. It will not be long before Iola will notice the offishness of girls of her own age, and the scornful glances which, even now, I think, are leveled at her. Yesterday Harry came crying to me, and told me that one of the neighbor's boys had called him 'nigger.'"

A shadow flitted over Leroy's face, as he answered, somewhat soberly, "Oh, Marie, do not meet trouble half way. I have manumitted you, and the children will follow your condition. I have made you all legatees of my will. Except my cousin, Alfred Lorraine, I have only distant relatives, whom I scarcely know and who hardly know me."

"Your cousin Lorraine? Are you sure our interests would be safe in his hands?"

"I think so; I don't think Alfred would do anything dishonorable."

"He might not with his equals. But how many men would be bound by a sense of honor where the rights of a colored woman are in question? Your cousin was bitterly opposed to our marriage, and I would not trust any important interests in his hands. I do hope that in providing for our future you will make assurance doubly sure."

"I certainly will, and all that human foresight can do shall be done for you and our children."

"Oh," said Marie, pressing to her heart a beautiful child of six summers, "I think it would almost make me turn over in my grave to know that every grace and charm which this child possesses would only be so much added to her value as an article of merchandise."

As Marie released the child from her arms she looked wonderingly into her mother's face and clung closely to her, as if to find refuge from some unseen evil. Leroy noticed this, and sighed unconsciously, as an expression of pain flitted over his face.

"Now, Marie," he continued, "stop tormenting yourself with useless fears. Although, with all her faults, I still love the South, I will make arrangements either to live North or go to France. There life will be brighter for us all. Now, Marie, seat yourself at the piano and sing :—

> 'Sing me the songs that to me were so dear,
> Long, long ago.
> Sing me the songs I delighted to hear,
> Long, long ago."

As Marie sang the anxiety faded from her face, a sense of security stole over her, and she sat among her loved ones a happy wife and mother. What if no one recognized her on that lonely plantation! Her world was, nevertheless, there. The love and devotion of her husband brightened every avenue of her life, while her children filled her home with music, mirth, and sunshine.

Marie had undertaken their education, but she could not give them the culture which comes from the attrition of thought, and from contact with the ideas of others. Since her school-days she had read extensively and thought much, and in solitude her thoughts had ripened. But for her children there were no companions except the young slaves of the plantation, and she dreaded the effect of such intercourse upon their lives and characters.

Leroy had always been especially careful to conceal from his children the knowledge of their connection with the negro race. To Marie this silence was oppressive.

One day she said to him, "I see no other way of finishing the education of these children than by sending them to some Northern school."

"I have come," said Leroy, "to the same conclusion. We had better take Iola and Harry North and make arrangements for them to spend several years in being educated. Riches take wings to themselves and fly away, but a good education is an investment on which the law can place no attachment. As there is a possibility of their origin being discovered, I will find a teacher to whom I can confide our story, and upon whom I can enjoin secrecy. I want them well fitted for any emergency in life. When I discover for what they have the most aptitude I will give them especial training in that direction."

A troubled look passed over the face of Marie, as she hesitatingly said: "I am so afraid that you will regret our marriage when you fully realize the complications it brings."

"No, no," said Leroy, tenderly, "it is not that I regret our marriage, or feel the least disdain for our children on account of the blood in their veins; but I do not wish them to grow up under the contracting influence of this race prejudice. I do not wish them to feel that they have been born under a proscription from which no valor can redeem them, nor that any social advancement or individual development can wipe off the ban which clings to them. No, Marie, let them go North, learn all they can, aspire all they may. The painful knowledge will come all too soon. Do not forestall it. I want them simply to grow up as other children; not being patronized by friends nor disdained by foes."

"My dear husband, you may be perfectly right, but are you not preparing our children for a fearful awakening? Are you not acting on the plan, 'After me the deluge?'"

"Not at all, Marie. I want our children to grow up without having their self-respect crushed in the bud. You know that the North is not free from racial prejudice."

"I know it," said Marie, sadly, "and I think one of the great mistakes of our civilization is that which makes color, and not character, a social test."

"I think so, too," said Leroy. "The strongest men and women of a down-trodden race may bare their bosoms to an adverse fate and develop courage in the midst of opposition, but we have no right to subject our children to such crucial tests before their characters are formed. For years, when I lived abroad, I had an opportunity to see and hear of men of African descent who had distinguished themselves and obtained a recognition in European circles, which they never could have gained in this country. I now recall the name of Ira Aldridge, a colored man from New York City, who was covered with princely honors as a successful tragedian. Alexander Dumas was not forced to conceal his origin to succeed as a novelist. When I was in St. Petersburg I was shown the works of Alexander Sergevitch, a Russian poet, who was spoken of as the Byron of Russian literature, and reckoned one of the finest poets that Russia has produced in this century. He was also a prominent figure in fashionable society, and yet he was of African lineage. One of his paternal ancestors was a negro who had been ennobled by Peter the

Great. I can't help contrasting the recognition which these men had received with the treatment which has been given to Frederick Douglass and other intelligent colored men in this country. With me the wonder is not that they have achieved so little, but that they have accomplished so much. No, Marie, we will have our children educated without being subjected to the depressing influences of caste feeling. Perhaps by the time their education is finished I will be ready to wind up my affairs and take them abroad, where merit and ability will give them entrance into the best circles of art, literature, and science."

After this conversation Leroy and his wife went North, and succeeded in finding a good school for their children. In a private interview he confided to the principal the story of the cross in their blood, and, finding him apparently free from racial prejudice, he gladly left the children in his care. Gracie, the youngest child, remained at home, and her mother spared no pains to fit her for the seminary against the time her sister should have finished her education.

CHAPTER XI.

THE PLAGUE AND THE LAW.

YEARS passed, bringing no special change to the life of Leroy and his wife. Shut out from the busy world, its social cares and anxieties, Marie's life flowed peacefully on. Although removed by the protecting care of Leroy from the condition of servitude, she still retained a deep sympathy for the enslaved, and was ever ready to devise plans to ameliorate their condition.

Leroy, although in the midst of slavery, did not believe in the rightfulness of the institution. He was in favor of gradual emancipation, which would prepare both master and slave for a moral adaptation to the new conditions of freedom. While he was willing to have the old rivets taken out of slavery, politicians and planters were devising plans to put in new screws. He was desirous of having it ended in the States; they were clamorous to have it established in the Territories.

But so strong was the force of habit, combined with the feebleness of his moral resistance and the nature of his environment, that instead of being an athlete, armed for a glorious strife, he had learned to drift where he should have steered, to float with the current instead of nobly breasting the tide. He conducted his plantation with as much lenity as it was possible to infuse into a system darkened with the shadow of a million crimes.

Leroy had always been especially careful not to allow his children to spend their vacations at home. He and Marie generally spent that time with them at some summer resort.

"I would like," said Marie, one day, "to have our children spend their vacations at home. Those summer resorts are pleasant, yet, after all, there is no place like home. But," and her voice became tremulous, "our children would now notice their social isolation and inquire the cause." A faint sigh arose to the lips of Leroy, as she added: "Man is a social being; I've known it to my sorrow."

There was a tone of sadness in Leroy's voice, as he replied: "Yes, Marie, let them stay North. We seem to be entering on a period fraught with great danger. I cannot help thinking and fearing that we are on the eve of a civil war."

"A civil war!" exclaimed Marie, with an air of astonishment. "A civil war about what?"

"Why, Marie, the thing looks to me so wild and foolish I hardly know how to explain. But some of our leading men have come to the conclusion that North and South had better separate, and instead of having one to have two independent governments. The spirit of secession is rampant in the land. I do not know what the result will be, and I fear it will bode no good to the country. Between the fire-eating Southerners and the meddling Abolitionists we are about to be plunged into a great deal of trouble. I fear there are breakers ahead. The South is dissatisfied with the state of public opinion in the North. We are realizing that we are two peoples in the midst of one nation. William H. Seward has proclaimed that the conflict between freedom and slavery is irrepressible, and that the country cannot remain half free and half slave."

"How will *you* go?" asked Marie.

"My heart is with the Union. I don't believe in secession. There has been no cause sufficient to justify a rupture. The North has met us time and again in the spirit of concession and compromise. When we wanted the continuance of the African slave trade the North conceded that we should have twenty years of slave-trading for the benefit of our plantations. When we wanted more territory she conceded to our desires and gave us land enough to carve out four States, and there yet remains enough for four more. When we wanted power to recapture our slaves when they fled North for refuge, Daniel Webster told Northerners to conquer their prejudices, and they gave us the whole Northern States as a hunting ground for our slaves. The Presidential chair has been filled the greater number of years by Southerners, and the majority of offices has been shared by our men. We wanted representation in Congress on a basis which would include our slaves, and the North, whose suffrage represents only men, gave us a three-fifths representation for our slaves, whom we count as property. I think the step will be suicidal. There are extremists in both sections, but I hope, between them both, wise counsels and measures will prevail."

Just then Alfred Lorraine was ushered into the room. Occasionally he visited Leroy, but he always came alone. His wife was the only daughter of an enterprising slave-trader, who had left her a large amount of property.

Her social training was deficient, her education limited, but she was too proud of being a pure white woman to enter the home of Leroy, with Marie as its presiding genius. Lorraine tolerated Marie's presence as a necessary evil, while to her he always seemed like a presentiment of trouble. With his coming a shadow fell upon her home, hushing its music and darkening its sunshine. A sense of dread oppressed her. There came into her soul an intuitive feeling that somehow his coming was fraught with danger. When not peering around she would often catch his eyes bent on her with a baleful expression.

Leroy and his cousin immediately fell into a discussion on the condition of the country. Lorraine was a rank Secessionist, ready to adopt the most extreme measures of the leaders of the movement, even to the reopening of the slave trade. Leroy thought a dissolution of the Union would involve a fearful expenditure of blood and treasure for which, before the eyes of the world, there could be no justification. The debate lasted late into the night, leaving both Lorraine and Leroy just as set in their opinions as they were before they began. Marie listened attentively awhile, then excused herself and withdrew.

After Lorraine had gone Marie said: "There is something about your cousin that fills me with nameless dread. I always feel when he enters the room as if some one were walking over my grave. I do wish he would stay at home."

"I wish so, too, since he disturbs you. But, Marie, you are growing nervous. How cold your hands are. Don't you feel well?"

"Oh, yes; I am only a little faint. I wish he would never come. But, as he does, I must make the best of it."

"Yes, Marie, treat him well for my sake. He is the only relative I have who ever darkens our doors."

"I have no faith in his friendship for either myself or my children. I feel that while he makes himself agreeable to you he hates me from the bottom of his heart, and would do anything to get me out of the way. Oh, I am *so* glad I am your lawful wife, and that you married me before you brought me back to this State! I believe that if you were gone he wouldn't have the least scruple against trying to prove our marriage invalid and remanding us to slavery."

Leroy looked anxiously and soberly at his wife, and said: "Marie, I do not think so. Your life is too lonely here. Write your orders to New Orleans, get what you need for the journey, and let us spend the summer somewhere in the North."

Just then Marie's attention was drawn to some household matters, and it was a short time before she returned.

"Tom," continued Leroy, "has just brought the mail, and here is a letter from Iola."

Marie noticed that he looked quite sober as he read, and that an expression of vexation was lingering on his lips.

"What is the matter?" asked Marie.

"Nothing much; only a tempest in a teapot. The presence of a colored girl in Mr. Galen's school has caused a breeze of excitement. You know Mr. Galen is quite an Abolitionist, and, being true to his principles, he could not consistently refuse when a colored woman applied for her daughter's admission. Of course, when he took her he was compelled to treat her as any other pupil. In so doing he has given mortal offense to the mother of two Southern boys. She has threatened to take them away if the colored girl remains."

"What will he do about it?" asked Marie, thoughtfully.

"Oh, it is a bitter pill, but I think he will have to swallow it. He is between two fires. He cannot dismiss her from the school and be true to his Abolition principles; yet if he retains her he will lose his Southern customers, and I know he cannot afford to do that."

"What does Iola say?"

"He has found another boarding place for her, but she is to remain in the school. He had to throw that sop to the whale."

"Does she take sides against the girl?"

"No, I don't think she does. She says she feels sorry for her, and that she would hate to be colored. 'It is so hard to be looked down on for what one can't help.'"

"Poor child! I wish we could leave the country. I never would consent to her marrying any one without first revealing to him her connection with the negro race. This is a subject on which I am not willing to run any risks."

"My dear Marie, when you shall have read Iola's letter you will see it is more than a figment of my imagination that has made me so loth to have our children know the paralyzing power of caste."

Leroy, always liberal with his wife and children, spared neither pains nor expense to have them prepared for their summer outing. Iola was to graduate in a few days. Harry was attending a school in the State of Maine, and his father had written to him, apprising him of his intention to come North that season. In a few days Leroy and his wife started North, but before they reached Vicksburg they were met by the intelligence that the yellow fever was spreading in the Delta, and that pestilence was breathing its bane upon the morning air and distilling its poison upon the midnight dews.

"Let us return home," said Marie.

"It is useless," answered Leroy. "It is nearly two days since we left home. The fever is spreading south of us with fearful rapidity. To return home is to walk into the jaws of death. It was my intention to have stopped at Vicksburg, but now I will go on as soon as I can make the connections."

Early next morning Leroy and his wife started again on their journey. The cars were filled with terror-stricken people who were fleeing from death, when death was everywhere. They fled from the city only to meet the dreaded apparition in the country. As they journeyed on Leroy grew restless and feverish. He tried to brace himself against the infection which was creeping slowly but insidiously into his life, dulling his brain, fevering his blood, and prostrating his strength. But vain were all his efforts. He had no armor strong enough to repel the invasion of death. They stopped at a small town on the way and obtained the best medical skill and most careful nursing, but neither skill nor art availed. On the third day death claimed Leroy as a victim, and Marie wept in hopeless agony over the grave of her devoted husband, whose sad lot it was to die from home and be buried among strangers.

But before he died he placed his will in Marie's hands, saying: "I have left you well provided for. Kiss the children for me and bid them good-bye."

He tried to say a parting word to Gracie, but his voice failed, and he fainted into the stillness of death. A mortal paleness overspread his countenance, on which had already gathered the shadows that never deceive. In speechless agony Marie held his hand until it released its pressure in death, and then she stood alone beside her dead, with all the bright sunshine of her life fading into the shadows of the grave. Heart-broken and full of fearful forebodings, Marie left her cherished dead in the quiet village of H—— and returned to her death-darkened home.

It was a lovely day in June, birds were singing their sweetest songs, flowers were breathing their fragrance on the air, when Mam Liza, sitting at her cabin-door, talking with some of the house servants, saw a carriage approaching, and wondered who was coming.

"I wonder," she said, excitedly, "whose comin' to de house when de folks is done gone."

But her surprise was soon changed to painful amazement, when she saw Marie, robed in black, alighting from the carriage, and holding Gracie by the hand. She caught sight of the drooping head and grief-stricken face, and rushed to her, exclaiming:—

"Whar's Marse Eugene?"

"Dead," said Marie, falling into Mammy Liza's arms, sobbing out, "dead! *he died* of yellow fever."

A wild burst of sorrow came from the lips of the servants, who had drawn near.

"Where is he?" said Mam Liza, speaking like one suddenly bewildered.

"He is buried in H——. I could not bring him home," said Marie.

"My pore baby," said Mam Liza, with broken sobs. "I'se dreffal sorry. My heart's most broke into two." Then, controlling herself, she dismissed the servants who stood around, weeping, and led Marie to her room.

"Come, honey, lie down an' lem'me git yer a cup ob tea."

"Oh, no; I don't want anything," said Marie, wringing her hands in bitter agony.

"Oh, honey," said Mam Liza, "yer musn't gib up. Yer knows whar to put yer trus'. Yer can't lean on de arm of flesh in dis tryin' time." Kneeling by the side of her mistress she breathed out a prayer full of tenderness, hope, and trust.

Marie grew calmer. It seemed as if that earnest, trustful prayer had breathed into her soul a feeling of resignation.

Gracie stood wonderingly by, vainly trying to comprehend the great sorrow which was overwhelming the life of her mother.

After the first great burst of sorrow was over, Marie sat down to her desk and wrote a letter to Iola, informing her of her father's death. By the time she had finished it she grew dizzy and faint, and fell into a swoon. Mammy Liza tenderly laid her on the bed, and helped restore her to consciousness.

Lorraine, having heard of his cousin's death, came immediately to see Marie. She was too ill to have an interview with him, but he picked up the letter she had written and obtained Iola's address.

Lorraine made a careful investigation of the case, to ascertain whether Marie's marriage was valid. To his delight he found there was a flaw in the marriage and an informality in the manumission. He then determined to invalidate Marie's claim, and divide the inheritance among Leroy's white relations. In a short time strangers, distant relatives of her husband, became frequent visitors at the plantation, and made themselves offensively familiar. At length the dreadful storm burst.

Alfred Lorraine entered suit for his cousin's estate, and for the remanding of his wife and children to slavery. In a short time he came armed with legal authority, and said to Marie:—

"I have come to take possession of these premises."

"By what authority?" she gasped, turning deathly pale. He hesitated a moment, as if his words were arrested by a sense of shame.

"By what authority?" she again demanded.

"By the authority of the law," answered Lorraine, "which has decided that Leroy's legal heirs are his white blood relations, and that your marriage is null and void."

"But," exclaimed Marie, "I have our marriage certificate. I was Leroy's lawful wife."

"Your marriage certificate is not worth the paper it is written on."

"Oh, you must be jesting, cruelly jesting. It can't be so."

"Yes; it is so. Judge Starkins has decided that your manumission is unlawful; your marriage a bad precedent, and inimical to the welfare of society; and that you and your children are remanded to slavery."

Marie stood as one petrified. She seemed a statue of fear and despair. She tried to speak, reached out her hand as if she were groping in the dark, turned pale as death as if all the blood in her veins had receded to her heart, and, with one heart-rending cry of bitter agony, she fell senseless to the floor. Her servants, to whom she had been so kind in her days of prosperity, bent pityingly over her, chafed her cold hands, and did what they could to restore her to consciousness. For awhile she was stricken with brain fever, and her life seemed trembling on its frailest cord.

Gracie was like one perfectly dazed. When not watching by her mother's bedside she wandered aimlessly about the house, growing thinner day by day. A slow fever was consuming her life. Faithfully and carefully Mammy Liza watched over her, and did all she could to bring smiles to her lips and light to her fading eyes, but all in vain. Her only interest in life was to sit where she could watch her mother as she tossed to and fro in delirium, and to wonder what had brought the change in her once happy home. Finally she, too, was stricken with brain fever, which intervened as a mercy between her and the great sorrow that was overshadowing her young life. Tears would fill the servants' eyes as they saw the dear child drifting from them like a lovely vision, too bright for earth's dull cares and weary, wasting pain.

CHAPTER XII.

SCHOOL-GIRL NOTIONS.

DURING Iola's stay in the North she found a strong tide of opposition against slavery. Arguments against the institution had entered the Church and made legislative halls the arenas of fierce debate. The subject had become part of the social converse of the fireside, and had enlisted the best brain and heart of the country. Anti-slavery discussions were pervading the strongest literature and claiming a place on the most popular platforms.

Iola, being a Southern girl and a slave-holder's daughter, always defended slavery when it was under discussion.

"Slavery can't be wrong," she would say, "for my father is a slave-holder, and my mother is as good to our servants as she can be. My father often tells her that she spoils them, and lets them run over her. I never saw my father strike one of them. I love my mammy as much as I do my own mother, and I believe she loves us just as if we were her own children. When we are sick I am sure that she could not do anything more for us than she does."

"But, Iola," responded one of her school friends, "after all, they are not free. Would you be satisfied to have the most beautiful home, the costliest jewels, or the most elegant wardrobe if you were a slave?"

"Oh, the cases are not parallel. Our slaves do not

want their freedom. They would not take it if we gave it to them."

"That is not the case with them all. My father has seen men who have encountered almost incredible hardships to get their freedom. Iola, did you ever attend an anti-slavery meeting?"

"No; I don't think these Abolitionists have any right to meddle in our affairs. I believe they are prejudiced against us, and want to get our property. I read about them in the papers when I was at home. I don't want to hear my part of the country run down. My father says the slaves would be very well contented if no one put wrong notions in their heads."

"I don't know," was the response of her friend, "but I do not think that that slave mother who took her four children, crossed the Ohio River on the ice, killed one of the children and attempted the lives of the other two, was a contented slave. And that other one, who, running away and finding herself pursued, threw herself over the Long Bridge into the Potomac, was evidently not satisfied. I do not think the numbers who are coming North on the Underground Railroad can be very contented. It is not natural for people to run away from happiness, and if they are so happy and contented, why did Congress pass the Fugitive Slave Bill?"

"Well, I don't think," answered Iola, "any of our slaves would run away. I know mamma don't like slavery very much. I have often heard her say that she hoped the time would come when there would not be a slave in the land. My father does not think as she does. He thinks slavery is not wrong if you treat them well and don't sell them from their families. I intend, after I have graduated, to persuade pa to buy a house in New Orleans, and spend the winter there. You know this will be my first season out, and I hope that you will come and spend the winter with me. We will have such gay times, and you will so fall in love with our sunny South that you will never want to come back to shiver amid the snows and cold of the North. I think one winter in the South would cure you of your Abolitionism."

"Have you seen her yet?"

This question was asked by Louis Bastine, an attorney who had come North in the interests of Lorraine. The scene was the New England village where Mr. Galen's academy was located, and which Iola was attending. This question was addressed to Camille Lecroix, Bastine's intimate friend, who had lately come North. He was the son of a planter who lived near Leroy's plantation, and was familiar with Iola's family history. Since his arrival North, Bastine had met him and communicated to him his intentions.

"Yes; just caught a glimpse of her this morning as she was going down the street," was Camille's reply.

"She is a most beautiful creature," said Louis Bastine. "She has the proud poise of Leroy, the most splendid eyes I ever saw in a woman's head, lovely complexion, and a glorious wealth of hair. She would bring $2000 any day in a New Orleans market."

"I always feel sorry," said Camille, "when I see one of those Creole girls brought to the auction block. I have known fathers who were deeply devoted to their daughters, but who through some reverse of fortune were forced to part with them, and I always think the blow has been equally terrible on both sides. I had a friend who had two beautiful daughters whom he had educated in the North. They were cultured, and really belles in society. They were entirely ignorant of their lineage, but when their father died it was discovered that their mother had been a slave. It was a fearful blow. They would have faced poverty, but the knowledge of their tainted blood was more than they could bear."

"What became of them?"

"They both died, poor girls. I believe they were as much killed by the blow as if they had been shot. To tell you the truth, Bastine, I feel sorry for this girl. I don't believe she has the least idea of her negro blood."

"No, Leroy has been careful to conceal it from her," replied Bastine.

"Is that so?" queried Camille. "Then he has made a great mistake."

"I can't help that," said Bastine; "business is business."

"How can you get her away?" asked Camille. "You will have to be very cautious, because if these pesky Abolitionists get an inkling of what you're doing they will balk your game double quick. And when you come to look at it, isn't it a shame to attempt to reduce that girl to slavery? She is just as white as we are, as good as any girl in the land, and better educated than thousands of white girls. A girl with her apparent refinement and magnificent beauty, were it not for the cross in her blood, I would be proud to introduce to our set. She would be the sensation of the season. I believe to-day it would be easier for me to go to the slums and take a young girl from there, and have her introduced as my wife, than to have society condone the offense if I married that lovely girl. There is not a social circle in the South that would not take it as a gross insult to have her introduced into it."

"Well," said Bastine, "my plan is settled. Leroy has never allowed her to spend her vacations at home. I understand she is now very anxious to get home, and, as Lorraine's attorney, I have come on his account to take her home."

"How will you do it?"

"I shall tell her her father is dangerously ill, and desires her to come as quickly as possible."

"And what then?"

"Have her inventoried with the rest of the property."

"Don't she know that her father is dead?"

"I think not," said Bastine." "She is not in mourning, but appeared very light-hearted this morning, laughing and talking with two other girls. I was struck with her great beauty, and asked a gentleman who she was. He said, 'Miss Leroy, of Mississippi.' I think Lorraine has managed the affair so as to keep her in perfect ignorance of her father's death. I don't like the job, but I never let sentiment interfere with my work."

Poor Iola! When she said slavery was not a bad thing, little did she think that she was destined to drink to its bitter dregs the cup she was so ready to press to the lips of others.

"How do you think she will take to her situation?" asked Camille.

"O, I guess," said Bastine, "she will sulk and take it pretty hard at first; but if she is managed right she will soon get over it. Give her plenty of jewelry, fine clothes, and an easy time."

"All this business must be conducted with the utmost secrecy and speed. Her mother could not have written to her, for she has been suffering with brain fever and nervous prostration since Leroy's death. Lorraine knows her market value too well, and is too shrewd to let so much property pass out of his hands without making an effort to retain it."

"Has she any brothers or sisters?"

"Yes, a brother," replied Bastine; "but he is at another school, and I have no orders from Lorraine in reference to him. If I can get the girl I am willing to let well enough alone. I dread the interview with the principal more than anything else. I am afraid he will hem and haw, and have his doubts. Perhaps, when he sees my letters and hears my story, I can pull the wool over his eyes."

"But, Louis, this is a pitiful piece of business. I should hate to be engaged in it."

A deep flush of shame overspread for a moment the face of Lorraine's attorney, as he replied: "I don't like the job, but I have undertaken it, and must go through with it."

"I see no '*must*' about it. Were I in your place I would wash my hands of the whole business."

"I can't afford it," was Bastine's hard, business-like reply. On the next morning after this conversation between these two young men, Louis Bastine presented himself to the principal of the academy, with the request that Iola be permitted to leave immediately to attend the sick-bed of her father, who was dangerously ill. The principal hesitated, but while he was deliberating, a telegram, purporting to come from Iola's mother, summoned Iola to her father's bedside without delay. The principal, set at rest in regard to the truthfulness of the dispatch, not only permitted but expedited her departure.

Iola and Bastine took the earliest train, and traveled without pausing until they reached a large hotel in a Southern city. There they were obliged to wait a few hours until they could resume their journey, the train having failed to make connection. Iola sat in a large, lonely parlor, waiting for the servant to show her to a private room. She had never known a great sorrow. Never before had the shadows of death mingled with the sunshine of her life.

Anxious, travel-worn, and heavy-hearted, she sat in an easy chair, with nothing to divert her from the grief and anxiety which rendered every delay a source of painful anxiety.

"Oh, I hope that he will be alive and growing better!" was the thought which kept constantly revolving in her mind, until she fell asleep. In her dreams she was at home, encircled in the warm clasp of her father's arms, feeling her mother's kisses lingering on her lips, and hearing the joyous greetings of the servants and Mammy Liza's glad welcome as she folded her to her heart. From this dream of bliss she was awakened by a burning kiss pressed on her lips, and a strong arm encircling her. Gazing around and taking in the whole situation, she sprang from her seat, her eyes flashing with rage and scorn, her face flushed to the roots of her hair, her voice shaken with excitement, and every nerve trembling with angry emotion.

"How dare you do such a thing! Don't you know if my father were here he would crush you to the earth?"

"Not so fast, my lovely tigress," said Bastine, "your father knew what he was doing when he placed you in my charge."

"My father made a great mistake, if he thought he had put me in charge of a gentleman."

"I am your guardian for the present," replied Bastine. "I am to see you safe home, and then my commission ends."

"I wish it were ended now," she exclaimed, trembling with anger and mortification. Her voice was choked by emotion, and broken by smothered sobs. Louis Bastine thought to himself, "she is a real spitfire, but beautiful even in her wrath."

During the rest of her journey Iola preserved a most freezing reserve towards Bastine. At length the journey was ended. Pale and anxious she rode up the avenue which led to her home.

A strange silence pervaded the place. The servants moved sadly from place to place, and spoke in subdued tones. The windows were heavily draped with crape, and a funeral air pervaded the house.

Mammy Liza met her at the door, and, with streaming eyes and convulsive sobs, folded her to her heart, as Iola exclaimed, in tones of hopeless anguish :—

"Oh, papa's dead!"

"Oh, my pore baby!" said mammy, "ain't you hearn tell 'bout it? Yore par's dead, an' your mar's bin drefful sick. She's better now."

Mam Liza stepped lightly into Mrs. Leroy's room, and gently apprised her of Iola's arrival. In a darkened room lay the stricken mother, almost distracted by her late bereavement.

"Oh, Iola," she exclaimed, as her daughter entered, "is this you? I am so sorry you came."

Then, burying her head in Iola's bosom, she wept convulsively. "Much as I love you," she continued, between her sobs, "and much as I longed to see you, I am sorry you came."

"Why, mother," replied Iola, astonished, "I received your telegram last Wednesday, and I took the earliest train I could get."

"My dear child, I never sent you a telegram. It was a trick to bring you down South and reduce you to slavery."

Iola eyed her mother curiously. What did she mean? Had grief dethroned her reason? Yet her eye was clear, her manner perfectly rational.

Marie saw the astounded look on Iola's face, and nerving herself to the task, said: "Iola, I must tell you what your father always enjoined me to be silent about. I did not think it was the wisest thing, but I yielded to his desires. I have negro blood in my veins. I was your father's slave before I married him. His relatives have set aside his will. The courts have declared our marriage null and void and my manumission illegal, and we are all to be remanded to slavery."

An expression of horror and anguish swept over Iola's face, and, turning deathly pale, she exclaimed, "Oh, mother, it can't be so! you must be dreaming!"

"No, my child; it is a terrible reality."

Almost wild with agony, Iola paced the floor, as the fearful truth broke in crushing anguish upon her mind.

Then bursting into a paroxysm of tears succeeded by peals of hysterical laughter, said:—

"I used to say that slavery is right. I didn't know what I was talking about." Then growing calmer, she said, "Mother, who is at the bottom of this downright robbery?"

"Alfred Lorraine; I have always dreaded that man, and what I feared has come to pass. Your father had faith in him; I never had."

"But, mother, could we not contest his claim. You have your marriage certificate and papa's will."

"Yes, my dear child, but Judge Starkins has decided that we have no standing in the court, and no testimony according to law."

"Oh, mother, what can I do?"

"Nothing, my child, unless you can escape to the North."

"And leave you?"

"Yes."

"Mother, I will never desert you in your hour of trial. But can nothing be done? Had father no friends who would assist us?"

"None that I know of. I do not think he had an acquaintance who approved of our marriage. The neighboring planters have stood so aloof from me that I do not know where to turn for either help or sympathy. I believe it was Lorraine who sent the telegram. I wrote to you as soon as I could after your father's death, but fainted just as I finished directing the letter. I do not think he knows where your brother is, and, if possible, he must not know. If you can by any means, *do* send a letter to Harry and warn him not to attempt to come home. I don't know how you will succeed, for Lorraine has us all under surveillance. But it is according to law."

"What law, mother?"

"The law of the strong against the weak."

"Oh, mother, it seems like a dreadful dream, a fearful nightmare! But I cannot shake it off. Where is Gracie?"

"The dear child has been running down ever since her papa's death. She clung to me night and day while I had the brain fever, and could not be persuaded to leave me. She hardly ate anything for more than a week. She has been dangerously ill for several days, and the doctor says she cannot live. The fever has exhausted all her rallying power, and yet, dear as she is to me, I would rather consign her to the deepest grave than see her forced to be a slave."

"So would I. I wish I could die myself."

"Oh, Iola, do not talk so. Strive to be a Christian, to have faith in the darkest hour. Were it not for my hope of heaven I couldn't stand all this trouble."

"Mother, are these people Christians who made these laws which are robbing us of our inheritance and reducing us to slavery? If this is Christianity I hate and despise it. Would the most cruel heathen do worse?"

"My dear child, I have not learned my Christianity from them. I have learned it at the foot of the cross, and from this book," she said, placing a New Testament in Iola's hands. "Some of the most beautiful lessons of faith and trust I have ever learned were from among our lowly people in their humble cabins."

"Mamma!" called a faint voice from the adjoining room. Marie immediately arose and went to the bedside of her sick child, where Mammy Liza was holding her faithful vigils. The child had just awakened from a fitful sleep.

"I thought," she said, "that I heard Iola's voice. Has she come?"

"Yes, darling; do you want to see her?"

"Oh, yes," she said, as a bright smile broke over her dying features.

Iola passed quickly into the room. Gracie reached out her thin, bloodless hand, clasped Iola's palm in hers, and said: "I am so glad you have come. Dear Iola, stand by mother. You and Harry are all she has. It is not hard to die. You and mother and Harry must meet me in heaven."

Swiftly the tidings went through the house that Gracie was dying. The servants gathered around her with tearful eyes, as she bade them all good-bye. When she had finished, and Mammy had lowered the pillow, an unwonted radiance lit up her eye, and an expression of ineffable gladness overspread her face, as she murmured: "It is beautiful, so beautiful!" Fainter and fainter grew her voice, until, without a struggle or sigh, she passed away beyond the oower of oppression and prejudice.

CHAPTER XIII.

A REJECTED SUITOR.

VERY unexpected was Dr. Gresham's proposal to Iola. She had heartily enjoyed his society and highly valued his friendship, but he had never been associated in her mind with either love or marriage. As he held her hand in his a tell-tale flush rose to her cheek, a look of grateful surprise beamed from her eye, but it was almost immediately succeeded by an air of inexpressible sadness, a drooping of her eyelids, and an increasing pallor of her cheek. She withdrew her hand from his, shook her head sadly, and said:—

"No, Doctor; that can never be. I am very grateful to you for your kindness. I value your friendship, but neither gratitude nor friendship is love, and I have nothing more than those to give."

"Not at present," said Dr. Gresham; "but may I not hope your friendship will ripen into love?"

"Doctor, I could not promise. I do not think that I should. There are barriers between us that I cannot pass. Were you to know them I think you would say the same."

Just then the ambulance brought in a wounded scout, and Iola found relief from the wounds of her own heart in attending to his.

Dr. Gresham knew the barrier that lay between them. It was one which his love had surmounted. But he was too noble and generous to take advantage of her loneliness to press his suit. He had lived in a part of the country where he had scarcely ever seen a colored person, and around the race their misfortunes had thrown a halo of romance. To him the negro was a picturesque being, over whose woes he had wept when a child, and whose wrongs he was ready to redress when a man. But when he saw the lovely girl who had been rescued by the commander of the post from the clutches of slavery, all the manhood and chivalry in his nature arose in her behalf, and he was ready to lay on the altar of her heart his first grand and overmastering love. Not discouraged by her refusal, but determined to overcome her objections, Dr. Gresham resolved that he would abide his time.

Iola was not indifferent to Dr. Gresham. She admired his manliness and respected his character. He was tall and handsome, a fine specimen of the best brain and heart of New England. He had been nurtured under grand and ennobling influences. His father was a devoted Abolitionist. His mother was kind-hearted, but somewhat exclusive and aristocratic. She would have looked upon his marriage with Iola as a mistake and feared that such an alliance would hurt the prospects of her daughters.

During Iola's stay in the North, she had learned enough of the racial feeling to influence her decision in reference to Dr. Gresham's offer. Iola, like other girls, had had her beautiful day-dreams before she was rudely awakened by the fate which had dragged her into the depths of slavery. In the chambers of her imagery were pictures of noble deeds; of high, heroic men, knightly, tender, true, and brave. In Dr. Gresham she saw the ideal of her soul exemplified. But in her lonely condition, with all its background of terrible sorrow and deep abasement, she had never for a moment thought of giving or receiving love from one of that race who had been so lately associated in her mind with horror, aversion, and disgust. His kindness to her had been a new experience. His companionship was an unexpected pleasure. She had learned to enjoy his presence and to miss him when absent, and when she began to question her heart she found that unconsciously it was entwining around him.

"Yes," she said to herself, "I do like him; but I can never marry him. To the man I marry my heart must be as open as the flowers to the sun. I could not accept his hand and hide from him the secret of my birth; and I could not consent to choose the happiest lot on earth without first finding my poor heart-stricken and desolate mother. Perhaps some day I may have the courage to tell him my sad story, and then make my heart the sepulchre in which to bury all the love which might have gladdened and brightened my whole life."

During the sad and weary months which ensued while the war dragged its slow length along, Dr. Gresham and Iola often met by the bedsides of the wounded and dying, and sometimes he would drop a few words at which her heart would beat quicker and her cheek flush more vividly. But he was so kind, tender, and respectful, that Iola had no idea he knew her race affiliations. She knew from unmistakable signs that Dr. Gresham had learned to love her, and that he had power to call forth the warmest affection of her soul; but she fought with her own heart and repressed its rising love. She felt that it was best for his sake that they should not marry. When she saw the evidences of his increasing love she regretted that she had not informed him at the first of the barrier that lay between them; it might have saved him unnecessary suffering. Thinking thus, Iola resolved, at whatever cost of pain it might be to herself, to explain to Dr. Gresham what she meant by the insurmountable barrier. Iola, after a continuous strain upon her nervous system for months, began to suffer from general debility and nervous depression. Dr. Gresham saw the increasing pallor on Iola's cheek and the loss of buoyancy in her step. One morning, as she turned from the bed of a young soldier for whom she had just written a letter to his mother, there was such a look of pity and sorrow on her face that Dr. Gresham's whole heart went out in sympathy for her, and he resolved to break the silence he had imposed upon himself.

"Iola," he said, and there was a depth of passionate tenderness in his voice, a volume of unexpressed affection in his face, "you are wronging yourself. You are sinking beneath burdens too heavy for you to bear. It seems to me that besides the constant drain upon your sympathies there is some great sorrow preying upon your life; some burden that ought to be shared." He gazed upon her so ardently that each cord of her heart seemed to vibrate, and unbidden tears sprang to her lustrous eyes, as she said, sadly:—

"Doctor, you are right."

"Iola, my heart is longing to lift those burdens from your life. Love, like faith, laughs at impossibilities. I can conceive of no barrier too high for my love to surmount. Consent to be mine, as nothing else on earth is mine."

"Doctor, you know not what you ask," replied Iola. "Instead of coming into this hospital a self-sacrificing woman, laying her every gift and advantage upon the altar of her country, I came as a rescued slave, glad to find a refuge from a fate more cruel than death; a fate from which I was rescued by the intervention of my dear dead friend, Thomas Anderson. I was born on a lonely plantation on the Mississippi River, where the white population was very sparse. We had no neighbors who ever visited us; no young white girls with whom I ever played in my childhood; but, never having enjoyed such companionship, I was unconscious of any sense of privation. Our parents spared no pains to make the lives of their children (we were three) as bright and pleasant as they could. Our home was so happy. We had a large number of servants, who were devoted to us. I never had the faintest suspicion that there was any wrongfulness in slavery, and I never dreamed of the dreadful fate which broke in a storm of fearful anguish over our devoted heads. Papa used to take us to New Orleans to see the Mardi Gras, and while there we visited the theatres and other places of amusement and interest. At home we had books, papers, and magazines to beguile our time. Perfectly ignorant of my racial connection, I was sent to a Northern academy, and soon made many friends among my fellow-students. Companionship with girls of my own age was a new experience, which I thoroughly enjoyed. I spent several years in New England, and was busily preparing for my commencement exercises when my father was snatched away—died of yellow fever on his way North to witness my graduation. Through a stratagem, I was brought hurriedly from the North, and found that my father was dead; that his nearest kinsman had taken possession of our property; that my mother's marriage had been declared illegal, because of an imperceptible infusion of negro blood in her veins; and that she and her children had been remanded to slavery. I was torn from my mother, sold as a slave, and subjected to cruel indignities, from which I was rescued and a place given to me in this hospital. Doctor, I did not choose my lot in life, but I have no other alternative than to accept it. The intense horror and agony I felt when I was first told the story are over. Thoughts and purposes have come to me in the shadow I should never have learned in the sunshine. I am constantly rousing myself up to suffer and be strong. I intend, when this conflict is over, to cast my lot with the freed people as a helper, teacher, and friend. I have passed through a fiery ordeal, but this ministry of suffering will not be in vain. I feel that my mind has matured beyond my years. I am a wonder to myself. It seems as if years had been compressed into a few short months. In telling you this, do you not, can you not, see that there is an insurmountable barrier between us?"

"No, I do not," replied Dr. Gresham. "I love you for your own sake. And with this the disadvantages of birth have nothing to do."

"You say so now, and I believe that you are perfectly sincere. To-day your friendship springs from compassion, but, when that subsides, might you not look on me as an inferior?"

"Iola, you do not understand me. You think too meanly of me. You must not judge me by the worst of my race. Surely our country has produced a higher type of manhood than the men by whom you were tried and tempted."

"Tried, but not tempted," said Iola, as a deep flush overspread her face; "I was never tempted. I was sold from State to State as an article of merchandise. I had outrages heaped on me which might well crimson the cheek of honest womanhood with shame, but I never fell into the clutches of an owner for whom I did not feel the utmost loathing and intensest horror. I have heard men talk glibly of the degradation of the negro, but there is a vast difference between abasement of condition and degradation of character. I was abased, but the men who trampled on me were the degraded ones."

"But, Iola, you must not blame all for what a few have done."

"A few have done? Did not the whole nation consent to our abasement?" asked Iola, bitterly.

"No, Miss Iola, we did not all consent to it. Slavery drew a line of cleavage in this country. Although we were under one government we were farther apart in our sentiments than if we had been divided by lofty mountains and separated by wide seas. And had not Northern sentiment been brought to bear against the institution, slavery would have been intact until to-day."

"But, Doctor, the negro is under a social ban both North and South. Our enemies have the ear of the world, and they can depict us just as they please."

"That is true; but the negro has no other alternative than to make friends of his calamities. Other men have plead his cause, but out of the race must come its own defenders. With them the pen must be mightier than the sword. It is the weapon of civilization, and they must use it in their own defense. We cannot tell what is in them until they express themselves."

"Yes, and I think there is a large amount of latent and undeveloped ability in the race, which they will learn to use for their own benefit. This my hospital experience has taught me."

"But," said Dr. Gresham, "they must learn to struggle, labor, and achieve. By facts, not theories, they will be judged in the future. The Anglo-Saxon race is proud, domineering, aggressive, and impatient of a rival, and, as I think, has more capacity for dragging down a weaker race than uplifting it. They have been a conquering and achieving people, marvelous in their triumphs of mind over matter. They have manifested the traits of character which are developed by success and victory."

"And yet," said Iola, earnestly, "I believe the time will come when the civilization of the negro will assume a better phase than you Anglo-Saxons possess. You will prove unworthy of your high vantage ground if you only use your superior ability to victimize feebler races and minister to a selfish greed of gold and a love of domination."

"But, Iola," said Dr. Gresham, a little impatiently, "what has all this to do with our marriage? Your complexion is as fair as mine. What is to hinder you from sharing my Northern home, from having my mother to be your mother?" The tones of his voice grew tender, as he raised his eyes to Iola's face and anxiously awaited her reply.

"Dr. Gresham," said Iola, sadly, "should the story of my life be revealed to your family, would they be willing to ignore all the traditions of my blood, forget all the terrible humiliations through which I have passed? I have too much self-respect to enter your home under a veil of concealment. I have lived in New England. I love the sunshine of her homes and the freedom of her institutions. But New England is not free from racial prejudice, and I would never enter a family where I would be an unwelcome member."

"Iola, dear, you have nothing to fear in that direction."

"Doctor," she said, and a faint flush rose to her cheek, "suppose we should marry, and little children in after years should nestle in our arms, and one of them show unmistakable signs of color, would you be satisfied?"

She looked steadfastly into his eyes, which fell beneath her truth-seeking gaze. His face flushed as if the question had suddenly perplexed him. Iola saw the irresolution on his face, and framed her answer accordingly.

"Ah, I see," she said, "that you are puzzled. You had not taken into account what might result from such a marriage. I will relieve you from all embarrassment by simply saying I cannot be your wife. When the war is over I intend to search the country for my mother. Doctor, were you to give me a palace-like home, with velvet carpets to hush my tread, and magnificence to surround my way, I should miss her voice amid all other tones, her presence amid every scene. Oh, you do not know how hungry my heart is for my mother! Were I to marry you I would carry an aching heart into your home and dim its brightness. I have resolved never to marry until I have found my mother. The hope of finding her has colored all my life since I regained my freedom. It has helped sustain me in the hour of fearful trial. When I see her I want to have the proud consciousness that I bring her back a heart just as loving, faithful, and devoted as the last hour we parted."

"And is this your final answer?"

"It is. I have pledged my life to that resolve, and I believe time and patience will reward me."

There was a deep shadow of sorrow and disappointment on the face of Dr. Gresham as he rose to leave. For a moment he held her hand as it lay limp in his own. If she wavered in her determination it was only for a moment. No quivering of her lip or paling of her cheek betrayed any struggle of her heart. Her resolve was made, and his words were powerless to swerve her from the purpose of her soul.

After Dr. Gresham had gone Iola went to her room and sat buried in thought. It seemed as if the fate of Tantalus was hers, without his crimes. Here she was lonely and heart-stricken, and unto her was presented the offer of love, home, happiness, and social position; the heart and hand of a man too noble and generous to refuse her companionship for life on account of the blood in her veins. Why should she refuse these desirable boons? But, mingling with these beautiful visions of manly love and protecting care she saw the anguish of her heart-stricken mother and the pale, sweet face of her dying sister, as with her latest breath she had said, "Iola, stand by mamma!"

"No, no," she said to herself; "I was right to refuse Dr. Gresham. How dare I dream of happiness when my poor mamma's heart may be slowly breaking? I should be ashamed to live and ashamed to die were I to choose a happy lot for myself and leave poor mamma to struggle alone. I will never be satisfied till I get tidings of her. And when I have found her I will do all I can to cheer and brighten the remnant of her life."

CHAPTER XIV.

HARRY LEROY.

IT was several weeks after Iola had written to her brother that her letter reached him. The trusty servant to whom she delivered it watched his opportunity to mail it. At last he succeeded in slipping it into Lorraine's mail and dropping them all into the post-office together. Harry was studying at a boys' academy in Maine. His father had given that State the preference because, while on a visit there, he had been favorably impressed with the kindness and hospitality of the people. He had sent his son a large sum of money, and given him permission to spend awhile with some school-chums till he was ready to bring the family North, where they could all spend the summer together. Harry had returned from his visit, and was looking for letters and remittances from home, when a letter, all crumpled, was handed him by the principal of the academy. He recognized his sister's handwriting and eagerly opened the letter. As he read, he turned very pale; then a deep flush overspread his face and an angry light flashed from his eyes. As he read on, his face became still paler; he gasped for breath and fell into a swoon. Appalled at the sudden change which had swept over him like a deadly sirocco, the principal rushed to the fallen boy, picked up the missive that lay beside him, and immediately rang for help and dispatched for the doctor. The doctor came at once and was greatly puzzled. Less than an hour before, he had seen him with a crowd of merry, laughter-loving boys, apparently as light-hearted and joyous as any of them; now he lay with features drawn and pinched, his face deadly pale, as if some terrible suffering had sent all the blood in his veins to stagnate around his heart. Harry opened his eyes, shuddered, and relapsed into silence. The doctor, all at sea in regard to the cause of the sudden attack, did all that he could to restore him to consciousness and quiet the perturbation of his spirit. He succeeded, but found he was strangely silent. A terrible shock had sent a tremor through every nerve, and the doctor watched with painful apprehension its effect upon his reason. Giving him an opiate and enjoining that he should be kept perfectly quiet, the doctor left the room, sought the principal, and said:—

"Mr. Bascom, here is a case that baffles my skill. I saw that boy pass by my window not more than half an hour ago, full of animation, and now he lies hovering between life and death. I have great apprehension for his reason. Can you throw any light on the subject?"

Mr. Bascom hesitated.

"I am not asking you as a matter of idle curiosity, but as a physician. I must have all the light I can get in making my diagnosis of the case."

The principal arose, went to his desk, took out the letter which he had picked up from the floor, and laid it in the physician's hand. As the doctor read, a look of indignant horror swept over his face. Then he said: "Can it be possible! I never suspected such a thing. It must be a cruel, senseless hoax."

"Doctor," said Mr. Bascom, "I have been a life-long Abolitionist and have often read of the cruelties and crimes of American slavery, but never before did I realize the low moral tone of the social life under which such shameless cruelties could be practiced on a defenseless widow and her orphaned children. Let me read the letter again. Just look at it, all tear-blotted and written with a trembling hand:—

'DEAR BROTHER:—I have dreadful news for you and I hardly know how to tell it. Papa and Gracie are both dead. He died of yellow fever. Mamma is almost distracted. Papa's cousin has taken possession of our property, and instead of heirs we are chattels. Mamma has explained the whole situation to me. She was papa's slave before she married. He loved her, manumitted, educated, and married her. When he died Mr. Lorraine entered suit for his property and Judge Starkins has decided in his favor. The decree of the court has made their marriage invalid, robbed us of our inheritance, and remanded us all to slavery. Mamma is too wretched to attempt to write herself, but told me to entreat you not to attempt to come home. You can do us no good, and that mean, cruel Lorraine may do you much harm. Don't attempt, I beseech you, to come home. Show this letter to Mr. Bascom and let him advise you what to do. But don't, for our sake, attempt to come home.

'Your heart-broken sister,

'IOLA LEROY.'"

"This," said the doctor, "is a very awkward affair. The boy is too ill to be removed. It is doubtful if the nerves which have trembled with such fearful excitement will ever recover their normal condition. It is simply a work of mercy to watch over him with the tenderest care."

Fortunately for Harry he had fallen into good hands, and the most tender care and nursing were bestowed upon him. For awhile Harry was strangely silent, never referring to the terrible misfortune which had so suddenly overshadowed his life. It seemed as if the past were suddenly blotted out of his memory. But he was young and of an excellent constitution, and in a few months he was slowly recovering.

"Doctor," said he one day, as the physician sat at his bedside, "I seem to have had a dreadful dream, and to have dreamt that my father was dead, and my mother and sister were in terrible trouble, but I could not help them. Doctor, was it a dream, or was it a reality? It could not have been a dream, for when I fell asleep the grass was green and the birds were singing, but now the winds are howling and the frost is on the ground. Doctor, tell me how it is? How long have I been here?"

Sitting by his bedside, and taking his emaciated hand in his, the doctor said, in a kind, fatherly tone: "My dear boy, you have been very ill, and everything depends on your keeping quiet, very quiet."

As soon as he was strong enough the principal gave him his letter to read.

"But, Mr. Bascom," Harry said, "I do not understand this. It says my mother and father were legally married. How could her marriage be set aside and her children robbed of their inheritance? This is not a heathen country. I hardly think barbarians would have done any worse; yet this is called a Christian country."

"Christian in name," answered the principal. "When your father left you in my care, knowing that I was an Abolitionist, he confided his secret to me. He said that life was full of vicissitudes, and he wished you to have a good education. He wanted you and your sister to be prepared for any emergency. He did not wish you to know that you had negro blood in your veins. He knew that the spirit of caste pervaded the nation, North and South, and he was very anxious to have his children freed from its depressing influences. He did not intend to stay South after you had finished your education."

"But," said Harry, "I cannot understand. If my mother was lawfully married, how could they deprive her of her marital rights?"

"When Lorraine," continued Mr. Bascom, "knew your father was dead, all he had to do was to find a flaw in her manumission, and, of course, the marriage became illegal. She could not then inherit property nor maintain her freedom; and her children followed her condition."

Harry listened attentively. Things which had puzzled him once now became perfectly clear. He sighed heavily, and, turning to the principal, said: "I see things in a new light. Now I remember that none of the planters' wives ever visited my mother; and we never went to church except when my father took us to the Cathedral in New Orleans. My father was a Catholic, but I don't think mamma is."

"Now, Harry," said the principal, "life is before you. If you wish to stay North, I will interest friends in your behalf, and try to get you a situation. Going South is out of the question. It is probable that by this time your mother and sister are removed from their home. You are powerless to fight against the law that enslaved them. Should you fall into the clutches of Lorraine, he might give you a great deal of trouble. You would be pressed into the Confederate service to help them throw up barricades, dig trenches, and add to the strength of those who enslaved your mother and sister."

"Never! never!" cried Harry. "I would rather die than do it! I should despise myself forever if I did."

"Numbers of our young men," said Mr. Bascom, "have gone to the war which is now raging between North and South. You have been sick for several months, and much has taken place of which you are unaware. Would you like to enlist?"

"I certainly would; not so much for the sake of fighting for the Government, as with the hope of finding my mother and sister, and avenging their wrongs. I should like to meet Lorraine on the battle-field."

"What kind of a regiment would you prefer, white or colored?"

Harry winced when the question was asked. He felt the reality of his situation as he had not done before. It was as if two paths had suddenly opened before him, and he was forced to choose between them. On one side were strength, courage, enterprise, power of achievement, and memories of a wonderful past. On the other side were weakness, ignorance, poverty, and the proud world's social scorn. He knew nothing of colored people except as slaves, and his whole soul shrank from equalizing himself with them. He was fair enough to pass unchallenged among the fairest in the land, and yet a Christless prejudice had decreed that he should be a social pariah. He sat, thoughtful and undecided, as if a great struggle were going on in his mind. Finally the principal said, "I do not think that you should be assigned to a colored regiment because of the blood in your veins, but you will have, in such a regiment, better facilities for finding your mother and sister."

"You are right, Mr. Bascom. To find my mother and sister I call no task too heavy, no sacrifice too great."

Since Harry had come North he had learned to feel profound pity for the slave. But there is a difference between looking on a man as an object of pity and protecting him as such, and being identified with him and forced to share his lot. To take his place with them on the arena of life was the test of his life, but love was stronger than pride.

His father was dead. His mother and sister were enslaved by a mockery of justice. It was more than a matter of choice where he should stand on the racial question. He felt that he must stand where he could strike the most effective blow for their freedom. With that thought strong in his mind, and as soon as he recovered, he went westward to find a colored regiment. He told the recruiting officer that he wished to be assigned to a colored regiment.

"Why do you wish that," said the officer, looking at Harry with an air of astonishment.

"Because I am a colored man."

The officer look puzzled. It was a new experience. He had seen colored men with fair complexions anxious to lose their identity with the colored race and pose as white men, but here was a man in the flush of his early manhood, to whom could come dreams of promotion from a simple private to a successful general, deliberately turning his back upon every gilded hope and dazzling opportunity, to cast his lot with the despised and hated negro.

"I do not understand you," said the officer. "Surely you are a white man, and, as such, I will enlist you in a white regiment."

"No," said Harry, firmly, "I am a colored man, and unless I can be assigned to a colored regiment I am not willing to enter the army."

"Well," said the officer, "you are the d—d'st fool I ever saw—a man as white as you are turning his back upon his chances of promotion! But you can take your choice."

So Harry was permitted to enter the army. By his promptness and valor he soon won the hearts of his superior officers, and was made drill sergeant. Having nearly all of his life been used to colored people, and being taught by his mother to be kind and respectful to them, he was soon able to gain their esteem. He continued in the regiment until Grant began the task of opening the Mississippi. After weeks of fruitless effort, Grant marched his army down the west side of the river, while the gunboats undertook the perilous task of running the batteries. Men were found for the hour. The volunteers offered themselves in such numbers that lots were cast to determine who should have the opportunity to enlist in an enterprise so fraught with danger. Harry was one on whom the lot fell.

Grant crossed the river below, coiled his forces around Vicksburg like a boa-constrictor, and held it in his grasp. After forty-seven days of endurance the city surrendered to him. Port Hudson, after the surrender of Vicksburg, gave up the unequal contest, and the Mississippi was open to the Gulf.

CHAPTER XV.

ROBERT AND HIS COMPANY.

"GOOD morning, gentlemen," said Robert Johnson, as he approached Colonel Robinson, the commander of the post, who was standing at the door of his tent, talking with Captain Sybil.

"Good morning," responded Colonel Robinson, "I am glad you have come. I was just about to send for you. How is your company getting on?"

"First rate, sir," replied Robert.

"In good health?"

"Excellent. They are all in good health and spirits. Our boys are used to hardship and exposure, and the hope of getting their freedom puts new snap into them."

"I am glad of it," said Colonel Robinson. "They make good fighters and very useful allies. Last night we received very valuable intelligence from some fugitives who had escaped through the Rebel lines. I do not think many of the Northern people realize the service they have been to us in bringing information and helping our boys when escaping from Rebel prisons. I never knew a full-blooded negro to betray us. A month ago, when we were encamped near the Rebel lines, a colored woman managed admirably to keep us posted as to the intended movements of the enemy. She was engaged in laundry work, and by means of hanging her sheets in different ways gave us the right signals."

"I hope," said Captain Sybil, "that the time will come when some faithful historian will chronicle all the deeds of daring and service these people have performed during this struggle, and give them due credit therefor."

"Our great mistake," said Colonel Robinson, "was our long delay in granting them their freedom, and even what we have done is only partial. The border States still retain their slaves. We ought to have made a clean sweep of the whole affair. Slavery is a serpent which we nourished in its weakness, and now it is stinging us in its strength."

"I think so, too," said Captain Sybil. "But in making his proclamation of freedom, perhaps Mr. Lincoln went as far as he thought public opinion would let him."

"It is remarkable," said Colonel Robinson, "how these Secesh hold out. It surprises me to see how poor white men, who, like the negroes, are victims of slavery, rally around the Stripes and Bars. These men, I believe, have been looked down on by the aristocratic slaveholders, and despised by the well-fed and comfortable slaves, yet they follow their leaders into the very jaws of death; face hunger, cold, disease, and danger; and all for what? What, under heaven, are they fighting for? Now, the negro, ignorant as he is, has learned to regard our flag as a banner of freedom, and to look forward to his deliverance as a consequence of the overthrow of the Rebellion."

"I think," said Captain Sybil "that these ignorant white men have been awfully deceived. They have had presented to their imaginations utterly false ideas of the results of Secession, and have been taught that its success would bring them advantages which they had never enjoyed in the Union."

"And I think," said Colonel Robinson, "that the women and ministers have largely fed and fanned the fires of this Rebellion, and have helped to create a public opinion which has swept numbers of benighted men into the conflict. Well might one of their own men say, 'This is a rich man's war and a poor man's fight.' They were led into it through their ignorance, and held in it by their fears."

"I think," said Captain Sybil, "that if the public school had been common through the South this war would never have occurred. Now things have reached such a pass that able-bodied men must report at headquarters, or be treated as deserters. Their leaders are desperate men, of whom it has been said: 'They have robbed the cradle and the grave.'"

"They are fighting against fearful odds," said Colonel Robinson, "and their defeat is only a question of time."

"As soon," said Robert, "as they fired on Fort Sumter, Uncle Daniel, a dear old father who had been praying and hoping for freedom, said to me: 'Dey's fired on Fort Sumter, an' mark my words, Bob, de Norf 's boun' ter whip.'"

"Had we freed the slaves at the outset," said Captain Sybil, "we wouldn't have given the Rebels so much opportunity to strengthen themselves by means of slave labor in raising their crops, throwing up their entrenchments, and building their fortifications. Slavery was a deadly cancer eating into the life of the nation; but, somehow, it had cast such a glamour over us that we have acted somewhat as if our national safety were better preserved by sparing the cancer than by cutting it out."

"Political and racial questions have sadly complicated this matter," said Colonel Robinson. "The North is not wholly made up of anti-slavery people. At the beginning of this war we were not permeated with justice, and so were not ripe for victory. The battle of Bull Run inaugurated the war by a failure. Instead of glory we gathered shame, and defeat in place of victory."

"We have been slow," said Captain Sybil, "to see our danger and to do our duty. Our delay has cost us thousands of lives and millions of dollars. Yet it may be it is all for the best. Our national wound was too deep to be lightly healed. When the President issued his Emancipation Proclamation my heart overflowed with joy, and I said: 'This is the first bright rift in the war cloud.'"

"And did you really think that they would accept the terms of freedom and lay down their arms?" asked Robert.

"I hardly thought they would," continued Captain Sybil. "I did not think that their leaders would permit it. I believe the rank and file of their army are largely composed of a mass of ignorance, led, manipulated, and moulded by educated and ambitious wickedness. In attempting to overthrow the Union, a despotism and reign of terror were created which encompassed them as fetters of iron, and they will not accept the conditions until they have reached the last extremity. I hardly think they are yet willing to confess that such extremity has been reached."

"Captain," said Robert, as they left Colonel Robinson's tent, "I have lived all my life where I have had a chance to hear the 'Secesh' talk, and when they left their papers around I used to read everything I could lay my hands on. It seemed to me that the big white men not only ruled over the poor whites and made laws for them, but over the whole nation."

"That was so," replied Captain Sybil. "The North was strong but forbearing. It was busy in trade and commerce, and permitted them to make the Northern States hunting-grounds for their slaves. When we sent back Simms and Burns from beneath the shadow of Bunker Hill Monument and Faneuil Hall, they mistook us; looked upon us as a lot of money-grabbers, who would be willing to purchase peace at any price. I do not believe when they fired on the 'Star of the West' that they had the least apprehension of the fearful results which were to follow their madness and folly."

"Well, Captain," asked Robert, "if the free North would submit to be called on to help them catch their slaves, what could be expected of us, who all our lives had known no other condition than that of slavery? How much braver would you have been, if your first recollections had been those of seeing your mother maltreated, your father cruelly beaten, or your fellow-servants brutally murdered? I wonder why they never enslaved the Indians!"

"You are mistaken, Robert, if you think the Indians were never enslaved. I have read that the Spaniards who visited the coasts of America kidnapped thousands of Indians, whom they sent to Europe and the West Indies as slaves. Columbus himself, we are informed, captured five hundred natives, and sent them to Spain. The Indian had the lesser power of endurance, and Las Cassas suggested the enslavement of the negro, because he seemed to possess greater breadth of physical organization and stronger power of endurance. Slavery was an old world's crime which, I have heard, the Indians never practiced among themselves. Perhaps it would have been harder to reduce them to slavery and hold them in bondage when they had a vast continent before them, where they could hide in the fastnesses of its mountains or the seclusion of its forests, than it was for white men to visit the coasts of Africa and, with their superior knowledge, obtain cargoes of slaves, bring them across the ocean, hem them in on the plantations, and surround them with a pall of dense ignorance."

"I remember," said Robert, "in reading a history I once came across at our house, that when the Africans first came to this country they did not all speak one language. Some had only met as mutual enemies. They were not all one color, their complexions ranging from tawny yellow to deep black."

"Yes," said Captain Sybil, "and in dealing with the negro we wanted his labor; in dealing with the Indian we wanted his lands. For one we had weapons of war; for the other we had real and invisible chains, the coercion of force, and the terror of the unseen world."

"That's exactly so, Captain! When I was a boy I used to hear the old folks tell what would happen to bad people in another world; about the devil pouring hot lead down people's throats and stirring them up with a pitch-fork; and I used to get so scared that I would be afraid to go to bed at night. I don't suppose the Indians ever heard of such things, or, if they had, I never heard of them being willing to give away all their lands on earth, and quietly wait for a home in heaven."

"But, surely, Robert, you do not think religion has degraded the negro?"

"Oh, I wouldn't say that. But a man is in a tight fix when he takes his part, like Nat Turner or Denmark Veasy, and is made to fear that he will be hanged in this world and be burned in the next. And, since I come to think of it, we colored folks used to get mightily mixed up about our religion. Mr. Gundover had on his plantation a real smart man. He was religious, but he would steal."

"Oh, Robert," queried Sybil, "how could he be religious and steal?"

"He didn't think," retorted Robert, "it was any harm to steal from his master. I guess he thought it was right to get from his master all he could. He would have thought it wrong to steal from his fellow-servants. He thought that downright mean, but I wouldn't have insured the lives of Gundover's pigs and chickens, if Uncle Jack got them in a tight place. One day there was a minister stopping with Mr. Gundover. As a matter of course, in speaking of his servants, he gave Jack's sins an airing. He would much rather confess Jack's sins than his own. Now Gundover wanted to do two things, save his pigs and poultry, and save Jack's soul. He told the minister that Jack was a liar and a thief, and gave the minister a chance to talk with Uncle Jack about the state of his soul. Uncle Jack listened very quietly, and when taxed with stealing his master's wheat he was ready with an answer. 'Now

Massa Parker,' said Jack, 'lem'me tell yer jis' how it war 'bout dat wheat. Wen ole Jack com'd down yere, dis place war all growed up in woods. He go ter work, clared up de groun' an' plowed, an' planted, an' riz a crap, an' den wen it war all done, he hadn't a dollar to buy his ole woman a gown; an' he jis' took a bag ob wheat.'"

"What did Mr. Parker say?" asked Sybil.

"I don't know, though I reckon he didn't think it was a bad steal after all, but I don't suppose he told Jack so. When he came to the next point, about Jack's lying, I suppose he thought he had a clear case; but Jack was equal to the occasion."

"How did he clear up that charge?" interrogated Captain Sybil.

"Finely. I think if he had been educated he would have made a first-rate lawyer. He said, 'Marse Parker, dere's old Joe. His wife don't lib on dis plantation. Old Joe go ober ter see her, but he stayed too long, an' didn't git back in time fer his work. Massa's oberseer kotched him an' cut him all up. When de oberseer went inter de house, pore old Joe war all tired an' beat up, an' so he lay down by de fence corner and go ter sleep. Bimeby Massa oberseer com'd an' axed, "all bin a workin' libely?" I say "Yes, Massa."' Then said Mr. Parker, 'You were lying, Joe had been sleeping, not working.' 'I know's dat, but ef I tole on Joe, Massa oberseer cut him all up again, and Massa Jesus says, "Blessed am de Peacemaker."' I heard, continued Robert, that Mr. Parker said to Gundover, 'You seem to me like a man standing in a stream where the blood of Jesus can reach you, but you are standing between it and your slaves. How will you answer that in the Day of Judgment?'"

"What did Gundover say?" asked Captain Sybil.

"He turned pale, and said, 'For God's sake don't speak of the Day of Judgment in connection with slavery.'"

Just then a messenger brought a communication to Captain Sybil. He read it attentively, and, turning to Robert, said, "Here are orders for an engagement at Five Forks to-morrow. Oh, this wasting of life and scattering of treasure might have been saved had we only been wiser. But the time is passing. Look after your company, and see that everything is in readiness as soon as possible."

Carefully Robert superintended the arrangements for the coming battle of a strife which for years had thrown its crimson shadows over the land. The Rebels fought with a valor worthy of a better cause. The disaster of Bull Run had been retrieved. Sherman had made his famous march to the sea. Fighting Joe Hooker had scaled the stronghold of the storm king and won a victory in the palace chamber of the clouds; the Union soldiers had captured Columbia, replanted the Stars and Stripes in Charleston, and changed that old sepulchre of slavery into the cradle of a new-born freedom. Farragut had been as triumphant on water as the other generals had been victorious on land, and New Orleans had been wrenched from the hands of the Confederacy. The Rebel leaders were obstinate. Misguided hordes had followed them to defeat and death. Grant was firm and determined to fight it out if it took all summer. The closing battles were fought with desperate courage and firm resistance, but at last the South was forced to succumb. On the ninth day of April, 1865, General Lee surrendered to General Grant. The lost cause went down in blood and tears, and on the brows of a ransomed people God poured the chrism of a new era, and they stood a race newly anointed with freedom.

CHAPTER XVI.

AFTER THE BATTLE.

VERY sad and heart-rending were the scenes with which Iola came in constant contact. Well may Christian men and women labor and pray for the time when nations shall learn war no more; when, instead of bloody conflicts, there shall be peaceful arbitration. The battle in which Robert fought, after his last conversation with Captain Sybil, was one of the decisive struggles of the closing conflict. The mills of doom and fate had ground out a fearful grist of agony and death,

> "And lives of men and souls of States
> Were thrown like chaff beyond the gates."

Numbers were taken prisoners. Pale, young corpses strewed the earth; manhood was stricken down in the flush of its energy and prime. The ambulances brought in the wounded and dying. Captain Sybil laid down his life on the altar of freedom. His prediction was fulfilled. Robert was brought into the hospital, wounded, but not dangerously. Iola remembered him as being the friend of Tom Anderson, and her heart was drawn instinctively towards him. For awhile he was delirious, but her presence had a soothing effect upon him. He sometimes imagined that she was his mother, and he would tell her how he had missed her; and then at times he would call her sister. Iola, tender and compassionate, humored his fancies, and would sing to him in low, sweet tones some of the hymns she had learned in her old home in Mississippi. One day she sang a few verses of the hymn beginning with the words—

> "Drooping souls no longer grieve,
> Heaven is propitious;
> If on Christ you do believe,
> You will find Him precious."

"That," said he, looking earnestly into Iola's face, "was my mother's hymn. I have not heard it for years. Where did you learn it?"

Iola gazed inquiringly upon the face of her patient, and saw, by his clear gaze and the expression of his face, that his reason had returned.

"In my home, in Mississippi, from my own dear mother," was Iola's reply.

"Do you know where she learned it?" asked Robert.

"When she was a little girl she heard her mother sing it. Years after, a Methodist preacher came to our house, sang this hymn, and left the book behind him. My father was a Catholic, but my mother never went to any church. I did not understand it then, but I do now. We used to sing together, and read the Bible when we were alone."

"Do you remember where she came from, and who was her mother?" asked Robert, anxiously.

"My dear friend, you must be quiet. The fever has left you, but I will not answer for the consequences if you get excited."

Robert lay quiet and thoughtful for awhile and, seeing he was wakeful, Iola said, "Have you any friends to whom you would like to send a letter?"

A pathetic expression flitted over his face, as he sadly replied, "I haven't, to my knowledge, a single relation in the world. When I was about ten years old my mother and sister were sold from me. It is more than twenty years since I have heard from them. But that hymn which you were singing reminded me so much of my mother! She used to sing it when I was a child. Please sing it again."

Iola's voice rose soft and clear by his bedside, till he fell into a quiet slumber. She remembered that her mother had spoken of her brother before they had parted, and her interest and curiosity were awakened by Robert's story. While he slept, she closely scrutinized Robert's features, and detected a striking resemblance between him and her mother.

"Oh, I *do* wonder if he can be my mother's brother, from whom she has been separated so many years!"

Anxious as she was to ascertain if there was any relationship between Robert and her mother, she forebore to question him on the subject which lay so near her heart. But one day, when he was so far recovered as to be able to walk around, he met Iola on the hospital grounds, and said to her:—

"Miss Iola, you remind me so much of my mother and sister that I cannot help wondering if you are the daughter of my long-lost sister."

"Do you think," asked Iola, "if you saw the likeness of your sister you would recognize her?"

"I am afraid not. But there is one thing I can remember about her: she used to have a mole on her cheek, which mother used to tell her was her beauty spot."

"Look at this," said Iola, handing him a locket which contained her mother's picture.

Robert grasped the locket eagerly, scanned the features attentively, then, handing it back, said: "I have only a faint remembrance of my sister's features; but I never could recognize in that beautiful woman the dear little sister with whom I used to play. Oh, the cruelty of slavery! How it wrenched and tore us apart! Where is *your* mother now?"

"Oh, I cannot tell," answered Iola. "I left her in Mississippi. My father was a wealthy Creole planter, who fell in love with my mother. She was his slave, but he educated her in the North, freed, and married her. My father was very careful to have the fact of our negro blood concealed from us. I had not the slightest suspicion of it. When he was dead the secret was revealed. His white relations set aside my father's will, had his marriage declared invalid, and my mother and her children were remanded to slavery." Iola shuddered as she pronounced the horrid word, and grew deadly pale; but, regaining her self-possession, continued: "Now, that freedom has come, I intend to search for my mother until I find her."

"I do not wonder," said Robert, "that we had this war. The nation had sinned enough to suffer."

"Yes," said Iola, "if national sins bring down national judgments, then the nation is only reaping what it sowed."

"What are your plans for the future, or have you any?" asked Robert.

"I intend offering myself as a teacher in one of the schools which are being opened in different parts of the country," replied Iola. "As soon as I am able I will begin my search for my dear mother. I will advertise for her in the papers, hunt for her in the churches, and use all the means in my power to get some tidings of her and my brother Harry. What a cruel thing it was to separate us!"

CHAPTER XVII.

FLAMES IN THE SCHOOL-ROOM.

"Good morning," said Dr. Gresham, approaching Robert and Iola. "How are you both? You have mended rapidly," turning to Robert, "but then it was only a flesh wound. Your general health being good, and your blood in excellent condition, it was not hard for you to rally."

"Where have you been, Doctor? I have a faint recollection of having seen you on the morning I was brought in from the field, but not since."

"I have been on a furlough. I was running down through exhaustion and overwork, and I was compelled to go home for a few weeks' rest. But now, as they are about to close the hospital, I shall be permanently relieved. I am glad that this cruel strife is over. It seemed as if I had lived through ages during these last few years. In the early part of the war I lost my arm by a stray shot, and my armless sleeve is one of the mementos of battle I shall carry with me through life. Miss Leroy," he continued, turning respectfully to Iola, "would you permit me to ask you, as I would have some one ask my sister under the same circumstances, if you have matured any plans for the future, or if I can be of the least service to you? If so, I would be pleased to render you any service in my power."

"My purpose," replied Iola, "is to hunt for my

mother, and to find her if she is alive. I am willing to go anywhere and do anything to find her. But I will need a standpoint from whence I can send out lines of inquiry. It must take time, in the disordered state of affairs, even to get a clue by which I may discover her whereabouts."

"How would you like to teach?" asked the Doctor. "Schools are being opened all around us. Numbers of excellent and superior women are coming from the North to engage as teachers of the freed people. Would you be willing to take a school among these people? I think it will be uphill work. I believe it will take generations to get over the duncery of slavery. Some of these poor fellows who came into our camp did not know their right hands from their left, nor their ages, nor even the days of the month. It took me some time, in a number of cases, to understand their language. It saddened my heart to see such ignorance. One day I asked one a question, and he answered, "I no shum'."

"What did he mean?" asked Iola."

"That he did not see it," replied the doctor. "Of course, this does not apply to all of them. Some of them are wide-awake and sharp as steel traps. I think some of that class may be used in helping others."

"I should be very glad to have an opportunity to teach," said Iola. "I used to be a great favorite among the colored children on my father's plantation."

In a few days after this conversation the hospital was closed. The sick and convalescent were removed, and Iola obtained a position as a teacher. Very soon Iola realized that while she was heartily appreciated by the freedmen, she was an object of suspicion and dislike to their former owners. The North had conquered by the supremacy of the sword, and the South had bowed to the inevitable. But here was a new army that had come with an invasion of ideas, that had come to supplant ignorance with knowledge, and it was natural that its members should be unwelcome to those who had made it a crime to teach their slaves to read the name of the ever blessed Christ. But Iola had found her work, and the freedmen their friend.

When Iola opened her school she took pains to get acquainted with the parents of the children, and she gained their confidence and co-operation. Her face was a passport to their hearts. Ignorant of books, human faces were the scrolls from which they had been reading for ages. They had been the sunshine and shadow of their lives.

Iola had found a school-room in the basement of a colored church, where the doors were willingly opened to her. Her pupils came from miles around, ready and anxious to get some "book larnin'." Some of the old folks were eager to learn, and it was touching to see the eyes which had grown dim under the shadows of slavery, donning spectacles and trying to make out the words. As Iola had nearly all of her life been accustomed to colored children she had no physical repulsions to overcome, no prejudices to conquer in dealing with parents and children. In their simple childish fashion they would bring her fruits and flowers, and gladden her lonely heart with little tokens of affection.

One day a gentleman came to the school and wished to address the children. Iola suspended the regular order of the school, and the gentleman essayed to talk to them on the achievements of the white race, such as building steamboats and carrying on business. Finally, he asked how they did it?

"They've got money," chorused the children.

"But how did they get it?"

"They took it from us," chimed the youngsters. Iola smiled, and the gentleman was nonplussed; but he could not deny that one of the powers of knowledge is the power of the strong to oppress the weak.

The school was soon overcrowded with applicants, and Iola was forced to refuse numbers, because their quarters were too cramped. The school was beginning to lift up the home, for Iola was not satisfied to teach her children only the rudiments of knowledge. She had tried to lay the foundation of good character. But the elements of evil burst upon her loved and cherished work. One night the heavens were lighted with lurid flames, and Iola beheld the school, the pride and joy of her pupils and their parents, a smouldering ruin. Iola gazed with sorrowful dismay on what seemed the cruel work of an incendiary's torch. While she sat, mournfully contemplating the work of destruction, her children formed a procession, and, passing by the wreck of their school, sang:—

> "Oh, do not be discouraged,
> For Jesus is your friend."

As they sang, the tears sprang to Iola's eyes, and she said to herself, "I am not despondent of the future of my people; there is too much elasticity in their spirits, too much hope in their hearts, to be crushed out by unreasoning malice."

CHAPTER XVIII.

SEARCHING FOR LOST ONES.

To BIND anew the ties which slavery had broken and gather together the remnants of his scattered family became the earnest purpose of Robert's life. Iola, hopeful that in Robert she had found her mother's brother, was glad to know she was not alone in *her* search. Having sent out lines of inquiry in different directions, she was led to hope, from some of the replies she had received, that her mother was living somewhere in Georgia.

Hearing that a Methodist conference was to convene in that State, and being acquainted with the bishop of that district, she made arrangements to accompany him thither. She hoped to gather some tidings of her mother through the ministers gathered from different parts of that State.

From her brother she had heard nothing since her father's death. On his way to the conference, the bishop had an engagement to dedicate a church, near the city of C——, in North Carolina. Iola was quite willing to stop there a few days, hoping to hear something of Robert Johnson's mother. Soon after she had seated herself in the cars she was approached by a gentleman, who reached out his hand to her, and greeted her with great cordiality. Iola looked up, and recognized him immediately as one of her last patients at the hospital. It was none other than Robert Johnson.

"I am so glad to meet you," he said. "I am on my

way to C—— in search of my mother. I want to see the person who sold her last, and, if possible, get some clew to the direction in which she went."

"And I," said Iola, "am in search of *my* mother. I am convinced that when we find those for whom we are searching they will prove to be very nearly related. Mamma said, before we were parted, that her brother had a red spot on his temple. If I could see that spot I should rest assured that my mother is your sister."

"Then," said Robert, "I can give you that assurance," and smilingly he lifted his hair from his temple, on which was a large, red spot.

"I am satisfied," exclaimed Iola, fixing her eyes, beaming with hope and confidence, on Robert. "Oh, I am so glad that I can, without the least hesitation, accept your services to join with me in the further search. What are your plans?"

"To stop for awhile in C——," said Robert, "and gather all the information possible from those who sold and bought my mother. I intend to leave no stone unturned in searching for her."

"Oh, I *do* hope that you will succeed. I expect to stop over there a few days, and I shall be *so* glad if, before I leave, I hear your search has been crowned with success, or, a least, that you have been put on the right track. Although I was born and raised in the midst of slavery, I had not the least idea of its barbarous selfishness till I was forced to pass through it. But we lived so much alone I had no opportunity to study it, except on our own plantation. My father and mother were very kind to their slaves. But it was slavery, all the same, and I hate it, root and branch."

Just then the conductor called out the station.

"We stop here," said Robert. "I am going to see Mrs. Johnson, and hunt up some of my old acquaintances. Where do you stop?"

"I don't know," replied Iola. "I expect that friends will be here to meet us. Bishop B——, permit me to introduce you to Mr. Robert Johnson, whom I have every reason to believe is my mother's brother. Like myself, he is engaged in hunting up his lost relatives."

"And I," said Robert, "am very much pleased to know that we are not without favorable clues."

"Bishop," said Iola, "Mr. Johnson wishes to know where I am to stop. He is going on an exploring expedition, and wishes to let me know the result."

"We stop at Mrs. Allston's, 313 New Street," said the bishop. "If I can be of any use to you, I am at your service."

"Thank you," said Robert, lifting his hat, as he left them to pursue his inquiries about his long-lost mother.

Quickly he trod the old familiar streets which led to his former home. He found Mrs. Johnson, but she had aged very fast since the war. She was no longer the lithe, active woman, with her proud manner and resolute bearing. Her eye had lost its brightness, her step its elasticity, and her whole appearance indicated that she was slowly sinking beneath a weight of sorrow which was heavier far than her weight of years. When she heard that Robert had called to see her she was going to receive him in the hall, as she would have done any of her former slaves, but her mind immediately changed when she saw him. He was not the light-hearted, careless, mischief-loving Robby of former days, but a handsome man, with heavy moustache, dark, earnest eyes, and proud military bearing. He smiled, and reached out his hand to her. She hardly knew how to address him. To her colored people were either boys and girls, or "aunties and uncles." She had never in her life addressed a colored person as "Mr. or Mrs." To do so now was to violate the social customs of the place. It would be like learning a new language in her old age. Robert immediately set her at ease by addressing her under the old familiar name of "Miss Nancy." This immediately relieved her of all embarrassment. She invited him into the sitting-room, and gave him a warm welcome.

"Well, Robby," she said, "I once thought that you would have been the last one to leave me. You know I never ill-treated you, and I gave you everything you needed. People said that I was spoiling you. I thought you were as happy as the days were long. When I heard of other people's servants leaving them I used to say to myself, 'I can trust my Bobby; he will stick to me to the last.' But I fooled myself that time. Soon as the Yankee soldiers got in sight you left me without saying a word. That morning I came down into the kitchen and asked Linda, 'Where's Robert? Why hasn't he set the table?' She said 'she hadn't seen you since the night before.' I thought maybe you were sick, and I went to see, but you were not in your room. I couldn't believe at first that you were gone. Wasn't I always good to you?"

"Oh, Miss Nancy," replied Robert; "you were good, but freedom was better."

"Yes," she said, musingly, "I suppose I would have done the same. But, Robby, it did go hard with me at first. However, I soon found out that my neighbors had been going through the same thing. But its all over now. Let by-gones be by-gones. What are you doing now, and where are you living?"

"I am living in the city of P——. I have opened a hardware store there. But just now I am in search of my mother and sister."

"I hope that you may find them."

"How long," asked Robert, "do you think it has been since they left here?"

"Let me see; it must have been nearly thirty years. You got my letter?"

"Yes, ma'am; thank you."

"There have been great changes since you left here," Mrs. Johnson said. "Gundover died, and a number of colored men have banded together, bought his plantation, and divided it among themselves. And I hear they have a very nice settlement out there. I hope, since the Government has set them free, that they will succeed."

After Robert's interview with Mrs. Johnson he thought he would visit the settlement and hunt up his old friends. He easily found the place. It was on a clearing in Gundover's woods, where Robert and Uncle Daniel had held their last prayer-meeting. Now the gloomy silence of those woods was broken by the hum of industry, the murmur of cheerful voices, and the merry laughter of happy children. Where they had trodden with fear and misgiving, freedmen walked with light and bounding hearts. The school-house had taken the place of the slave-pen and auction-block.

"How is yer, ole boy?" asked one laborer of another.

"Everything is lobly," replied the other. The blue sky arching overhead and the beauty of the scenery justified the expression.

Gundover had died soon after the surrender. Frank Anderson had grown reckless and drank himself to death. His brother Tom had been killed in battle. Their mother, who was Gundover's daughter, had died insane. Their father had also passed away. The defeat of the Confederates, the loss of his sons, and the emancipation of his slaves, were blows from which he never recovered. As Robert passed leisurely along, delighted with the evidences of thrift and industry which constantly met his eye, he stopped to admire a garden filled with beautiful flowers, clambering vines, and rustic adornments.

On the porch sat an elderly woman, darning stockings, the very embodiment of content and good humor. Robert looked inquiringly at her. On seeing him, she almost immediately exclaimed, "Shore as I'se born, dat's Robert! Look yere, honey, whar did yer come from? I'll gib my head fer a choppin' block ef dat ain't Miss Nancy's Bob. Ain't yer our Bobby? Shore yer is."

"Of course I am," responded Robert. "It isn't anybody else. How did you know me?"

"How did I know yer? By dem mischeebous eyes, ob course. I'd a knowed yer if I had seed yer in Europe."

"In Europe, Aunt Linda? Where's that?"

"I don't know. I specs its some big city, somewhar. But yer looks jis' splendid. Yer looks good 'nuff ter kiss."

"Oh, Aunt Linda, don't say that. You make me blush."

"Oh you go 'long wid yer. I specs yer's got a nice little wife up dar whar yer comes from, dat kisses yer ebery day, an' Sunday, too."

"Is that the way your old man does you?"

"Oh, no, not a bit. He isn't one ob de kissin' kine. But sit down," she said, handing Robert a chair. "Won't yer hab a glass ob milk? Boy, I'se a libin' in clover. Neber 'spected ter see sich good times in all my born days."

"Well, Aunt Linda," said Robert, seating himself near her, and drinking the glass of milk which she had handed him, "how goes the battle? How have you been getting on since freedom?"

"Oh, fust rate, fust rate! Wen freedom com'd I jist lit out ob Miss Johnson's kitchen soon as I could. I wanted ter re'lize I war free, an' I couldn't, tell I got out er de sight and soun' ob ole Miss. When de war war ober an' de sogers war still stopping' yere, I made pies an' cakes, sole em to de sogers, an' jist made money han' ober fist. An' I kep' on a workin' an' a savin' till my ole man got back from de war wid his wages and his bounty money. I felt right set up an' mighty big wen we counted all dat money. We had neber seen so much money in our lives befo', let alone hab it fer ourselbs. An' I sez, 'John, you take dis money an' git a nice place wid it.' An' he sez, 'Dere's no use tryin', kase dey don't want ter sell us any lan'.' Ole Gundover said, 'fore he died, dat he would let de lan' grow up in trees 'fore he'd sell it to us. An' dere war Mr. Brayton; he buyed some lan' and sole it to some cullud folks, an' his ole frien's got so mad wid him dat dey wouldn't speak ter him, an' he war borned down yere. I tole ole Miss Anderson's daughter dat we wanted ter git some homes ob our ownselbs. She sez, 'Den you won't want ter work for us?' Jis' de same as ef we could eat an' drink our houses. I tell yer, Robby, dese white folks don't know eberything."

"That's a fact, Aunt Linda."

"Den I sez ter John, 'wen one door shuts anoder opens.' An' shore 'nough, ole Gundover died, an' his place war all in debt, an' had to be sole. Some Jews bought it, but dey didn't want to farm it, so dey gib us a chance to buy it. Dem Jews hez been right helpful to cullud people wen dey hab lan' to sell. I reckon dey don't keer who buys it so long as dey gits de money. Well, John didn't gib in at fust; didn't want to let on his wife knowed more dan he did, an' dat he war ruled ober by a woman. Yer know he is an' ole Firginian, an' some ob dem ole Firginians do so lub to rule a woman. But I kep' naggin at him, till I specs he got tired of my tongue, an' he went and buyed dis piece ob lan'. Dis house war on it, an' war all gwine to wrack. It used to belong to John's ole marster. His wife died right in dis house, an' arter dat her husband went right to de dorgs; an' now he's in de pore-house. My! but ain't dem tables turned. When we knowed it war our own, warn't my ole man proud! I seed it in him, but he wouldn't let on. Ain't you men powerful 'ceitful?"

"Oh, Aunt Linda, don't put me in with the rest!"

"I don't know 'bout dat. Put you all in de bag for 'ceitfulness, an' I don't know which would git out fust."

"Well, Aunt Linda, I suppose by this time you know how to read and write?"

"No, chile, sence freedom's com'd I'se bin scratchin' too hard to get a libin' to put my head down to de book."

"But, Aunt Linda, it would be such company when your husband is away, to take a book. Do you never get lonesome?"

"Chile, I ain't got no time ter get lonesome. Ef you had eber so many chickens to feed, an' pigs squealin' fer somethin' ter eat, an' yore ducks an' geese squakin' 'roun' yer, yer wouldn't hab time ter git lonesome."

"But, Aunt Linda, you might be sick for months, and think what a comfort it would be if you could read your Bible."

"Oh, I could hab prayin' and singin'. Dese people is mighty good 'bout prayin' by de sick. Why, Robby, I think it would gib me de hysterics ef I war to try to git book larnin' froo my pore ole head. How long is yer gwine to stay? An' whar is yer stoppin?"

"I got here to-day," said Robert, "but I expect to stay several days."

"Well, I wants yer to meet my ole man, an' talk 'bout ole times. Couldn't yer come an' stop wid me, or isn't my house sniptious 'nuff?"

"Yes, thank you; but there is a young lady in town whom I think is my niece, my sister's daughter, and I want to be with her all I can."

"Your niece! Whar did you git any niece from?"

"Don't you remember," asked Robert, "that my mother had a little daughter, when Mrs. Johnson sold her? Well, I believe this young lady is that daughter's child."

"Laws a marcy!" exclaimed Aunt Linda, "yer don't tell me so! Whar did yer ketch up wid her?"

"I met her first," said Robert, "at the hospital here, when our poor Tom was dying; and when I was wounded at Five Forks she attended me in the field hospital there. She was just as good as gold."

"Well, did I eber! You jis' fotch dat chile to see me, ef she ain't too fine. I'se pore, but I'se clean, an' I ain't forgot how ter git up good dinners. Now, I wants ter hab a good talk 'bout our feller-sarvants."

"Yes, and I," said Robert, "want to hear all about Uncle Daniel, and Jennie, and Uncle Ben Tunnel."

"Well, I'se got lots an' gobs ter tell yer. I'se kep' track ob dem all. Aunt Katie died an' went ter hebben in a blaze ob glory. Uncle Dan'el stayed on de place till Marse Robert com'd back. When de war war ober he war smashed all ter pieces. I did pity him from de bottom ob my heart. When he went ter de war he looked so brave an' han'some; an' wen he com'd back he looked orful. 'Fore he went he gib Uncle Dan'el a bag full ob money ter take kere ob. 'An wen he com'd back Uncle Dan'el gibed him ebery cent ob it. It warn't ebery white pusson he could hab trusted wid it. 'Cause yer know, Bobby, money's a mighty temptin' thing. Dey tells me dat Marster Robert los' a heap ob property by de war; but Marse Robert war always mighty good ter Uncle Dan'el and Aunt Katie. He war wid her wen she war dyin' an' she got holt his han' an' made him promise dat he would meet her in glory. I neber seed anybody so happy in my life. She singed an' prayed ter de last. I tell you dis ole time religion is good 'nuff fer me. Mr. Robert didn't stay yere long arter her, but I beliebs he went all right. But 'fore he went he looked out fer Uncle Dan'el. Did you see dat nice little cabin down dere wid de green shutters an' nice little garden in front? Well, 'fore Marse Robert died he gib Uncle Dan'el dat place, an' Miss Mary and de chillen looks arter him yet; an' he libs jis' as snug as a bug in a rug. I'se gwine ter axe him ter take supper wid you. He'll be powerful glad ter see you."

"Do you ever go to see old Miss?" asked Robert.

"Oh, yes; I goes ebery now and den. But she's jis' fell froo. Ole Johnson jis' drunk hisself to death. He war de biggest guzzler I eber seed in my life. Why, dat man he drunk up ebery thing he could lay his han's on. Sometimes he would go 'roun' tryin' to borrer money from pore cullud folks. 'Twas rale drefful de way dat pore feller did frow hisself away. But drink did it all. I tell you, Bobby, dat drink's a drefful thing wen it gits de upper han' ob you. You'd better steer clar ob it."

"That's so," assented Robert.

"I know'd Miss Nancy's fadder and mudder. Dey war mighty rich. Some ob de real big bugs. Marse Jim used to know dem, an' come ober ter de plantation, an' eat an' drink wen he got ready, an' stay as long as he choose. Ole Cousins used to have wine at dere table ebery day, an' Marse Jim war mighty fon' ob dat wine, an' sometimes he would drink till he got quite boozy. Ole Cousins liked him bery well, till he foun' out he wanted his darter, an' den he didn't want him fer rags nor patches. But Miss Nancy war mighty headstrong, an' allers liked to hab her own way; an' dis time she got it. But didn't she step her foot inter it? Ole Johnson war mighty han'some, but when dat war said all war said. She run'd off an' got married, but wen she got down she war too spunkey to axe her pa for anything. Wen you war wid her, yer know she only took big bugs. But wen de war com'd 'roun' it tore her all ter pieces, an' now she's as pore as Job's turkey. I feel's right sorry fer her. Well, Robby, things is turned 'roun' mighty quare. Ole Mistus war up den, an' I war down; now, she's down, an' I'se up. But I pities her, 'cause she warn't so bad arter all. De wuss thing she eber did war to sell your mudder, an' she wouldn't hab done dat but she snatched de whip out ob her han' an gib her a lickin'. Now I belieb in my heart she war 'fraid ob your mudder arter dat. But we women had ter keep 'em from whippin' us, er dey'd all de time been libin' on our bones. She had no man ter whip us 'cept dat ole drunken husband ob hern, an' he war allers too drunk ter whip hisself. He jis' wandered off, an' I reckon he died in somebody's pore-house. He warn't no 'count nohow you fix it. Weneber I goes to town I carries her some garden sass, er a little milk an' butter. An' she's mighty glad ter git it. I ain't got nothin' agin her. She neber struck me a lick in her life, an' I belieb in praising de bridge dat carries me ober. Dem Yankees set me free, an' I thinks a powerful heap ob dem. But it does rile me ter see dese mean white men comin' down yere an' settin' up dere grog-shops, tryin' to fedder dere nests sellin' licker to pore culled people. Deys de bery kine ob men dat used ter keep dorgs to ketch de runaways. I'd be chokin' fer a drink 'fore I'd eber spen' a cent wid dem, a spreadin' dere traps to git de black folks' money. You jis' go down town 'fore sun up to-morrer mornin' an' you see ef dey don't hab dem bars open to sell dere drams to dem hard workin' culled people 'fore dey goes ter work. I thinks some niggers is mighty big fools."

"Oh, Aunt Linda, don't run down your race. Leave that for the white people."

"I ain't runnin' down my people. But a fool's a fool, wether he's white or black. An' I think de nigger who will spen' his hard-earned money in dese yere new grog-shops is de biggest kine ob a fool, an' I sticks ter dat. You know we didn't hab all dese low places in slave times. An' what is dey fer, but to get the people's money. An' its a shame how dey do sling de licker 'bout 'lection times."

"But don't the temperance people want the colored people to vote the temperance ticket?"

"Yes, but some ob de culled people gits mighty skittish ef dey tries to git em to vote dare ticket 'lection time, an' keeps dem at a proper distance wen de 'lection's ober. Some ob dem say dere's a trick behine it, an' don't want to tech it. Dese white folks could do a heap wid de culled folks ef dey'd only treat em right."

"When our people say there is a trick behind it, said Robert," I only wish they could see the trick before it—the trick of worse than wasting their money, and of keeping themselves and families poorer and more ignorant than there is any need for them to be."

"Well, Bobby, I beliebs we might be a people ef it warn't for dat mizzable drink. An' Robby, I jis' tells yer what I wants; I wants some libe man to come down yere an' splain things ter dese people. I don't mean a politic man, but a man who'll larn dese people how to bring up dere chillen, to keep our gals straight, an' our boys from runnin' in de saloons an' gamblin' dens."

"Don't your preachers do that?" asked Robert.

"Well, some ob dem does, an' some ob dem doesn't. An' wen dey preaches, I want dem to practice wat dey preach. Some ob dem says dey's called, but I jis' thinks laziness called some ob dem. An' I thinks since freedom come deres some mighty pore sticks set up for preachers. Now dere's John Anderson, Tom's brudder; you 'member Tom."

"Yes; as brave a fellow and as honest as ever stepped in shoe leather."

"Well, his brudder war mighty diff'rent. He war down in de lower kentry wen de war war ober. He war mighty smart, an' had a good head-piece, an' a orful glib tongue. He set up store an' sole whisky, an' made a lot ob money. Den he wanted ter go to de legislatur. Now what should he do but make out he'd got 'ligion, an' war called to preach. He had no more 'ligion dan my ole dorg. But he had money an' built a meetin' house, whar he could hole meeting, an' hab funerals; an' you know cullud folks is mighty great on funerals. Well dat jis' tuck wid de people, an' he got 'lected to de legislatur. Den he got a fine house, an' his ole wife warn't good 'nuff for him. Den dere war a young school-teacher, an' he begun cuttin' his eyes at her. But she war as deep in de mud as he war in de mire, an' he jis' gib up his ole wife and married her, a fusty thing. He war a mean ole hypocrit, an' I wouldn't sen' fer him to bury my cat. Robby, I'se down on dese kine ob preachers like a thousand bricks."

"Well, Aunt Linda, all the preachers are not like him."

"No; I knows dat; not by a jug full. We's got some mighty good men down yere, an' we's glad when dey comes, an' orful sorry when dey goes 'way. De las preacher we had war a mighty good man. He didn't like too much hollerin'."

"Perhaps," said Robert, "he thought it were best for only one to speak at a time."

"I specs so. His wife war de nicest and sweetest lady dat eber I did see. None ob yer airish, stuck up folks, like a tarrapin carryin' eberything on its back. She used ter hab meetins fer de mudders, an' larn us how to raise our chillen, an' talk so putty to de chillen. I sartinly did lub dat woman."

"Where is she now?" asked Robert.

"De Conference moved dem 'bout thirty miles from yere. Deys gwine to hab a big meetin' ober dere next Sunday. Don't you 'member dem meetins we used to hab in de woods? We don't hab to hide like we did den. But it don't seem as ef de people had de same good 'ligion we had den. 'Pears like folks is took up wid makin' money an' politics."

"Well, Aunt Linda, don't you wish those good old days would come back?"

"No, chile; neber! neber! Wat fer you take me? I'd ruther lib in a corn-crib. Freedom needn't keep me outer heben; an' ef I'se sich a fool as ter lose my 'ligion cause I'se free, I oughtn' ter git dere."

"But, Aunt Linda, if old Miss were able to take care of you, wouldn't you just as leave be back again?"

There was a faint quiver of indignation in Aunt Linda's voice, as she replied :—

"Don't yer want yer freedom? Well I wants ter pat my free foot. Halleluyah! But, Robby, I wants yer ter go ter dat big meetin' de wuss kine."

"How will I get there?" asked Robert.

"Oh, dat's all right. My ole man's got two ob de nicest mules you eber set yer eyes on. It'll jis' do yer good ter look at dem. I 'spect you'll see some ob yer ole frens dere. Dere's a nice settlemen' of cullud folks ober dere, an' I wants yer to come an' bring dat young lady. I wants dem folks to see wat nice folks I kin bring to de meetin'. I hope's yer didn't lose all your 'ligion in de army."

"Oh, I hope not," replied Robert.

"Oh, chile, yer mus' be shore 'bout dat. I don't want yer to ride hope's hoss down to torment. Now be shore an' come to-morrer an' bring dat young lady, an' take supper wid me. I'se all on nettles to see dat chile."

CHAPTER XIX.

STRIKING CONTRASTS.

THE next day, Robert, accompanied by Iola, went to the settlement to take supper with Aunt Linda, and a very luscious affair it was. Her fingers had not lost their skill since she had tasted the sweets of freedom. Her biscuits were just as light and flaky as ever. Her jelly was as bright as amber, and her preserves were perfectly delicious. After she had set the table she stood looking in silent admiration, chuckling to herself: "Ole Mistus can't set sich a table as dat. She ought'er be yere to see it. Specs 'twould make her mouf water. Well, I mus' let bygones be bygones. But dis yere freedom's mighty good."

Aunt Linda had invited Uncle Daniel, and, wishing to give him a pleasant surprise, she had refrained from telling him that Robert Johnson was the one she wished him to meet.

"Do you know dis gemmen?" said Aunt Linda to Uncle Daniel, when the latter arrived.

"Well, I can't say's I do. My eyes is gittin dim, an I disremembers him."

"Now jis' you look right good at him. Don't yer 'member him?"

Uncle Daniel looked puzzled and, slowly scanning Robert's features, said: "He do look like somebody I used ter know, but I can't make him out ter save my life. I don't know whar to place him. Who is de gemmen, ennyhow?"

"Why, Uncle Dan'el," replied Aunt Linda, "dis is Robby; Miss Nancy's bad, mischeebous Robby, dat war allers playin' tricks on me."

"Well, shore's I'se born, ef dis ain't our ole Bobby!" exclaimed Uncle Daniel, delightedly. "Why, chile, whar did yer come from? Thought you war dead an' buried long 'go."

"Why, Uncle Daniel, did you send anybody to kill me?" asked Robert, laughingly.

"Oh, no'n 'deed, chile! but I yeard dat you war killed in de battle, an' I never 'spected ter see you agin."

"Well, here I am," replied Robert, "large as life, and just as natural. And this young lady, Uncle Daniel, I believe is my niece." As he spoke he turned to Iola. "Do you remember my mother?"

"Oh, yes," said Uncle Daniel, looking intently at Iola as she stepped forward and cordially gave him her hand.

"Well, I firmly believe," continued Robert, "that this is the daughter of the little girl whom Miss Nancy sold away with my mother."

"Well, I'se rale glad ter see her. She puts me mighty much in mine ob dem days wen we war all young togedder; wen Miss Nancy sed, 'Harriet war too high fer her.' It jis' seems like yisterday wen I yeard Miss Nancy say, 'No house could flourish whar dere war two mistresses.' Well, Mr. Robert——"

"Oh, no, no, Uncle Daniel," interrupted Robert, "don't say that! Call me Robby or Bob, just as you used to."

"Well, Bobby, I'se glad klar from de bottom of my heart ter see yer."

"Even if you wouldn't go with us when we left?"

"Oh, Bobby, dem war mighty tryin' times. You boys didn't know it, but Marster Robert hab giben me a bag ob money ter take keer ob, an' I promised him I'd do it an' I had ter be ez good ez my word."

"Oh, Uncle Daniel, why didn't you tell us boys all about it? We could have helped you take care of it."

"Now, wouldn't dat hab bin smart ter let on ter you chaps, an' hab you huntin' fer it from Dan ter Barsheba? I specs some ob you would bin a rootin' fer it yit!"

"Well, Uncle Daniel, we were young then; I can't tell what we would have done if we had found it. But we are older now."

"Yes, yer older, but I wouldn't put it pas' yer eben now, ef yer foun' out whar it war."

"Yes," said Iola, laughing, "they say 'caution is the parent of safety.'"

"Money's a mighty tempting thing," said Robert, smiling.

"But, Robby, dere's nothin' like a klar conscience; a klar conscience, Robby!"

Just then Aunt Linda, who had been completing the preparations for her supper, entered the room with her husband, and said, "Salters, let me interdoos you ter my fren', Mr. Robert Johnson, an' his niece, Miss Leroy."

"Why, is it possible," exclaimed Robert, rising, and shaking hands, "that you are Aunt Linda's husband?"

"Dat's what de parson sed," replied Salters.

"I thought," pursued Robert, "that your name was John Andrews. It was such when you were in my company."

"All de use I'se got fer dat name is ter git my money

wid it; an' wen dat's done, all's done. Got 'nuff ob my ole Marster in slave times, widout wearin' his name in freedom. Wen I got done wid him, I got done wid his name. Wen I 'listed, I war John Andrews; and wen I gits my pension, I'se John Andrews; but now Salters is my name, an' I likes it better."

"But how came you to be Aunt Linda's husband? Did you get married since the war?"

"Lindy an' me war married long 'fore de war. But my ole Marster sole me away from her an' our little gal, an' den sole her chile ter somebody else. Arter freedom, I hunted up our little gal, an' foun' her. She war a big woman den. Den I com'd right back ter dis place an' foun' Lindy. She hedn't married agin, nuther hed I; so we jis' let de parson marry us out er de book; an' we war mighty glad ter git togedder agin, an' feel hitched togedder fer life."

"Well, Uncle Daniel," said Robert, turning the conversation toward him, "you and Uncle Ben wouldn't go with us, but you came out all right at last."

"Yes, indeed," said Aunt Linda, "Ben got inter a stream of luck. Arter freedom com'd, de people had a heap of fath in Ben; an' wen dey wanted some one to go ter Congress dey jist voted for Ben ter go. An' he went, too. An' wen Salters went to Washin'ton to git his pension, who should he see dere wid dem big men but our Ben, lookin' jist as big as any ob dem."

"An' it did my ole eyes good jist ter see it," broke in Salters; "if I couldn't go dere myself, I war mighty glad to see some one ob my people dat could. I felt like de boy who, wen somebody said he war gwine to slap off his face, said, 'Yer kin slap off my face, but I'se got a big brudder, an' you can't slap off his face.' I went to see him 'fore I lef', and he war jist de same as he war wen we war boys togedder. He hadn't got de big head a bit."

"I reckon Mirandy war mighty sorry she didn't stay wid him. I know I should be," said Aunt Linda.

"Uncle Daniel," asked Robert, "are you still preaching?"

"Yes, chile, I'se still firing off de Gospel gun."

"I hear some of the Northern folks are down here teaching theology, that is, teaching young men how to preach. Why don't you study theology?"

"Look a yere, boy, I'se been a preachin' dese thirty years, an' you come yere a tellin' me 'bout studying yore ologies. I larn'd my 'ology at de foot ob de cross. You bin dar?"

"Dear Uncle Daniel," said Iola, "the moral aspect of the nation would be changed if it would learn at the same cross to subordinate the spirit of caste to the spirit of Christ."

"Does yer 'member Miss Nancy's Harriet," asked Aunt Linda, "dat she sole away kase she wouldn't let her whip her? Well, we think dis is Harriet's gran'-chile. She war sole away from her mar, an' now she's a lookin' fer her."

"Well, I hopes she may fine her," replied Salters. "I war sole 'way from my mammy wen I war eighteen mont's ole, an' I wouldn't know her now from a bunch ob turnips."

"I," said Iola, "am on my way South seeking for my mother, and I shall not give up until I find her."

"Come," said Aunt Linda, "we mustn't stan' yer

talkin', or de grub'll git cole. Come, frens, sit down, an' eat some ob my pore supper."

Aunt Linda sat at the table in such a flutter of excitement that she could hardly eat, but she gazed with intense satisfaction on her guests. Robert sat on her right hand, contrasting Aunt Linda's pleasant situation with the old days in Mrs. Johnson's kitchen, where he had played his pranks upon her, and told her the news of the war.

Over Iola there stole a spirit of restfulness. There was something so motherly in Aunt Linda's manner that it seemed to recall the bright, sunshiny days when she used to nestle in Mam Liza's arms, in her own happy home. The conversation was full of army reminiscences and recollections of the days of slavery. Uncle Daniel was much interested, and, as they rose from the table, exclaimed :—

"Robby, seein' yer an' hearin' yer talk, almos' puts new springs inter me. I feel 'mos' like I war gittin' younger."

After the supper, Salters and his guests returned to the front room, which Aunt Linda regarded with so much pride, and on which she bestowed so much care.

"Well, Captin," said Salters, "I neber 'spected ter see you agin. Do you know de las' time I seed yer? Well, you war on a stretcher, an' four ob us war carryin' you ter de hospital. War you much hurt?

"No," replied Robert, "it was only a flesh wound; and this young lady nursed me so carefully that I soon got over it."

"Is dat de way you foun' her?"

"Yes, Andrews,"——

"Salters, ef you please," interrupted Salters. I'se only Andrews wen I gits my money."

"Well, Salters," continued Robert, "our freedom was a costly thing. Did you know that Captain Sybil was killed in one of the last battles of the war? These young chaps, who are taking it so easy, don't know the hardships through which we older ones passed. But all the battles are not fought, nor all the victories won. The colored man has escaped from one slavery, and I don't want him to fall into another. I want the young folks to keep their brains clear, and their right arms strong, to fight the battles of life manfully, and take their places alongside of every other people in this country. And I cannot see what is to hinder them if they get a chance."

"I don't nuther," said Salters. "I don't see dat dey drinks any more dan anybody else, nor dat dere is any meanness or debilment dat a black man kin do dat a white man can't keep step wid him."

"Yes," assented Robert, "but while a white man is stealing a thousand dollars, a black man is getting into trouble taking a few chickens."

"All that may be true," said Iola, "but there are some things a white man can do that we cannot afford to do."

"I beliebs eberybody, Norf and Souf, is lookin' at us; an' some ob dem ain't got no good blood fer us, nohow you fix it," said Salters.

"I specs cullud folks mus' hab done somethin'," interposed Aunt Linda.

"O, nonsense," said Robert. "I don't think they are any worse than the white people. I don't believe, if we had the power, we would do any more lynching, burning, and murdering than they do."

"Dat's so," said Aunt Linda, "it's ralely orful how our folks hab been murdered sence de war. But I don't think dese young folks is goin' ter take things as we's allers done."

"We war cowed down from the beginnin'," said Uncle Daniel, "but dese young folks ain't comin' up dat way."

"No," said Salters, "fer one night arter some ob our pore people had been killed, an' some ob our women had run'd away 'bout seventeen miles, my gran'son, looking me squar in de face, said: 'Ain't you got five fingers? Can't you pull a trigger as well as a white man?' I tell yer, Cap, dat jis' got to me, an' I made up my mine dat my boy should neber call me a coward."

"It is not to be expected," said Robert, "that these young people are going to put up with things as we did, when we weren't permitted to hold a meeting by ourselves, or to own a club or learn to read."

"I tried," said Salters, "to git a little out'er de book wen I war in de army. On Sundays I sometimes takes a book an' tries to make out de words, but my eyes is gittin' dim an' de letters all run togedder, an' I gits sleepy, an' ef yer wants to put me to sleep jis' put a book in my han'. But wen it comes to gittin' out a stan' ob cotton, an' plantin' corn, I'se dere all de time. But dat gran'son ob mine is smart as a steel trap. I specs he'll be a preacher."

Salters looked admiringly at his grandson, who sat grinning in the corner, munching a pear he had brought from the table.

"Yes," said Aunt Linda, "his fadder war killed by

the Secesh, one night, comin' home from a politic meetin', an' his pore mudder died a few weeks arter, an' we mean to make a man ob him."

"He's got to larn to work fust," said Salters, "an' den ef he's right smart I'se gwine ter sen' him ter college. An' ef he can't get a libin' one way, he kin de oder."

"Yes," said Iola, "I hope he will turn out an excellent young man, for the greatest need of the race is noble, earnest men, and true women."

"Job," said Salters, turning to his grandson, "tell Jake ter hitch up de mules, an' you stay dere an' help him. We's all gwine ter de big meetin'. Yore grandma hab set her heart on goin', an' it'll be de same as a spell ob sickness ef she don't hab a chance to show her bes' bib an' tucker. That ole gal's as proud as a peacock."

"Now, John Salters," exclaimed Aunt Linda, "ain't you 'shamed ob yourself? Allers tryin' to poke fun at yer pore wife. Never mine; wait till I'se gone, an' you'll miss me."

"Ef I war single," said Salters, "I could git a putty young gal, but it wouldn't be so easy wid you."

"Why not?" said Iola, smiling.

"'Cause young men don't want ole hens, an' ole men want young pullets," was Salter's reply.

"Robby, honey," said Aunt Linda, "when you gits a wife, don't treat her like dat man treats me."

"Oh, his head's level," answered Robert; "at least it was in the army."

"Dat's jis' de way; you see dat, Miss Iola? One man takin' up for de oder. But I'll be eben wid you bof. I must go now an' git ready."

Iola laughed. The homely enjoyment of that evening was very welcome to her after the trying scenes through which she had passed. Further conversation was interrupted by the appearance of the wagon, drawn by two fine mules. John Salters stopped joking his wife to admire his mules.

"Jis' look at dem," he said. "Ain't dey beauties? I bought 'em out ob my bounty-money. Arter de war war ober I had a little money, an' I war gwine ter rent a plantation on sheers an' git out a good stan' ob cotton. Cotton war bringin' orful high prices den, but Lindy said to me, 'Now, John, you'se got a lot ob money, an' you'd better salt it down. I'd ruther lib on a little piece ob lan' ob my own dan a big piece ob somebody else's. Well, I says to Lindy, I dun know nuthin' 'bout buyin' lan', an' I'se 'fraid arter I'se done buyed it an' put all de marrer ob dese bones in it, dat somebody's far-off cousin will come an' say de title ain't good, an' I'll lose it all."

"You're right thar, John," said Uncle Daniel. "White man's so unsartain, black man's nebber safe."

"But somehow," continued Salters, "Lindy warn't satisfied wid rentin', so I buyed a piece ob lan', an' I'se glad now I'se got it. Lindy's got a lot ob gumption; knows most as much as a man. She ain't got dat long head fer nuffin. She's got lots ob sense, but I don't like to tell her so."

"Why not?" asked Iola. "Do you think it would make her feel too happy?"

"Well, it don't do ter tell you women how much we thinks ob you. It sets you up too much. Ole Gundover's overseer war my marster, an' he used ter lib in dis bery house. I'se fixed it up sence I'se got it. Now I'se better off dan he is, 'cause he tuck to drink, an' all his frens is gone, an' he's in de pore-house."

Just then Linda came to the door with her baskets.

"Now, Lindy, ain't you ready yet? Do hurry up."

"Yes, I'se ready, but things wouldn't go right ef you didn't hurry me."

"Well, put your chicken fixins an' cake right in yere. Captin, you'll ride wid me, an' de young lady an' my ole woman'll take de back seat. Uncle Dan'el, dere's room for you ef you'll go."

"No, I thank you. It's time fer ole folks to go to bed. Good night! An', Bobby, I hopes to see you agin'."

CHAPTER XX.

A REVELATION.

IT was a lovely evening for the journey. The air was soft and balmy. The fields and hedges were redolent with flowers. Not a single cloud obscured the brightness of the moon or the splendor of the stars. The ancient trees were festooned with moss, which hung like graceful draperies. Ever and anon a startled hare glided over the path, and whip-poor-wills and crickets broke the restful silence of the night. Robert rode quietly along, quaffing the beauty of the scene and thinking of his boyish days, when he gathered nuts and wild plums in those woods; he also indulged pleasant reminiscences of later years, when, with Uncle Daniel and Tom Anderson, he attended the secret prayer-meetings. Iola rode along, conversing with Aunt Linda, amused and interested at the quaintness of her speech and the shrewdness of her intellect. To her the ride was delightful.

"Does yer know dis place, Robby," asked Aunt Linda, as they passed an old resort.

"I should think I did," replied Robert. "It is the place where we held our last prayer-meeting."

"An' dere's dat ole broken pot we used, ter tell 'bout de war. But warn't ole Miss hoppin' wen she foun' out you war goin' to de war! I thought she'd go almos' wile. Now, own up, Robby, didn't you feel kine ob mean to go off widout eben biddin' her good bye? An'

I ralely think ole Miss war fon' ob yer. Now, own up, honey, didn't yer feel a little down in de mouf wen yer lef' her."

"Not much," responded Robert. "I only thought she was getting paid back for selling my mother."

"Dat's so, Robby! yore mudder war a likely gal, wid long black hair, an' kine ob ginger-bread color. An' you neber hearn tell ob her sence dey sole her to Georgia?"

"Never," replied Robert, "but I would give everything I have on earth to see her once more. I *do* hope, if she is living, that I may meet her before I die."

"You's right, boy, cause she lub'd you as she lub'd her own life. Many a time hes she set in my ole cabin an' cried 'bout yer wen you war fas' asleep. It's all ober now, but I'se gwine to hole up fer dem Yankees dat gib me my freedom, an' sent dem nice ladies from de Norf to gib us some sense. Some ob dese folks calls em nigger teachers, an' won't hab nuffin to do wid 'em, but I jis' thinks dey's splendid. But dere's some triflin' niggers down yere who'll sell der votes for almost nuffin. Does you 'member Jake Williams an' Gundover's Tom? Well dem two niggers is de las' ob pea-time. Dey's mighty small pertaters an' few in a hill."

"Oh, Aunt Linda," said Robert, "don't call them niggers. They are our own people."

"Dey ain't my kine ob people. I jis' calls em niggers, an' niggers I means; an' de bigges' kine ob niggers. An' if my John war sich a nigger I'd whip him an' leave him."

"An' what would I be a doin'," queried John, suddenly rousing up at the mention of his name.

"Standing still and taking it, I suppose," said Iola, who had been quietly listening to and enjoying the conversation.

"Yes, an' I'd ketch myself stan'in' still an' takin' it," was John's plucky response.

"Well, you oughter, ef you's mean enough to wote dat ticket ter put me back inter slavery," was Aunt Linda's parting shot. "Robby," she continued, "you 'member Miss Nancy's Jinnie?"

"Of course I do," said Robert.

"She married Mr. Gundover's Dick. Well, dere warn't much git up an' go 'bout him. So, wen 'lection time com'd, de man he war workin' fer tole him ef he woted de radical ticket he'd turn him off. Well, Jinnie war so 'fraid he'd do it, dat she jis' follered him fer days."

"Poor fellow!" exclaimed Robert. "How did he come out?"

"He certainly was between two fires," interposed Iola.

"Oh, Jinnie gained de day. She jis' got her back up, and said, 'Now ef yer wote dat ticket ter put me back inter slavery, you take yore rags an' go.' An' Dick jis' woted de radical ticket. Jake Williams went on de Secesh side, woted whar he thought he'd git his taters, but he got fooled es slick es greese."

"How was that?" asked Robert.

"Some ob dem folks, dat I 'spects buyed his wote, sent him some flour an' sugar. So one night his wife hab company ter tea. Dey made a big spread, an' put a lot ob sugar on de table fer supper, an' Tom jis' went fer dat sugar. He put a lot in his tea. But somehow it didn't tase right, an' wen dey come ter fine out what war de matter, dey hab sent him a barrel ob san' wid some sugar on top, an' wen de sugar war all gone de san' war dare. Wen I yeard it, I jis' split my sides a larfin. It war too good to keep; an' wen it got roun', Jake war as mad as a March hare. But it sarved him right."

"Well, Aunt Linda, you musn't be too hard on Uncle Jake; you know he's getting old."

"Well he ain't too ole ter do right. He ain't no older dan Uncle Dan'el. An' I yered dey offered him $500 ef he'd go on dere side. An' Uncle Dan'el wouldn't tech it. An' dere's Uncle Job's wife; why didn't she go dat way? She war down on Job's meanness."

"What did she do?"

"Wen 'lection time 'rived, he com'd home bringing some flour an' meat; an' he says ter Aunt Polly, 'Ole woman, I got dis fer de wote.' She jis' picked up dat meat an' flour an' sent it sailin' outer doors, an' den com'd back an' gib him a good tongue-lashin'. 'Oder people,' she said, 'a wotin' ter lib good, an' you a sellin' yore wote! Ain't you got 'nuff ob ole Marster, an' ole Marster bin cuttin' you up? It shan't stay yere.' An' so she wouldn't let de things stay in de house."

"What did Uncle Job do?"

"He jis' stood dere an' cried."

"And didn't you feel sorry for him?" asked Iola.

"Not a bit! he hedn't no business ter be so shabby."

"But, Aunt Linda," pursued Iola, "if it were shabby for an ignorant colored man to sell his vote, wasn't it shabbier for an intelligent white man to buy it?"

"You see," added Robert, "all the shabbiness is not on our side."

"I knows dat," said Aunt Linda, "but I can't help it. I wants my people to wote right, an' to think somethin' ob demselves."

"Well, Aunt Linda, they say in every flock of sheep there will be one that's scabby," observed Iola.

"Dats so! But I ain't got no use fer scabby sheep."

"Lindy," cried John, "we's most dar! Don't you yere dat singin'? Dey's begun a'ready."

"Neber mine," said Aunt Linda, "sometimes de las' ob de wine is de bes'."

Thus discoursing they had beguiled the long hours of the night and made their long journey appear short.

Very soon they reached the church, a neat, commodious, frame building, with a blue ceiling, white walls within and without, and large windows with mahogany-colored facings. It was a sight full of pathetic interest to see that group which gathered from miles around. They had come to break bread with each other, relate their experiences, and tell of their hopes of heaven. In that meeting were remnants of broken families—mothers who had been separated from their children before the war, husbands who had not met their wives for years. After the bread had been distributed and the handshaking was nearly over, Robert raised the hymn which Iola had sung for him when he was recovering from his wounds, and Iola, with her clear, sweet tones, caught up the words and joined him in the strain. When the hymn was finished a dear old mother rose from her seat. Her voice was quite strong. With still a lingering light and fire in her eye, she said:—

"I rise, bredren an' sisters, to say I'm on my solemn march to glory."

"Amen!" "Glory!" came from a number of voices.

"I'se had my trials an' temptations, my ups an' downs; but I feels I'll soon be in one ob de many mansions. If it hadn't been for dat hope I 'spects I would have broken down long ago. I'se bin through de deep waters, but dey didn't overflow me; I'se bin in de fire, but de smell ob it isn't on my garments. Bredren an' sisters, it war a drefful time when I war tored away from my pore little chillen."

"Dat's so!" exclaimed a chorus of voices. Some of her hearers moaned, others rocked to and fro, as thoughts of similar scenes in their own lives arose before them.

"When my little girl," continued the speaker, "took hole ob my dress an' begged me ter let her go wid me, an' I couldn't do it, it mos' broke my heart. I had a little boy, an' wen my mistus sole me she kep' him. She carried on a boardin' house. Many's the time I hab stole out at night an' seen dat chile an' sleep'd wid him in my arms tell mos' day. Bimeby de people I libed wid got hard up fer money, an' dey sole me one way an' my pore little gal de oder; an' I neber laid my eyes on my pore chillen sence den. But, honeys, let de wind blow high or low, I 'spects to outwedder de storm an' anchor by'm bye in bright glory. But I'se bin a prayin' fer one thing, an' I beliebs I'll git it; an' dat is dat I may see my chillen 'fore I die. Pray fer me dat I may hole out an' hole on, an' neber make a shipwrack ob faith, an' at las' fine my way from earth to glory."

Having finished her speech, she sat down and wiped away the tears that flowed all the more copiously as she remembered her lost children. When she rose to speak her voice and manner instantly arrested Robert's attention. He found his mind reverting to the scenes of his childhood. As she proceeded his attention became riveted on her. Unbidden tears filled his eyes and great sobs shook his frame. He trembled in every limb. Could it be possible that after years of patient search through churches, papers, and inquiring friends, he had accidentally stumbled on his mother—the mother who, long years ago, had pillowed his head upon her bosom and left her parting kiss upon his lips? How should he reveal himself to her? Might not sudden joy do what years of sorrow had failed to accomplish? Controlling his feelings as best he could, he rose to tell his experience. He referred to the days when they used to hold their meetings in the lonely woods and gloomy swamps. How they had prayed for freedom and plotted to desert to the Union army; and continuing, he said: "Since then, brethren and sisters, I have had my crosses and trials, but I try to look at the mercies. Just think what it was then and what it is now! How many of us, since freedom has come, have been looking up our scattered relatives. I have just been over to visit my old mistress, Nancy Johnson, and to see if I could get some clue to my long-lost mother, who was sold from me nearly thirty years ago."

Again there was a chorus of moans.

On resuming, Robert's voice was still fuller of pathos. "When," he said, "I heard that dear old mother tell her experience it seemed as if some one had risen from the dead. She made me think of my own dear mother, who used to steal out at night to see me, fold me in her arms, and then steal back again to her work. After she was sold away I never saw her face again by daylight. I have been looking for her ever since the war, and I think at last I have got on the right track. If Mrs. Johnson, who kept the boarding-house in C——, is the one who sold that dear old mother from her son, then she is the one I am looking for, and I am the son she has been praying for."

The dear old mother raised her eyes. They were clear and tearless. An expression of wonder, hope, and love flitted over her face. It seemed as if her youth were suddenly renewed and, bounding from her seat, she rushed to the speaker in a paroxysm of joy. "Oh, Robby! Robby! is dis you? Is dat my pore, dear boy I'se been prayin' 'bout all dese years? Oh, glory! glory!" And overflowing with joyous excitement she threw her arms around him, looking the very impersonation of rapturous content. It was a happy time. Mothers whose children had been torn from them in the days of slavery knew how to rejoice in her joy. The young people caught the infection of the general happiness and rejoiced with them that rejoiced. There were songs of rejoicing and shouts of praise. The undertone of sadness which had so often mingled with their songs gave place to strains of exultation; and tears of tender sympathy flowed from eyes which had often been blurred by anguish. The child of many prayers and tears was restored to his mother.

Iola stood by the mother's side, smiling, and weeping tears of joy. When Robert's mother observed Iola, she said to Robert, "Is dis yore wife?"

"Oh, no," replied Robert, "but I believe she is your

grandchild, the daughter of the little girl who was sold away from you so long ago. She is on her way to the farther South in search of her mother."

"Is she? Dear chile! I hope she'll fine her! She puts me in mine ob my pore little Marie. Well, I'se got one chile, an' I means to keep on prayin' tell I fine my daughter. I'm *so* happy! I feel's like a new woman!"

"My dear mother," said Robert, "now that I have found you, I mean to hold you fast just as long as you live. Ever since the war I have been trying to find out if you were living, but all efforts failed. At last, I thought I would come and hunt you myself and, now that I have found you, I am going to take you home to live with me, and to be as happy as the days are long. I am living in the North, and doing a good business there. I want you to see joy according to all the days wherein you have seen sorrow. I do hope this young lady will find *her* ma and that, when found, she will prove to be your daughter!"

"Yes, pore, dear chile! I specs her mudder's heart's mighty hungry fer her. I does hope she's my gran'chile."

Tenderly and caressingly Iola bent over the happy mother, with her heart filled with mournful memories of her own mother.

Aunt Linda was induced to stay until the next morning, and then gladly assisted Robert's mother in arranging for her journey northward. The friends who had given her a shelter in their hospitable home, learned to value her so much that it was with great reluctance they resigned her to the care of her son. Aunt Linda was full of bustling activity, and her spirits overflowed with good humor.

"Now, Harriet," she said, as they rode along on their return journey, "you mus' jis' thank me fer finin' yore chile, 'cause I got him to come to dat big meetin' wid me."

"Oh, Lindy," she cried, "I'se glad from de bottom ob my heart ter see you's all. I com'd out dere ter git a blessin', an' I'se got a double po'tion. De frens I war libin' wid war mighty good ter me. Dey lib'd wid me in de lower kentry, an' arter de war war ober I stopped wid 'em and helped take keer ob de chillen; an' when dey com'd up yere dey brought me wid 'em. I'se com'd a way I didn't know, but I'se mighty glad I'se com'd."

"Does you know dis place?" asked Aunt Linda, as they approached the settlement.

"No'n 'deed I don't. It's all new ter me."

"Well, dis is whar I libs. Ain't you mighty tired? I feels a little stiffish. Dese bones is gittin' ole."

"Dat's so! But I'se mighty glad I'se lib'd to see my boy 'fore I crossed ober de riber. An' now I feel like ole Simeon."

"But, mother," said Robert, "if you are ready to go, I am not willing to let you. I want you to stay ever so long where I can see you."

A bright smile overspread her face. Robert's words reassured and gladdened her heart. She was well satisfied to have a pleasant aftermath from life on this side of the river.

After arriving home Linda's first thought was to prepare dinner for her guests. But, before she began her work of preparation, she went to the cupboard to get a cup of home-made wine.

"Here," she said, filling three glasses, "is some wine I made myself from dat grape-vine out dere. Don't it look nice and clar? Jist taste it. It's fus'-rate."

"No, thank you," said Robert. "I'm a temperance man, and never take anything which has alcohol in it."

"Oh, dis ain't got a bit ob alcohol in it. I made it myself."

"But, Aunt Linda, you didn't make the law which ferments grape-juice and makes it alcohol."

"But, Robby, ef alcohol's so bad, w'at made de Lord put it here?"

"Aunt Lindy," said Iola, "I heard a lady say that there were two things the Lord didn't make. One is sin, and the other alcohol."

"Why, Aunt Linda," said Robert, "there are numbers of things the Lord has made that I wouldn't touch with a pair of tongs."

"What are they?"

"Rattlesnakes, scorpions, and moccasins."

"Oh, sho!"

"Aunt Linda," said Iola, "the Bible says that the wine at last will bite like a serpent and sting like an adder."

"And, Aunt Linda," added Robert, "as I wouldn't wind a serpent around my throat, I don't want to put something inside of it which will bite like a serpent and sting as an adder."

"I reckon Robby's right," said his mother, setting down her glass and leaving the wine unfinished. "You young folks knows a heap more dan we ole folks."

"Well," declared Aunt Linda, "you all is temp'rence to de backbone. But what could I do wid my wine ef we didn't drink it?"

"Let it turn to vinegar, and sign the temperance pledge," replied Robert.

"I don't keer 'bout it myself, but I don't 'spect John would be willin' ter let it go, 'cause he likes it a heap."

"Then you must give it up for his sake and Job's," said Robert. "They may learn to like it too well."

"You know, Aunt Linda," said Iola, "people don't get to be drunkards all at once. And you wouldn't like to feel, if Job should learn to drink, that you helped form his appetite."

"Dat' so! I beliebs I'll let dis turn to winegar, an' not make any more."

"That's right, Aunt Linda. I hope you'll hold to it," said Robert, encouragingly.

Very soon Aunt Linda had an excellent dinner prepared. After it was over Robert went with Iola to C——, where her friend, the bishop, was awaiting her return. She told him the wonderful story of Robert's finding his mother, and of her sweet, childlike faith.

The bishop, a kind, fatherly man, said, "Miss Iola, I hope that such happiness is in store for you. My dear child, still continue to pray and trust. I am old-fashioned enough to believe in prayer. I knew an old lady living in Illinois, who was a slave. Her son got a chance to come North and beg money to buy his mother. The mother was badly treated, and made up her mind to run away. But before she started she thought she would kneel down to pray. And something, she said, reasoned within her, and whispered, 'Stand still and see what I am going to do for you.' So real was it to her that she unpacked her bundle and desisted from her flight. Strange as it may appear to you, her son returned, bringing with him money enough to purchase her freedom, and she was redeemed from bondage. Had she persisted in running away she might have been lost in the woods and have died, exhausted by starvation. But she believed, she trusted, and was delivered. Her son took her North, where she could find a resting place for the soles of her feet."

That night Iola and the bishop left for the South.

CHAPTER XXI.

A HOME FOR MOTHER.

AFTER Iola had left the settlement, accompanied by Robert as far as the town, it was a pleasant satisfaction for the two old friends to settle themselves down, and talk of times past, departed friends, and long-forgotten scenes.

"What," said Mrs. Johnson, as we shall call Robert's mother, "hab become ob Miss Nancy's husband? Is he still a libin'?"

"Oh, he drunk hisself to death,' 'responded Aunt Linda.

"He used ter be mighty handsome."

"Yes, but drink war his ruination."

"An' how's Miss Nancy?"

"Oh, she's com'd down migh'ly. She's pore as a church mouse. I thought 'twould com'd home ter her wen she sole yer 'way from yore chillen. Dere's nuffin goes ober de debil's back dat don't come under his belly. Do yo 'member Miss Nancy's fardder?"

"Ob course I does!"

"Well," said Aunt Linda, "he war a nice ole gemmen. Wen he died, I said de las' gemmen's dead, an' dere's noboddy ter step in his shoes."

"Pore Miss Nancy!" exclaimed Robert's mother. "I ain't nothin' agin her. But I wouldn't swap places wid her, 'cause I'se got my son; an' I beliebs he'll do a good part by me."

"Mother," said Robert, as he entered the room, "I've brought an old friend to see you. Do you remember Uncle Daniel?"

Uncle Daniel threw back his head, reached out his hand, and manifested his joy with "Well, Haryet! is dis you? I neber 'spected to see you in dese lower grouns! How does yer do? an' whar hab you bin all dis time?"

"O, I'se been tossin' roun' 'bout; but it's all com'd right at las'. I'se lib'd to see my boy 'fore I died."

"My wife an' boys is in glory," said Uncle Daniel. "But I 'spects to see 'em 'fore long. 'Cause I'se tryin' to dig deep, build sure, an' make my way from earth ter glory."

"Dat's de right kine ob talk, Dan'el. We ole folks ain't got long ter stay yere."

They chatted together until Job and Salters came home for supper. After they had eaten, Uncle Daniel said:—

"We'll hab a word ob prayer."

There, in that peaceful habitation, they knelt down, and mingled their prayers together, as they had done in bygone days, when they had met by stealth in lonely swamps or silent forests.

The next morning Robert and his mother started northward. They were well supplied with a bountiful luncheon by Aunt Linda, who had so thoroughly enjoyed their sojourn with her. On the next day he arrived in the city of P——, and took his mother to his boarding-house, until he could find a suitable home into which to install her. He soon came across one which just suited his taste, but when the agent discovered that Robert's mother was colored, he told him that the house had been previously engaged. In company with his mother he looked at several other houses in desirable neighborhoods, but they were constantly met with the answer, "The house is engaged," or, "We do not rent to colored people."

At length Robert went alone, and, finding a desirable house, engaged it, and moved into it. In a short time it was discovered that he was colored, and, at the behest of the local sentiment of the place, the landlord used his utmost endeavors to oust him, simply because he belonged to an unfashionable and unpopular race. At last he came across a landlord who was broad enough to rent him a good house, and he found a quiet resting place among a set of well-to-do and well-disposed people.

CHAPTER XXII.

FURTHER LIFTING OF THE VEIL.

In one of those fearful conflicts by which the Mississippi was freed from Rebel intrusion and opened to commerce Harry was severely wounded, and forced to leave his place in the ranks for a bed in the hospital.

One day, as he lay in his bed, thinking of his former home in Mississippi and wondering if the chances of war would ever restore him to his loved ones, he fell into a quiet slumber. When he awoke he found a lady bending over him, holding in her hands some fruit and flowers. As she tenderly bent over Harry's bed their eyes met, and with a thrill of gladness they recognized each other.

"Oh, my son, my son!" cried Marie, trying to repress her emotion, as she took his wasted hand in hers, and kissed the pale cheeks that sickness and suffering had blanched. Harry was very weak, but her presence was a call to life. He returned the pressure of her hand, kissed it, and his eyes grew full of sudden light, as he murmured faintly, but joyfully:—

"Mamma; oh, mamma! have I found you at last?"

The effort was too much, and he immediately became unconscious.

Anxious, yet hopeful, Marie sat by the bedside of her son till consciousness was restored. Caressingly she bent over his couch, murmuring in her happiness the tenderest, sweetest words of motherly love. In Harry's veins flowed new life and vigor, calming the restlessness of his nerves.

As soon as possible Harry was carried to his mother's home; a home brought into the light of freedom by the victories of General Grant. Nursed by his mother's tender, loving care, he rapidly recovered, but, being too disabled to re-enter the army, he was honorably discharged.

Lorraine had taken Marie to Vicksburg, and there allowed her to engage in confectionery and preserving for the wealthy ladies of the city. He had at first attempted to refugee with her in Texas, but, being foiled in the attempt, he was compelled to enlist in the Confederate Army, and met his fate by being killed just before the surrender of Vicksburg.

"My dear son," Marie would say, as she bent fondly over him, "I am deeply sorry that you are wounded, but I am glad that the fortunes of war have brought us together. Poor Iola! I *do* wonder what has become of her? Just as soon as this war is over I want you to search the country all over. Poor child! How my heart has ached for her!"

Time passed on. Harry and his mother searched and inquired for Iola, but no tidings of her reached them.

Having fully recovered his health, and seeing the great need of education for the colored people, Harry turned his attention toward them, and joined the new army of Northern teachers.

He still continued his inquiries for his sister, not knowing whether or not she had succumbed. to the cruel change in her life. He thought she might have passed into the white basis for the sake of bettering her fortunes. Hope deferred, which had sickened his mother's heart, had only roused him to renewed diligence.

A school was offered him in Georgia, and thither he repaired, taking his mother with him. They were soon established in the city of A——. In hope of finding Iola he visited all the conferences of the Methodist Church, but for a long time his search was in vain.

"Mamma," said Harry, one day during his vacation, "there is to be a Methodist Conference in this State in the city of S——, about one hundred and fifty miles from here. I intend to go and renew my search for Iola."

"Poor child!" burst out Marie, as the tears gathered in her eyes, "I wonder if she is living."

"I think so," said Harry, kissing the pale cheek of his mother; "I don't feel that Iola is dead. I believe we will find her before long."

"It seems to me my heart would burst with joy to see my dear child just once more. I am glad that you are going. When will you leave?"

"To-morrow morning."

"Well, my son, go, and my prayers will go with you," was Marie's tender parting wish.

Early next morning Harry started for the conference, and reached the church before the morning session was over. Near him sat two ladies, one fair, the other considerably darker. There was something in the fairer one that reminded him forcibly of his sister, but she was much older and graver than he imagined his sister to be. Instantly he dismissed the thought that had forced itself into his mind, and began to listen attentively to the proceedings of the conference.

When the regular business of the morning session was over the bishop arose and said :—

"I have an interesting duty to perform. I wish to introduce a young lady to the conference, who was the daughter of a Mississippi planter. She is now in search of her mother and brother, from whom she was sold a few months before the war. Her father married her mother in Ohio, where he had taken her to be educated. After his death they were robbed of their inheritance and enslaved by a distant relative named Lorraine. Miss Iola Leroy is the young lady's name. If any one can give the least information respecting the objects of her search it will be thankfully received."

"I can," exclaimed a young man, rising in the midst of the audience, and pressing eagerly, almost impetuously, forward. "I am her brother, and I came here to look for her."

Iola raised her eyes to his face, so flushed and bright with the glow of recognition, rushed to him, threw her arms around his neck, kissed him again and again, crying: "O, Harry!" Then she fainted from excitement. The women gathered around her with expressions of tender sympathy, and gave her all the care she needed. They called her the "dear child," for without any effort on her part she had slidden into their hearts and found a ready welcome in each sympathizing bosom.

Harry at once telegraphed the glad tidings to his mother, who waited their coming with joyful anticipation. Long before the cars reached the city, Mrs. Leroy was at the depot, restlessly walking the platform or eagerly peering into the darkness to catch the first glimpse of the train which was bearing her treasures.

At length the cars arrived, and, as Harry and Iola alighted, Marie rushed forward, clasped Iola in her arms and sobbed out her joy in broken words.

Very happy was the little family that sat together around the supper-table for the first time for years. They partook of that supper with thankful hearts and with eyes overflowing with tears of joy. Very touching were the prayers the mother uttered, when she knelt with her children that night to return thanks for their happy reunion, and to seek protection through the slumbers of the night.

The next morning, as they sat at the breakfast-table, Marie said :—

"My dear child, you are so changed I do not think I would have known you if I had met you in the street!"

"And I," said Harry, "can hardly realize that you are our own Iola, whom I recognized as sister a half dozen years ago."

"Am I so changed?" asked Iola, as a faint sigh escaped her lips.

"Why, Iola," said Harry, "you used to be the most harum-scarum girl I ever knew—laughing, dancing, and singing from morning until night."

"Yes, I remember," said Iola. "It all comes back to me like a dream. Oh, mamma! I have passed through a fiery ordeal of suffering since then. But it is useless," and as she continued her face assumed a brighter look, "to brood over the past. Let us be happy in the present. Let me tell you something which will please you. Do you remember telling me about your mother and brother?"

"Yes," said Marie, in a questioning tone."

"Well," continued Iola, with eyes full of gladness, "I think I have found them."

"Can it be possible!" exclaimed Marie, in astonishment. "It is more than thirty years since we parted. I fear you are mistaken."

"No, mamma; I have drawn my conclusions from good circumstantial evidence. After I was taken from you, I passed through a fearful siege of suffering, which would only harrow up your soul to hear. I often shudder at the remembrance. The last man in whose clutches I found myself was mean, brutal, and cruel. I was in his power when the Union army came into C——, where I was living. A number of colored men stampeded to the Union ranks, with a gentleman as a leader, whom I think is your brother. A friend of his reported my case to the commander of the post, who instantly gave orders for my release. A place was given me as nurse in the hospital. I attended that friend in his last illness. Poor fellow! he was the best friend I had in all the time I have been tossing about. The gentleman whom I think is your brother appeared to be very anxious about his friend's recovery, and was deeply affected by his death. In one of the last terrible battles of the war, that of Five Forks, he was wounded and put into the hospital ward where I was an attendant. For awhile he was delirious, and in his delirium he would sometimes think that I was his mother and at other times his sister. I humored his fancies, would often sing to him when he was restless, and my voice almost invariably soothed him to sleep. One day I sang to him that old hymn we used to sing on the plantation:—

"Drooping souls no longer grieve,
  Heaven is propitious;
If on Christ you do believe,
  You will find Him precious."

"I remember," said Marie, with a sigh, as memories of the past swept over her.

"After I had finished the hymn," continued Iola, "he looked earnestly and inquiringly into my face, and asked, 'Where did you learn that hymn? I have heard my mother sing it when I was a boy, but I have never heard it since.' I think, mamma, the words, 'I was lost but now I'm found; glory! glory! glory!' had imprinted themselves on his memory, and that his mind was assuming a higher state of intellectuality. He asked me to sing it again, which I did, until he fell asleep. Then I noticed a marked resemblance between him and Harry, and I thought, 'Suppose he should prove to be your long-lost brother?' During his convalescence we found that we had a common ground of sympathy. We were anxious to be reunited to our severed relations. We had both been separated from our mothers. He told me of his little sister, with whom he used to play. She had a mole on her cheek which he called her beauty spot. He had the red spot on his forehead which you told me of."

CHAPTER XXIII.

DELIGHTFUL REUNIONS.

VERY bright and happy was the home where Marie and her children were gathered under one roof. Mrs. Leroy's neighbors said she looked ten years younger. Into that peaceful home came no fearful forebodings of cruel separations. Harry and Iola were passionately devoted to their mother, and did all they could to flood her life with sunshine.

"Iola, dear," said Harry, one morning at the breakfast-table, "I have a new pleasure in store for you."

"What is it, brother mine?" asked Iola, assuming an air of interest.

"There is a young lady living in this city to whom I wish to introduce you. She is one of the most remarkable women I have ever met."

"Do tell me all about her," said Iola. "Is she young and handsome, brilliant and witty?

"She," replied Harry, "is more than handsome, she is lovely; more than witty, she is wise; more than brilliant, she is excellent."

"Well, Harry," said Mrs. Leroy, smiling, "if you keep on that way I shall begin to fear that I shall soon be supplanted by a new daughter."

"Oh, no, mamma," replied Harry, looking slightly confused, "I did not mean that."

"Well, Harry," said Iola, amused, "go on with your description; I am becoming interested. Tax your powers of description to give me her likeness."

"Well, in the first place," continued Harry, "I suppose she is about twenty-five years old."

"Oh, the idea," interrupted Iola, "of a gentleman talking of a lady's age. That is a tabooed subject."

"Why, Iola, that adds to the interest of my picture. It is her combination of earnestness and youthfulness which enhances her in my estimation."

"Pardon the interruption," said Iola; "I am anxious to hear more about her."

"Well, she is of medium height, somewhat slender, and well formed, with dark, expressive eyes, full of thought and feeling. Neither hair nor complexion show the least hint of blood admixture."

"I am glad of it," said Iola. "Every person of unmixed blood who succeeds in any department of literature, art, or science is a living argument for the capability which is in the race."

"Yes," responded Harry, "for it is not the white blood which is on trial before the world. Well, I will bring her around this evening."

In the evening Harry brought Miss Delany to call on his sister and mother. They were much pleased with their visitor. Her manner was a combination of suavity and dignity. During the course of the evening they learned that she was a graduate of the University of A——. One day she saw in the newspapers that colored women were becoming unfit to be servants for white people. She then thought that if they are not fit to be servants for white people, they are unfit to be mothers to their own children, and she conceived the idea of opening a school to train future wives and mothers. She began on a small scale, in a humble building, and her work was soon crowned with gratifying success. She had enlarged her quarters, increased her teaching force, and had erected a large and commodious school-house through her own exertions and the help of others.

Marie cordially invited her to call again, saying, as she rose to go: "I am very glad to have met you. Young women like you always fill my heart with hope for the future of our race. In you I see reflected some of the blessed possibilities which lie within us."

"Thank you," said Miss Delany, "I want to be classed among those of whom it is said, 'She has done what she could.'"

Very pleasant was the acquaintance which sprang up between Miss Delany and Iola. Although she was older than Iola, their tastes were so congenial, their views of life and duty in such unison, that their acquaintance soon ripened into strong and lasting friendship. There were no foolish rivalries and jealousies between them. Their lives were too full of zeal and earnestness for them to waste in selfishness their power to be moral and spiritual forces among a people who so much needed their helping hands. Miss Delany gave Iola a situation in her school; but before the term was quite over she was force to resign, her health having been so undermined by the fearful strain through which she had passed, that she was quite unequal to the task. She remained at home, and did what her strength would allow in assisting her mother in the work of canning and preserving fruits.

In the meantime, Iola had been corresponding with Robert. She had told him of her success in finding her mother and brother, and had received an answer congratulating her on the glad fruition of her hopes. He also said that his business was flourishing, that his mother was keeping house for him, and, to use her own expression, was as happy as the days are long. She was firmly persuaded that Marie was her daughter, and she wanted to see her before she died.

"There is one thing," continued the letter, "that your mother may remember her by. It was a little handkerchief on which were a number of cats' heads. She gave one to each of us."

"I remember it well," said Marie, "she must, indeed, be my mother. Now, all that is needed to complete my happiness is her presence, and my brother's. And I intend, if I live long enough, to see them both."

Iola wrote Robert that her mother remembered the incident of the handkerchief, and was anxious to see them.

In the early fall Robert started for the South in order to clear up all doubts with respect to their relationship. He found Iola, Harry, and their mother living cosily together. Harry was teaching and was a leader among the rising young men of the State. His Northern education and later experience had done much toward adapting him to the work of the new era which had dawned upon the South.

Marie was very glad to welcome Robert to her home, but it was almost impossible to recognize her brother in that tall, handsome man, with dark-brown eyes and wealth of chestnut-colored hair, which he readily lifted to show the crimson spot which lay beneath it.

But as they sat together, and recalled the long-forgotten scenes of their childhood, they concluded that they were brother and sister.

"Marie," said Robert, "how would you like to leave the South?"

"I should like to go North, but I hate to leave Harry. He's a splendid young fellow, although I say it myself. He is so fearless and outspoken that I am constantly anxious about him, especially at election time."

Harry then entered the room, and, being introduced to Robert, gave him a cordial welcome. He had just returned from school.

"We were talking of you, my son," said Marie.

"What were you saying? Nothing of the absent but good?" asked Harry.

"I was telling your uncle, who wants me to come North, that I would go, but I am afraid that you will get into trouble and be murdered, as many others have been."

"Oh, well, mother, I shall not die till my time comes. And if I die helping the poor and needy, I shall die at my post. Could a man choose a better place to die?"

"Were you aware of the virulence of caste prejudice and the disabilities which surround the colored people when you cast your lot with them?" asked Robert.

"Not fully," replied Harry; "but after I found out that I was colored, I consulted the principal of the school, where I was studying, in reference to the future. He said that if I stayed in the North, he had friends whom he believed would give me any situation I could fill, and I could simply take my place in the rank of workers, the same as any other man. Then he told me of the army, and I made up my mind to enter it, actuated by a desire to find my mother and sister; and at any rate I wanted to avenge their wrongs. I do not feel so now. Since I have seen the fearful ravages of war, I have learned to pity and forgive. The principal said he thought I would be more apt to find my family if I joined a colored regiment in the West than if I joined one of the Maine companies. I confess at first I felt a shrinking from taking the step, but love for my mother overcame all repugnance on my part. Now that I have linked my fortunes to the race I intend to do all I can for its elevation."

As he spoke Robert gazed admiringly on the young face, lit up by noble purposes and lofty enthusiasm.

"You are right, Harry. I think it would be treason, not only to the race, but to humanity, to have you ignoring your kindred and masquerading as a white man."

"I think so, too," said Marie.

"But, sister, I am anxious for you all to come North. If Harry feels that the place of danger is the post of duty, let him stay, and he can spend his vacations with us. I think both you and Iola need rest and change. Mother longs to see you before she dies. She feels that we have been the children of many prayers and tears, and I want to make her last days as happy as possible. The South has not been a paradise to you all the time, and I should think you would be willing to leave it."

"Yes, that is so. Iola needs rest and change, and she would be such a comfort to mother. I suppose, for her sake, I will consent to have her go back with you, at least for awhile."

In a few days, with many prayers and tears, Marie, half reluctantly, permitted Iola to start for the North in company with Robert Johnson, intending to follow as soon as she could settle her business and see Harry in a good boarding place.

Very joyful was the greeting of the dear grandmother. Iola soon nestled in her heart and lent additional sunshine to her once checkered life, and Robert, who had so long been robbed of kith and kin, was delighted with the new accession to his home life.

CHAPTER XXIV.

NORTHERN EXPERIENCE.

"UNCLE ROBERT," said Iola, after she had been North several weeks, "I have a theory that every woman ought to know how to earn her own living. I believe that a great amount of sin and misery springs from the weakness and inefficiency of women."

"Perhaps that's so, but what are you going to do about it?"

"I am going to join the great rank of bread-winners. Mr. Waterman has advertised for a number of saleswomen, and I intend to make application."

"When he advertises for help he means white women," said Robert.

"He said nothing about color," responded Iola.

"I don't suppose he did. He doesn't expect any colored girl to apply."

"Well, I think I could fill the place. At least I should like to try. And I do not think when I apply that I am in duty bound to tell him my great-grandmother was a negro."

"Well, child, there is no necessity for you to go out to work. You are perfectly welcome here, and I hope that you feel so."

"Oh, I certainly do. But still I would rather earn my own living."

That morning Iola applied for the situation, and, being prepossessing in her appearance, she obtained it.

For awhile everything went as pleasantly as a marriage bell. But one day a young colored lady, well-dressed and well-bred in her manner, entered the store. It was an acquaintance which Iola had formed in the colored church which she attended. Iola gave her a few words of cordial greeting, and spent a few moments chatting with her. The attention of the girls who sold at the same counter was attracted, and their suspicion awakened. Iola was a stranger in that city. Who was she, and who were her people? At last it was decided that one of the girls should act as a spy, and bring what information she could concerning Iola.

The spy was successful. She found out that Iola was living in a good neighborhood, but that none of the neighbors knew her. The man of the house was very fair, but there was an old woman whom Iola called "Grandma," and she was unmistakably colored. The story was sufficient. If that were true, Iola must be colored, and she should be treated accordingly.

Without knowing the cause, Iola noticed a chill in the social atmosphere of the store, which communicated itself to the cash-boys, and they treated her so insolently that her situation became very uncomfortable. She saw the proprietor, resigned her position, and asked for and obtained a letter of recommendation to another merchant who had advertised for a saleswoman.

In applying for the place, she took the precaution to inform her employer that she was colored. It made no difference to him; but he said:—

"Don't say anything about it to the girls. They might not be willing to work with you."

Iola smiled, did not promise, and accepted the situation. She entered upon her duties, and proved quite acceptable as a saleswoman.

One day, during an interval in business, the girls began to talk of their respective churches, and the question was put to Iola:—

"Where do you go to church?"

"I go," she replied, "to Rev. River's church, corner of Eighth and L Streets."

"Oh, no; you must be mistaken. There is no church there except a colored one."

"That is where I go."

"Why do you go there?"

"Because I liked it when I came here, and joined it."

"A member of a colored church? What under heaven possessed you to do such a thing?"

"Because I wished to be with my own people."

Here the interrogator stopped, and looked surprised and pained, and almost instinctively moved a little farther from her. After the store was closed, the girls had an animated discussion, which resulted in the information being sent to Mr. Cohen that Iola was a colored girl, and that they protested against her being continued in his employ. Mr. Cohen yielded to the pressure, and informed Iola that her services were no longer needed.

When Robert came home in the evening, he found that Iola had lost her situation, and was looking somewhat discouraged.

"Well, uncle," she said, "I feel out of heart. It seems as if the prejudice pursues us through every avenue of life, and assigns us the lowest places."

"That is so," replied Robert, thoughtfully.

"And yet I am determined," said Iola, "to win for myself a place in the fields of labor. I have heard of a place in New England, and I mean to try for it, even if I only stay a few months."

"Well, if you *will* go, say nothing about your color."

"Uncle Robert, I see no necessity for proclaiming that fact on the house-top. Yet I am resolved that nothing shall tempt me to deny it. The best blood in my veins is African blood, and I am not ashamed of it."

"Hurrah for you!" exclaimed Robert, laughing heartily.

As Iola wished to try the world for herself, and so be prepared for any emergency, her uncle and grandmother were content to have her go to New England. The town to which she journeyed was only a few hours' ride from the city of P——, and Robert, knowing that there is no teacher like experience, was willing that Iola should have the benefit of her teaching.

Iola, on arriving in H——, sought the firm, and was informed that her services were needed. She found it a pleasant and lucrative position. There was only one drawback—her boarding place was too far from her work. There was an institution conducted by professed Christian women, which was for the special use of respectable young working girls. This was in such a desirable location that she called at the house to engage board.

The matron conducted her over the house, and grew so friendly in the interview that she put her arm around her, and seemed to look upon Iola as a desirable accession to the home. But, just as Iola was leaving, she said to the matron: "I must be honest with you; I am a colored woman."

Swift as light a change passed over the face of the matron. She withdrew her arm from Iola, and said: "I must see the board of managers about it."

When the board met, Iola's case was put before them, but they decided not to receive her. And these women, professors of a religion which taught, "If ye have respect to persons ye commit sin," virtually shut the door in her face because of the outcast blood in her veins.

Considerable feeling was aroused by the action of these women, who, to say the least, had not put their religion in the most favorable light.

Iola continued to work for the firm until she received letters from her mother and uncle, which informed her that her mother, having arranged her affairs in the South, was ready to come North. She then resolved to return to the city of P——, to be ready to welcome her mother on her arrival.

Iola arrived in time to see that everything was in order for her mother's reception. Her room was furnished neatly, but with those touches of beauty that womanly hands are such adepts in giving. A few charming pictures adorned the walls, and an easy chair stood waiting to receive the travel-worn mother. Robert and Iola met her at the depot; and grandma was on her feet at the first sound of the bell, opened the door, clasped Marie to her heart, and nearly fainted for joy.

"Can it be possible dat dis is my little Marie?" she exclaimed.

It did seem almost impossible to realize that this faded woman, with pale cheeks and prematurely whitened hair, was the rosy-cheeked child from whom she had been parted more than thirty years.

"Well," said Robert, after the first joyous greeting was over, "love is a very good thing, but Marie has had a long journey and needs something that will stick by the ribs. How about dinner, mother?"

"It's all ready," said Mrs. Johnson.

After Marie had gone to her room and changed her dress, she came down and partook of the delicious repast which her mother and Iola had prepared for her.

In a few days Marie was settled in the home, and was well pleased with the change. The only drawback to her happiness was the absence of her son, and she expected him to come North after the closing of his school.

"Uncle Robert," said Iola, after her mother had been with them several weeks, "I am tired of being idle."

"What's the matter now?" asked Robert. "You are surely not going East again, and leave your mother?"

"Oh, I hope not," said Marie, anxiously. "I have been so long without you."

"No, mamma, I am not going East. I can get suitable employment here in the city of P——."

"But, Iola," said Robert, "you have tried, and been defeated. Why subject yourself to the same experience again?"

"Uncle Robert, I think that every woman should have some skill or art which would insure her at least a comfortable support. I believe there would be less unhappy marriages if labor were more honored among women."

"Well, Iola," said her mother, "what is your skill?"

"Nursing. I was very young when I went into the

hospital, but I succeeded so well that the doctor said I must have been a born nurse. Now, I see by the papers, that a gentleman who has an invalid daughter wants some one who can be a nurse and companion for her, and I mean to apply for the situation. I do not think, if I do my part well in that position, that the blood in my veins will be any bar to my success."

A troubled look stole over Marie's face. She sighed faintly, but made no remonstrance. And so it was decided that Iola should apply for the situation.

Iola made application, and was readily accepted. Her patient was a frail girl of fifteen summers, who was ill with a low fever. Iola nursed her carefully, and soon had the satisfaction of seeing her restored to health. During her stay, Mr. Cloten, the father of the invalid, had learned some of the particulars of Iola's Northern experience as a bread-winner, and he resolved to give her employment in his store when her services were no longer needed in the house. As soon as a vacancy occurred he gave Iola a place in his store.

The morning she entered on her work he called his employés together, and told them that Miss Iola had colored blood in her veins, but that he was going to employ her and give her a desk. If any one objected to working with her, he or she could step to the cashier's desk and receive what was due. Not a man remonstrated, not a woman demurred; and Iola at last found a place in the great army of bread-winners, which the traditions of her blood could not affect.

"How did you succeed?" asked Mrs. Cloten of her husband, when he returned to dinner.

"Admirably! 'Everything is lovely and the goose

hangs high.' I gave my employés to understand that they could leave if they did not wish to work with Miss Leroy. Not one of them left, or showed any disposition to rebel."

"I am very glad," said Mrs Cloten. "I am ashamed of the way she has been treated in our city, when seeking to do her share in the world's work. I am glad that you were brave enough to face this cruel prejudice, and give her a situation."

"Well, my dear, do not make me a hero for a single act. I am grateful for the care Miss Leroy gave our Daisy. Money can buy services, but it cannot purchase tender, loving sympathy. I was also determined to let my employés know that I, not they, commanded my business. So, do not crown me a hero until I have won a niche in the temple of fame. In dealing with Southern prejudice against the negro, we Northerners could do it with better grace if we divested ourselves of our own. We irritate the South by our criticisms, and, while I confess that there is much that is reprehensible in their treatment of colored people, yet if our Northern civilization is higher than theirs we should 'criticise by creation.' We should stamp ourselves on the South, and not let the South stamp itself on us. When we have learned to treat men according to the complexion of their souls, and not the color of their skins, we will have given our best contribution towards the solution of the negro problem."

"I feel, my dear," said Mrs. Cloten, "that what you have done is a right step in the right direction, and I hope that other merchants will do the same. We have numbers of business men, rich enough to afford themselves the luxury of a good conscience."

CHAPTER XXV.

AN OLD FRIEND.

"GOOD-MORNING, Miss Leroy," said a cheery voice in tones of glad surprise, and, intercepting her path, Dr. Gresham stood before Iola, smiling, and reaching out his hand.

"Why, Dr. Gresham, is this you?" said Iola, lifting her eyes to that well-remembered face. "It has been several years since we met. How have you been all this time, and where?"

"I have been sick, and am just now recovering from malaria and nervous prostration. I am attending a medical convention in this city, and hope that I shall have the pleasure of seeing you again."

Iola hesitated, and then replied: "I should be pleased to have you call."

"It would give me great pleasure. Where shall I call?"

"My home is 1006 South Street, but I am only at home in the evenings."

They walked together a short distance till they reached Mr. Cloten's store; then, bidding the doctor good morning, Iola left him repeating to himself the words of his favorite poet:—

> "Thou art too lovely and precious a gem
> To be bound to their burdens and sullied by them."

No one noticed the deep flush on Iola's face as she entered the store, nor the subdued, quiet manner with which she applied herself to her tasks. She was living over again the past, with its tender, sad, and thrilling reminiscences.

In the evening Dr. Gresham called on Iola. She met him with a pleasant welcome. Dr. Gresham gazed upon her with unfeigned admiration, and thought that the years, instead of detracting from, had only intensified, her loveliness. He had thought her very beautiful in the hospital, in her gray dress and white collar, with her glorious wealth of hair drawn over her ears. But now, when he saw her with that hair artistically arranged, and her finely-proportioned form arrayed in a dark crimson dress, relieved by a shimmer of lace and a bow of white ribbon at her throat, he thought her superbly handsome. The lines which care had written upon her young face had faded away. There was no undertone of sorrow in her voice as she stood up before him in the calm loveliness of her ripened womanhood, radiant in beauty and gifted in intellect. Time and failing health had left their traces upon Dr. Gresham. His step was less bounding, his cheek a trifle paler, his manner somewhat graver than it was when he had parted from Iola in the hospital, but his meeting with her had thrilled his heart with unexpected pleasure. Hopes and sentiments which long had slept awoke at the touch of her hand and the tones of her voice, and Dr. Gresham found himself turning to the past, with its sad memories and disappointed hopes. No other face had displaced her image in his mind; no other love had woven itself around every tendril of his soul. His heart and hand were just as free as they were the hour they had parted.

"To see you again," said Dr. Gresham, "is a great and unexpected pleasure."

"You had not forgotten me, then?" said Iola, smiling.

"Forget you! I would just as soon forget my own existence. I do not think that time will ever efface the impressions of those days in which we met so often. When last we met you were intending to search for your mother. Have you been successful?"

"More than successful," said Iola, with a joyous ring in her voice. "I have found my mother, brother, grandmother, and uncle, and, except my brother, we are all living together, and we are so happy. Excuse me a few minutes," she said, and left the room. Iola soon returned, bringing with her her mother and grandmother.

"These," said Iola, introducing her mother and grandmother, "are the once-severed branches of our family; and this gentleman you have seen before," continued Iola, as Robert entered the room.

Dr. Gresham looked scrutinizingly at him and said: "Your face looks familiar, but I saw so many faces at the hospital that I cannot just now recall your name."

"Doctor," said Robert Johnson, "I was one of your last patients, and I was with Tom Anderson when he died."

"Oh, yes," replied Dr. Gresham; "it all comes back to me. You were wounded at the battle of Five Forks, were you not?"

"Yes," said Robert.

"I saw you when you were recovering. You told me that you thought you had a clue to your lost relatives, from whom you had been so long separated. How have you succeeded?"

"Admirably! I have been fortunate in finding my mother, my sister, and her children."

"Ah, indeed! I am delighted to hear it. Where are they?"

"They are right here. This is my mother," said Robert, bending fondly over her, as she returned his recognition with an expression of intense satisfaction; "and this," he continued, "is my sister, and Miss Leroy is my niece."

"Is it possible! I am very glad to hear it. It has been said that every cloud has its silver lining, and the silver lining of our war cloud is the redemption of a race and the reunion of severed hearts. War is a dreadful thing; but worse than the war was the slavery which preceded it."

"Slavery," said Iola, "was a fearful cancer eating into the nation's heart, sapping its vitality, and undermining its life."

"And war," said Dr. Gresham, "was the dreadful surgery by which the disease was eradicated. The cancer has been removed, but for years to come I fear that we will have to deal with the effects of the disease. But I believe that we have vitality enough to outgrow those effects."

"I think, Doctor," said Iola, "that there is but one remedy by which our nation can recover from the evil entailed upon her by slavery."

"What is that?" asked Robert.

"A fuller comprehension of the claims of the Gospel of Jesus Christ, and their application to our national life."

"Yes," said Robert; "while politicians are stumbling

on the barren mountains of fretful controversy, and asking what shall we do with the negro, I hold that Jesus answered that question nearly two thousand years ago, when he said, 'Whatsoever ye would that men should do to you, do ye even so to them.'"

"Yes," said Dr. Gresham; "the application of that rule in dealing with the negro would solve the whole problem."

"Slavery," said Mrs. Leroy, "is dead, but the spirit which animated it still lives; and I think that a reckless disregard for human life is more the outgrowth of slavery than any actual hatred of the negro."

"The problem of the nation," continued Dr. Gresham, "is not what men will do with the negro, but what will they do with the reckless, lawless white men who murder, lynch, and burn their fellow-citizens. To me these lynchings and burnings are perfectly alarming. Both races have reacted on each other—men fettered the slave, and cramped their own souls; denied him knowledge, and darkened their spiritual insight; subdued him to the pliancy of submission, and in their turn became the thralls of public opinion. The negro came here from the heathenism of Africa; but the young colonies could not take into their early civilization a stream of barbaric blood without being affected by its influence, and the negro, poor and despised as he is, has laid his hands on our Southern civilization and helped mould its character."

"Yes," said Mrs. Leroy; "the colored nurse could not nestle her master's child in her arms, hold up his baby footsteps on their floors, and walk with him through the impressible and formative period of his young life without leaving upon him the impress of her hand."

"I am glad," said Robert, "for the whole nation's sake, that slavery has been destroyed."

"And our work," said Dr. Gresham, "is to build over the desolations of the past a better and brighter future. The great distinction between savagery and civilization is the creation and maintenance of law. A people cannot habitually trample on law and justice without retrograding toward barbarism. But I am hopeful that time will bring us changes for the better; that, as we get farther away from the war, we will outgrow the animosities and prejudices engendered by slavery. The short-sightedness of our fathers linked the negro's destiny to ours. We are feeling the friction of the ligatures which bind us together, but I hope that the time will speedily come when the best members of both races will unite for the maintenance of law and order and the progress and prosperity of the country, and that the intelligence and virtue of the South will be strong to grapple effectually with its ignorance and vice."

"I hope that time will speedily come," said Marie. "My son is in the South, and I am always anxious for his safety. He is not only a teacher, but a leading young man in the community where he lives."

"Yes," said Robert, "and when I see the splendid work he is doing in the South, I am glad that, instead of trying to pass for a white man, he has cast his lot with us."

"But," answered Dr. Gresham, "he would possess advantages as a white man which he could not if he were known to be colored."

"Doctor," said Iola, decidedly, "he has greater advantages as a colored man."

"I do not understand you," said Dr. Gresham, looking somewhat puzzled.

"Doctor," continued Iola, "I do not think life's highest advantages are those that we can see with our eyes or grasp with our hands. To whom to-day is the world most indebted—to its millionaires or to its martyrs?"

"Taking it from the ideal standpoint," replied the doctor, "I should say its martyrs."

"To be," continued Iola, "the leader of a race to higher planes of thought and action, to teach men clearer views of life and duty, and to inspire their souls with loftier aims, is a far greater privilege than it is to open the gates of material prosperity and fill every home with sensuous enjoyment."

"And I," said Mrs. Leroy, her face aglow with fervid feeling, "would rather—ten thousand times rather—see Harry the friend and helper of the poor and ignorant than the companion of men who, under the cover of night, mask their faces and ride the country on lawless raids."

"Dr. Gresham," said Robert, "we ought to be the leading nation of the earth, whose influence and example should give light to the world."

"Not simply," said Iola, "a nation building up a great material prosperity, founding magnificent cities, grasping the commerce of the world, or excelling in literature, art, and science, but a nation wearing sobriety as a crown and righteousness as the girdle of her loins."

Dr. Gresham gazed admiringly upon Iola. A glow of enthusiasm overspread her beautiful, expressive face. There was a rapt and far-off look in her eye, as if she were looking beyond the present pain to a brighter future for the race with which she was identified, and felt the grandeur of a divine commission to labor for its uplifting.

As Dr. Gresham was parting with Robert, he said: "This meeting has been a very unexpected pleasure. I have spent a delightful evening. I only regret that I had not others to share it with me. A doctor from the South, a regular Bourbon, is stopping at the hotel. I wish he could have been here to-night. Come down to the Concordia, Mr. Johnson, to-morrow night. If you know any colored man who is a strong champion of equal rights, bring him along. Good-night. I shall look for you," said the doctor, as he left the door.

When Robert returned to the parlor he said to Iola: "Dr. Gresham has invited me to come to his hotel to-morrow night, and to bring some wide-awake colored man with me. There is a Southerner whom he wishes me to meet. I suppose he wants to discuss the negro problem, as they call it. He wants some one who can do justice to the subject. I wonder whom I can take with me?"

"I will tell you who, I think, will be a capital one to take with you, and I believe he would go," said Iola.

"Who?" asked Robert.

"Rev. Carmicle, your pastor."

"He is just the one," said Robert, "courteous in his manner and very scholarly in his attainments. He is a man whom if everybody hated him no one could despise him."

CHAPTER XXVI.

OPEN QUESTIONS.

In the evening Robert and Rev. Carmicle called on Dr. Gresham, and found Dr. Latrobe, the Southerner, and a young doctor by the name of Latimer, already there. Dr. Gresham introduced Dr. Latrobe, but it was a new experience to receive colored men socially. His wits, however, did not forsake him, and he received the introduction and survived it.

"Permit me, now," said Dr. Gresham, "to introduce you to my friend, Dr. Latimer, who is attending our convention. He expects to go South and labor among the colored people. Don't you think that there is a large field of usefulness before him?"

"Yes," replied Dr. Latrobe, "if he will let politics alone."

"And why let politics alone?" asked Dr. Gresham.

"Because," replied Dr. Latrobe, "we Southerners will never submit to negro supremacy. We will never abandon our Caucasian civilization to an inferior race."

"Have you any reason," inquired Rev. Carmicle, "to dread that a race which has behind it the heathenism of Africa and the slavery of America, with its inheritance of ignorance and poverty, will be able, in less than one generation, to domineer over a race which has behind it ages of dominion, freedom, education, and Christianity?"

A slight shade of vexation and astonishment passed

over the face of Dr. Latrobe. He hesitated a moment, then replied:—

"I am not afraid of the negro as he stands alone, but what I dread is that in some closely-contested election ambitious men will use him to hold the balance of power and make him an element of danger. He is ignorant, poor, and clannish, and they may impact him as their policy would direct."

"Any more," asked Robert, "than the leaders of the Rebellion did the ignorant, poor whites during our late conflict?

"Ignorance, poverty, and clannishness," said Dr. Gresham, "are more social than racial conditions, which may be outgrown."

"And I think," said Rev. Carmicle, "that we are outgrowing them as fast as any other people would have done under the same conditions."

"The negro," replied Dr. Latrobe, "always has been and always will be an element of discord in our country."

"What, then, is your remedy?" asked Dr. Gresham.

"I would eliminate him from the politics of the country."

"As disfranchisement is a punishment for crime, is it just to punish a man before he transgresses the law?" asked Dr. Gresham.

"If," said Dr. Latimer, "the negro is ignorant, poor, and clannish, let us remember that in part of our land it was once a crime to teach him to read. If he is poor, for ages he was forced to bend to unrequited toil. If he is clannish, society has segregated him to himself."

"And even," said Robert, "has given him a negro pew in your churches and a negro seat at your communion table."

"Wisely, or unwisely," said Dr. Gresham, "the Government has put the ballot in his hands. It is better to teach him to use that ballot aright than to intimidate him by violence or vitiate his vote by fraud."

"To-day," said Dr. Latimer, "the negro is not plotting in beer-saloons against the peace and order of society. His fingers are not dripping with dynamite, neither is he spitting upon your flag, nor flaunting the red banner of anarchy in your face."

"Power," said Dr. Gresham, "naturally gravitates into the strongest hands. The class who have the best brain and most wealth can strike with the heaviest hand. I have too much faith in the inherent power of the white race to dread the competition of any other people under heaven."

"I think you Northerners fail to do us justice," said Dr. Latrobe. "The men into whose hands you put the ballot were our slaves, and we would rather die than submit to them. Look at the carpet-bag governments the wicked policy of the Government inflicted upon us. It was only done to humiliate us."

"Oh, no!" said Dr. Gresham, flushing, and rising to his feet. "We had no other alternative than putting the ballot in their hands."

"I will not deny," said Rev. Carmicle, "that we have made woeful mistakes, but with our antecedents it would have been miraculous if we had never committed any mistakes or made any blunders."

"They were allies in war," continued Dr. Gresham,

"and I am sorry that we have not done more to protect them in peace."

"Protect them in peace!" said Robert, bitterly. "What protection does the colored man receive from the hands of the Government? I know of no civilized country outside of America where men are still burned for real or supposed crimes."

"Johnson," said Dr. Gresham, compassionately, "it is impossible to have a policeman at the back of each colored man's chair, and a squad of soldiers at each cross-road, to detect with certainty, and punish with celerity, each invasion of his rights. We tried provisional governments and found them a failure. It seemed like leaving our former allies to be mocked with the name of freedom and tortured with the essence of slavery. The ballot is our weapon of defense, and we gave it to them for theirs."

"And there," said Dr. Latrobe, emphatically, "is where you signally failed. We are numerically stronger in Congress to-day than when we went out. You made the law, but the administration of it is in our hands, and we are a unit."

"But, Doctor," said Rev. Carmicle, "you cannot willfully deprive the negro of a single right as a citizen without sending demoralization through your own ranks."

"I think," said Dr. Latrobe, "that we are right in suppressing the negro's vote. This is a white man's government, and a white man's country. We own nineteen-twentieths of the land, and have about the same ratio of intelligence. I am a white man, and, right or wrong, I go with my race."

"But, Doctor," said Rev. Carmicle, "there are rights

more sacred than the rights of property and superior intelligence."

"What are they?" asked Dr. Latrobe.

"The rights of life and liberty," replied Rev. Carmicle.

"That is true," said Dr. Gresham; "and your Southern civilization will be inferior until you shall have placed protection to those rights at its base, not in theory but in fact."

"But, Dr. Gresham, we have to live with these people, and the North is constantly irritating us by its criticisms."

"The world," said Dr. Gresham, "is fast becoming a vast whispering gallery, and lips once sealed can now state their own grievances and appeal to the conscience of the nation, and, as long as a sense of justice and mercy retains a hold upon the heart of our nation, you cannot practice violence and injustice without rousing a spirit of remonstrance. And if it were not so I would be ashamed of my country and of my race."

"You speak," said Dr. Latrobe, "as if we had wronged the negro by enslaving him and being unwilling to share citizenship with him. I think that slavery has been of incalculable value to the negro. It has lifted him out of barbarism and fetich worship, given him a language of civilization, and introduced him to the world's best religion. Think what he was in Africa and what he is in America!"

"The negro," said Dr. Gresham, thoughtfully, "is not the only branch of the human race which has been low down in the scale of civilization and freedom, and which has outgrown the measure of his chains. Slavery, polygamy, and human sacrifices have been practiced among Europeans in bygone days; and when Tyndall tells us that out of savages unable to count to the number of their fingers and speaking only a language of nouns and verbs, arise at length our Newtons and Shakspeares, I do not see that the negro could not have learned our language and received our religion without the intervention of ages of slavery."

"If," said Rev. Carmicle, "Mohammedanism, with its imperfect creed, is successful in gathering large numbers of negroes beneath the Crescent, could not a legitimate commerce and the teachings of a pure Christianity have done as much to plant the standard of the Cross over the ramparts of sin and idolatry in Africa? Surely we cannot concede that the light of the Crescent is greater than the glory of the Cross, that there is less constraining power in the Christ of Calvary than in the Prophet of Arabia? I do not think that I underrate the difficulties in your way when I say that you young men are holding in your hands golden opportunities which it would be madness and folly to throw away. It is your grand opportunity to help build up a new South, not on the shifting sands of policy and expediency, but on the broad basis of equal justice and universal freedom. Do this and you will be blessed, and will make your life a blessing."

After Robert and Rev. Carmicle had left the hotel, Drs. Latimer, Gresham, and Latrobe sat silent and thoughtful awhile, when Dr. Gresham broke the silence by asking Dr. Latrobe how he had enjoyed the evening.

"Very pleasantly," he replied. "I was quite interested in that parson. Where was he educated?"

"In Oxford, I believe. I was pleased to hear him say that he had no white blood in his veins."

"I should think not," replied Dr. Latrobe, "from his looks. But one swallow does not make a summer. It is the exceptions which prove the rule."

"Don't you think," asked Dr. Gresham, "that we have been too hasty in our judgment of the negro? He has come handicapped into life, and is now on trial before the world. But it is not fair to subject him to the same tests that you would a white man. I believe that there are possibilities of growth in the race which we have never comprehended."

"The negro," said Dr. Latrobe, "is perfectly comprehensible to me. The only way to get along with him is to let him know his place, and make him keep it."

"I think," replied Dr. Gresham, "every man's place is the one he is best fitted for."

"Why," asked Dr. Latimer, "should any place be assigned to the negro more than to the French, Irish, or German?"

"Oh," replied Dr. Latrobe, "they are all Caucasians."

"Well," said Dr. Gresham, "is all excellence summed up in that branch of the human race?"

"I think," said Dr. Latrobe, proudly, "that we belong to the highest race on earth and the negro to the lowest."

"And yet," said Dr. Latimer, "you have consorted with them till you have bleached their faces to the whiteness of your own. Your children nestle in their bosoms; they are around you as body servants, and yet if one of them should attempt to associate with you your bitterest scorn and indignation would be visited upon them."

"I think," said Dr. Latrobe, "that feeling grows out of our Anglo-Saxon regard for the marriage relation. These white negroes are of illegitimate origin, and we would scorn to share our social life with them. Their blood is tainted."

"Who tainted it?" asked Dr. Latimer, bitterly. "You give absolution to the fathers, and visit the misfortunes of the mothers upon the children."

"But, Doctor, what kind of society would we have if we put down the bars and admitted everybody to social equality?"

"This idea of social equality," said Dr. Latimer, "is only a bugbear which frightens well-meaning people from dealing justly with the negro. I know of no place on earth where there is perfect social equality, and I doubt if there is such a thing in heaven. The sinner who repents on his death-bed cannot be the equal of St. Paul or the Beloved Disciple."

"Doctor," said Dr. Gresham, "I sometimes think that the final solution of this question will be the absorption of the negro into our race."

"Never! never!" exclaimed Dr. Latrobe, vehemently. "It would be a death blow to American civilization."

"Why, Doctor," said Dr. Latimer, "you Southerners began this absorption before the war. I understand that in one decade the mixed bloods rose from one-ninth to one-eighth of the population, and that as early as 1663 a law was passed in Maryland to prevent English women from intermarrying with slaves; and, even now, your laws against miscegenation presuppose that you apprehend danger from that source."

"Doctor, it is no use talking," replied Dr. Latrobe, wearily. "There are niggers who are as white as I am, but the taint of blood is there and we always exclude it."

"How do you know it is there?" asked Dr. Gresham.

"Oh, there are tricks of blood which always betray them. My eyes are more practiced than yours. I can always tell them. Now, that Johnson is as white as any man; but I knew he was a nigger the moment I saw him. I saw it in his eye."

Dr. Latimer smiled at Dr. Latrobe's assertion, but did not attempt to refute it; and bade him good-night.

"I think," said Dr. Latrobe, "that our war was the great mistake of the nineteenth century. It has left us very serious complications. We cannot amalgamate with the negroes. We cannot expatriate them. Now, what are we to do with them?"

"Deal justly with them," said Dr. Gresham, "and let them alone. Try to create a moral sentiment in the nation, which will consider a wrong done to the weakest of them as a wrong done to the whole community. Whenever you find ministers too righteous to be faithless, cowardly, and time serving; women too Christly to be scornful; and public men too noble to be tricky and too honest to pander to the prejudices of the people, stand by them and give them your moral support."

"Doctor," said Latrobe, "with your views you ought to be a preacher striving to usher in the millennium."

"It can't come too soon," replied Dr. Gresham.

CHAPTER XXVII.

DIVERGING PATHS.

On the eve of his departure from the city of P——, Dr. Gresham called on Iola, and found her alone. They talked awhile of reminiscences of the war and hospital life, when Dr. Gresham, approaching Iola, said:—

"Miss Leroy, I am glad the great object of your life is accomplished, and that you have found all your relatives. Years have passed since we parted, years in which I have vainly tried to get a trace of you and have been baffled, but I have found you at last!" Clasping her hand in his, he continued, "I would it were so that I should never lose you again! Iola, will you not grant me the privilege of holding this hand as mine all through the future of our lives? Your search for your mother is ended. She is well cared for. Are you not free at last to share with me my Northern home, free to be mine as nothing else on earth is mine." Dr. Gresham looked eagerly on Iola's face, and tried to read its varying expression. "Iola, I learned to love you in the hospital. I have tried to forget you, but it has been all in vain. Your image is just as deeply engraven on my heart as it was the day we parted."

"Doctor," she replied, sadly, but firmly, as she withdrew her hand from his, "I feel now as I felt then, that there is an insurmountable barrier between us."

"What is it, Iola?" asked Dr. Gresham, anxiously.

"It is the public opinion which assigns me a place with the colored people."

"But what right has public opinion to interfere with our marriage relations? Why should we yield to its behests?"

"Because it is stronger than we are, and we cannot run counter to it without suffering its penalties."

"And what are they, Iola? Shadows that you merely dread?"

"No! no! the penalties of social ostracism North and South, except here and there some grand and noble exceptions. I do not think that you fully realize how much prejudice against colored people permeates society, lowers the tone of our religion, and reacts upon the life of the nation. After freedom came, mamma was living in the city of A———, and wanted to unite with a Christian church there. She made application for membership. She passed her examination as a candidate, and was received as a church member. When she was about to make her first communion, she unintentionally took her seat at the head of the column. The elder who was administering the communion gave her the bread in the order in which she sat, but before he gave her the wine some one touched him on the shoulder and whispered a word in his ear. He then passed mamma by, gave the cup to others, and then returned to her. From that rite connected with the holiest memories of earth, my poor mother returned humiliated and depressed."

"What a shame!" exclaimed Dr. Gresham, indignantly.

"I have seen," continued Iola, "the same spirit manifested in the North. Mamma once attempted to do missionary work in this city. One day she found an outcast colored girl, whom she wished to rescue. She took her to an asylum for fallen women and made an application for her, but was refused. Colored girls were not received there. Soon after mamma found among the colored people an outcast white girl. Mamma's sympathies, unfettered by class distinction, were aroused in her behalf, and, in company with two white ladies, she went with the girl to that same refuge. For her the door was freely opened and admittance readily granted. It was as if two women were sinking in the quicksands, and on the solid land stood other women with life-lines in their hands, seeing the deadly sands slowly creeping up around the hapless victims. To one they readily threw the lines of deliverance, but for the other there was not one strand of salvation. Sometime since, to the same asylum, came a poor fallen girl who had escaped from the clutches of a wicked woman. For her the door would have been opened, had not the vile woman from whom she was escaping followed her to that place of refuge and revealed the fact that she belonged to the colored race. That fact was enough to close the door upon her, and to send her back to sin and to suffer, and perhaps to die as a wretched outcast. And yet in this city where a number of charities are advertised, I do not think there is one of them which, in appealing to the public, talks more religion than the managers of this asylum. This prejudice against the colored race environs our lives and mocks our aspirations."

"Iola, I see no use in your persisting that you are colored when your eyes are as blue and complexion as white as mine."

"Doctor, were I your wife, are there not people who would caress me as a white woman who would shrink from me in scorn if they knew I had one drop of negro blood in my veins? When mistaken for a white woman, I should hear things alleged against the race at which my blood would boil. No, Doctor, I am not willing to live under a shadow of concealment which I thoroughly hate as if the blood in my veins were an undetected crime of my soul."

"Iola, dear, surely you paint the picture too darkly."

"Doctor, I have painted it with my heart's blood. It is easier to outgrow the dishonor of crime than the disabilities of color. You have created in this country an aristocracy of color wide enough to include the South with its treason and Utah with its abominations, but too narrow to include the best and bravest colored man who bared his breast to the bullets of the enemy during your fratricidal strife. Is not the most arrant Rebel to-day more acceptable to you than the most faithful colored man?"

"No! no!" exclaimed Dr. Gresham, vehemently. "You are wrong. I belong to the Grand Army of the Republic. We have no separate State Posts for the colored people, and, were such a thing proposed, the majority of our members, I believe, would be against it. In Congress colored men have the same seats as white men, and the color line is slowly fading out in our public institutions."

"But how is it in the Church?" asked Iola.

"The Church is naturally conservative. It preserves old truths, even if it is somewhat slow in embracing new ideas. It has its social as well as its spiritual side.

Society is woman's realm. The majority of church members are women, who are said to be the aristocratic element of our country. I fear that one of the last strongholds of this racial prejudice will be found beneath the shadow of some of our churches. I think, on account of this social question, that large bodies of Christian temperance women and other reformers, in trying to reach the colored people even for their own good, will be quicker to form separate associations than our National Grand Army, whose ranks are open to black and white, liberals and conservatives, saints and agnostics. But, Iola, we have drifted far away from the question. No one has a right to interfere with our marriage if we do not infringe on the rights of others."

"Doctor," she replied, gently, "I feel that our paths must diverge. My life-work is planned. I intend spending my future among the colored people of the South."

"My dear friend," he replied, anxiously, "I am afraid that you are destined to sad disappointment. When the novelty wears off you will be disillusioned, and, I fear, when the time comes that you can no longer serve them they will forget your services and remember only your failings."

"But, Doctor, they need me; and I am sure when I taught among them they were very grateful for my services."

"I think," he replied, "these people are more thankful than grateful."

"I do not think so; and if I did it would not hinder me from doing all in my power to help them. I do not expect all the finest traits of character to spring from the hot-beds of slavery and caste. What matters it if they do forget the singer, so they don't forget the song? No, Doctor, I don't think that I could best serve my race by forsaking them and marrying you."

"Iola," he exclaimed, passionately, "if you love your race, as you call it, work for it, live for it, suffer for it, and, if need be, die for it; but don't marry for it. Your education has unfitted you for social life among them."

"It was," replied Iola, "through their unrequited toil that I was educated, while they were compelled to live in ignorance. I am indebted to them for the power I have to serve them. I wish other Southern women felt as I do. I think they could do so much to help the colored people at their doors if they would look at their opportunities in the light of the face of Jesus Christ. Nor am I wholly unselfish in allying myself with the colored people. All the rest of my family have done so. My dear grandmother is one of the excellent of the earth, and we all love her too much to ignore our relationship with her. I did not choose my lot in life, and the simplest thing I can do is to accept the situation and do the best I can."

"And is this your settled purpose?" he asked, sadly.

"It is, Doctor," she replied, tenderly but firmly. "I see no other. I must serve the race which needs me most."

"Perhaps you are right," he replied; "but I cannot help feeling sad that our paths, which met so pleasantly, should diverge so painfully. And yet, not only the freedmen, but the whole country, need such helpful, self-sacrificing teachers as you will prove; and if earnest prayers and holy wishes can brighten your path, your lines will fall in the pleasantest places."

As he rose to go, sympathy, love, and admiration were blended in the parting look he gave her; but he felt it was useless to attempt to divert her from her purpose. He knew that for the true reconstruction of the country something more was needed than bayonets and bullets, or the schemes of selfish politicians or plotting demagogues. He knew that the South needed the surrender of the best brain and heart of the country to build, above the wastes of war, more stately temples of thought and action.

CHAPTER XXVIII.

DR. LATROBE'S MISTAKE.

ON the morning previous to their departure for their respective homes, Dr. Gresham met Dr. Latrobe in the parlor of the Concordia.

"How," asked Dr. Gresham, "did you like Dr. Latimer's paper?"

"Very much, indeed. It was excellent. He is a very talented young man. He sits next to me at lunch and I have conversed with him several times. He is very genial and attractive, only he seems to be rather cranky on the negro question. I hope if he comes South that he will not make the mistake of mixing up with the negroes. It would be throwing away his influence and ruining his prospects. He seems to be well versed in science and literature and would make a very delightful accession to our social life."

"I think," replied Dr. Gresham, "that he is an honor to our profession. He is one of the finest specimens of our young manhood."

Just then Dr. Latimer entered the room. Dr. Latrobe arose and, greeting him cordially, said: "I was delighted with your paper; it was full of thought and suggestion."

"Thank you," answered Dr. Latimer, "it was my aim to make it so."

"And you succeeded admirably," replied Dr. Latrobe. "I could not help thinking how much we owe to heredity and environment."

"Yes," said Dr. Gresham. "Continental Europe yearly sends to our shores subjects to be developed into citizens. Emancipation has given us millions of new citizens, and to them our influence and example should be a blessing and not a curse."

"Well," said Dr. Latimer, "I intend to go South, and help those who so much need helpers from their own ranks."

"I hope," answered Dr. Latrobe, "that if you go South you will only sustain business relations with the negroes, and not commit the folly of equalizing yourself with them."

"Why not?" asked Dr. Latimer, steadily looking him in the eye.

"Because in equalizing yourself with them you drag us down; and our social customs must be kept intact."

"You have been associating with me at the convention for several days; I do not see that the contact has dragged you down, has it?"

"You! What has that got to do with associating with niggers?" asked Dr. Latrobe, curtly.

"The blood of that race is coursing through my veins. I am one of them," replied Dr. Latimer, proudly raising his head.

"You!" exclaimed Dr. Latrobe, with an air of profound astonishment and crimsoning face.

"Yes;" interposed Dr. Gresham, laughing heartily at Dr. Latrobe's discomfiture. "He belongs to that negro race both by blood and choice. His father's mother made overtures to receive him as her grandson and heir, but he has nobly refused to forsake his mother's people and has cast his lot with them."

"And I," said Dr. Latimer, "would have despised myself if I had done otherwise."

"Well, well," said Dr. Latrobe, rising, "I was never so deceived before. Good morning!"

Dr. Latrobe had thought he was clear-sighted enough to detect the presence of negro blood when all physical traces had disappeared. But he had associated with Dr. Latimer for several days, and admired his talent, without suspecting for one moment his racial connection. He could not help feeling a sense of vexation at the signal mistake he had made.

Dr. Frank Latimer was the natural grandson of a Southern lady, in whose family his mother had been a slave. The blood of a proud aristocratic ancestry was flowing through his veins, and generations of blood admixture had effaced all trace of his negro lineage. His complexion was blonde, his eye bright and piercing, his lips firm and well moulded; his manner very affable; his intellect active and well stored with information. He was a man capable of winning in life through his rich gifts of inheritance and acquirements. When freedom came, his mother, like Hagar of old, went out into the wide world to seek a living for herself and child. Through years of poverty she labored to educate her child, and saw the glad fruition of her hopes when her son graduated as an M. D. from the University of P——.

After his graduation he met his father's mother, who recognized him by his resemblance to her dear, departed son. All the mother love in her lonely heart awoke, and she was willing to overlook "the missing link of matrimony," and adopt him as her heir, if he would ignore his identity with the colored race.

Before him loomed all the possibilities which only birth and blood can give a white man in our Democratic country. But he was a man of too much sterling worth of character to be willing to forsake his mother's race for the richest advantages his grandmother could bestow.

Dr. Gresham had met Dr. Latimer at the beginning of the convention, and had been attracted to him by his frank and genial manner. One morning, when conversing with him, Dr. Gresham had learned some of the salient points of his history, which, instead of repelling him, had only deepened his admiration for the young doctor. He was much amused when he saw the pleasant acquaintanceship between him and Dr. Latrobe, but they agreed to be silent about his racial connection until the time came when they were ready to divulge it; and they were hugely delighted at his signal blunder.

CHAPTER XXIX.

VISITORS FROM THE SOUTH.

"MAMMA is not well," said Iola to Robert. "I spoke to her about sending for a doctor, but she objected and I did not insist."

"I will ask Dr. Latimer, whom I met at the Concordia, to step in. He is a splendid young fellow. I wish we had thousands like him."

In the evening the doctor called. Without appearing to make a professional visit he engaged Marie in conversation, watched her carefully, and came to the conclusion that her failing health proceeded more from mental than physical causes.

"I am so uneasy about Harry," said Mrs. Leroy. "He is so fearless and outspoken. I do wish the attention of the whole nation could be turned to the cruel barbarisms which are a national disgrace. I think the term 'bloody shirt' is one of the most heartless phrases ever invented to divert attention from cruel wrongs and dreadful outrages."

Just then Iola came in and was introduced by her uncle to Dr. Latimer, to whom the introduction was a sudden and unexpected pleasure.

After an interchange of courtesies, Marie resumed the conversation, saying: "Harry wrote me only last week that a young friend of his had lost his situation because he refused to have his pupils strew flowers on the streets through which Jefferson Davis was to pass."

"I think," said Dr. Latimer, indignantly, "that the Israelites had just as much right to scatter flowers over the bodies of the Egyptians, when the waves threw back their corpses on the shores of the Red Sea, as these children had to strew the path of Jefferson Davis with flowers. We want our boys to grow up manly citizens, and not cringing sycophants. When do you expect your son, Mrs. Leroy?"

"Some time next week," answered Marie.

"And his presence will do you more good than all the medicine in my chest."

"I hope, Doctor," said Mrs. Leroy, "that we will not lose sight of you, now that your professional visit is ended; for I believe your visit was the result of a conspiracy between Iola and her uncle."

Dr. Latimer laughed, as he answered, "Ah, Mrs. Leroy, I see you have found us all out."

"Oh, Doctor," exclaimed Iola, with pleasing excitement, "there is a young lady coming here to visit me next week. Her name is Miss Lucille Delany, and she is my ideal woman. She is grand, brave, intellectual, and religious."

"Is that so? She would make some man an excellent wife," replied Dr. Latimer.

"Now isn't that perfectly manlike," answered Iola, smiling. "Mamma, what do you think of that? Did any of you gentlemen ever see a young woman of much ability that you did not look upon as a flotsam all adrift until some man had appropriated her?"

"I think, Miss Leroy, that the world's work, if shared, is better done than when it is performed alone. Don't you think your life-work will be better done if some one shares it with you?" asked Dr. Latimer, slowly, and with a smile in his eyes.

"That would depend on the person who shared it," said Iola, faintly blushing.

"Here," said Robert, a few evenings after this conversation, as he handed Iola a couple of letters, "is something which will please you."

Iola took the letters, and, after reading one of them, said: "Miss Delany and Harry will be here on Wednesday; and this one is an invitation which also adds to my enjoyment."

"What is it?" asked Marie; "an invitation to a hop or a german?"

"No; but something which I value far more. We are all invited to Mr. Stillman's to a *conversazione*."

"What is the object?"

"His object is to gather some of the thinkers and leaders of the race to consult on subjects of vital interest to our welfare. He has invited Dr. Latimer, Professor Gradnor, of North Carolina, Mr. Forest, of New York, Hon. Dugdale, Revs. Carmicle, Cantnor, Tunster, Professor Langhorne, of Georgia, and a few ladies, Mrs. Watson, Miss Brown, and others."

"I am glad that it is neither a hop nor a german," said Iola, "but something for which I have been longing."

"Why, Iola," asked Robert, "don't you believe in young people having a good time?"

"Oh, yes," answered Iola, seriously, "I believe in young people having amusements and recreations; but the times are too serious for us to attempt to make our lives a long holiday."

"Well, Iola," answered Robert, "this is the first holiday we have had in two hundred and fifty years, and you shouldn't be too exacting."

"Yes," replied Marie, "human beings naturally crave enjoyment, and if not furnished with good amusements they are apt to gravitate to low pleasures."

"Some one," said Robert, "has said that the Indian belongs to an old race and looks gloomily back to the past, and that the negro belongs to a young race and looks hopefully towards the future."

"If that be so," replied Marie, "our race-life corresponds more to the follies of youth than the faults of maturer years."

On Dr. Latimer's next visit he was much pleased to see a great change in Marie's appearance. Her eye had grown brighter, her step more elastic, and the anxiety had faded from her face. Harry had arrived, and with him came Miss Delany.

"Good evening, Dr. Latimer," said Iola, cheerily, as she entered the room with Miss Lucille Delany. "This is my friend, Miss Delany, from Georgia. Were she not present I would say she is one of the grandest women in America."

"I am very much pleased to meet you," said Dr. Latimer, cordially; "I have heard Miss Leroy speak of you. We were expecting you," he added, with a smile.

Just then Harry entered the room, and Iola presented him to Dr. Latimer, saying, "This is my brother, about whom mamma was so anxious."

"Had you a pleasant journey?" asked Dr. Latimer, after the first greetings were over.

"Not especially," answered Miss Delany. "Southern

roads are not always very pleasant to travel. When Mr. Leroy entered the cars at A——, where he was known, had he taken his seat among the white people he would have been remanded to the colored car."

"But after awhile," said Harry, "as Miss Delany and myself were sitting together, laughing and chatting, a colored man entered the car, and, mistaking me for a white man, asked the conductor to have me removed, and I had to insist that I was colored in order to be permitted to remain. It would be ludicrous, if it were not vexatious, to be too white to be black, and too black to be white."

"Caste plays such fantastic tricks in this country," said Dr. Latimer.

"I tell Mr. Leroy," said Miss Delany, "that when he returns he must put a label on himself, saying, 'I am a colored man,' to prevent annoyance."

CHAPTER XXX.

FRIENDS IN COUNCIL.

On the following Friday evening, Mr. Stillman's pleasant, spacious parlors were filled to overflowing with a select company of earnest men and women deeply interested in the welfare of the race.

Bishop Tunster had prepared a paper on "Negro Emigration." Dr. Latimer opened the discussion by speaking favorably of some of the salient points, but said:—

"I do not believe self-exilement is the true remedy for the wrongs of the negro. Where should he go if he left this country?"

"Go to Africa," replied Bishop Tunster, in his bluff, hearty tones. "I believe that Africa is to be redeemed to civilization, and that the negro is to be gathered into the family of nations and recognized as a man and a brother."

"Go to Africa?" repeated Professor Langhorne, of Georgia. "Does the United States own one foot of African soil? And have we not been investing our blood in the country for ages?"

"I am in favor of missionary efforts," said Professor Gradnor, of North Carolina, "for the redemption of Africa, but I see no reason for expatriating ourselves because some persons do not admire the color of our skins."

"I do not believe," said Mr. Stillman, "in emptying on the shores of Africa a horde of ignorant, poverty-stricken people, as missionaries of civilization or Christianity. And while I am in favor of missionary efforts, there is need here for the best heart and brain to work in unison for justice and righteousness."

"America," said Miss Delany, "is the best field for human development. God has not heaped up our mountains with such grandeur, flooded our rivers with such majesty, crowned our valleys with such fertility, enriched our mines with such wealth, that they should only minister to grasping greed and sensuous enjoyment."

"Climate, soil, and physical environments," said Professor Gradnor, "have much to do with shaping national characteristics. If in Africa, under a tropical sun, the negro has lagged behind other races in the march of civilization, at least for once in his history he has, in this country, the privilege of using climatic advantages and developing under new conditions."

"Yes," replied Dr. Latimer, "and I do not wish our people to become restless and unsettled before they have tried one generation of freedom."

"I am always glad," said Mr. Forest, a tall, distinguished-looking gentleman from New York, "when I hear of people who are ill treated in one section of the country emigrating to another. Men who are deaf to the claims of mercy, and oblivious to the demands of justice, can feel when money is slipping from their pockets."

"The negro," said Hon. Dugdale, "does not present to my mind the picture of an effete and exhausted people, destined to die out before a stronger race. Gilbert Haven once saw a statue which suggested this thought, 'I am black, but comely; the sun has looked down upon me, but I will teach you who despise me to feel that I am your superior.' The men who are acquiring property and building up homes in the South show us what energy and determination may do even in that part of the country. I believe such men can do more to conquer prejudice than if they spent all their lives in shouting for their rights and ignoring their duties. No! as there are millions of us in this country, I think it best to settle down and work out our own salvation here."

"How many of us to-day," asked Professor Langhorne, "would be teaching in the South, if every field of labor in the North was as accessible to us as to the whites? It has been estimated that a million young white men have left the South since the war, and, had our chances been equal to theirs, would we have been any more willing to stay in the South with those who need us than they? But this prejudice, by impacting us together, gives us a common cause and brings our intellect in contact with the less favored of our race."

"I do not believe," said Miss Delany, "that the Southern white people themselves desire any wholesale exodus of the colored from their labor fields. It would be suicidal to attempt their expatriation."

"History," said Professor Langhorne, "tells that Spain was once the place where barbarian Europe came to light her lamp. Seven hundred years before there was a public lamp in London you might have gone through the streets of Cordova amid ten miles of lighted lamps, and stood there on solidly paved land, when hundreds of years afterwards, in Paris, on a rainy day you would have sunk to your ankles in the mud. But she who bore the name of the 'Terror of Nations,' and the 'Queen of the Ocean,' was not strong enough to dash herself against God's law of retribution and escape unscathed. She inaugurated a crusade of horror against a million of her best laborers and artisans. Vainly she expected the blessing of God to crown her work of violence. Instead of seeing the fruition of her hopes in the increased prosperity of her land, depression and paralysis settled on her trade and business. A fearful blow was struck at her agriculture; decay settled on her manufactories; money became too scarce to pay the necessary expenses of the king's exchequer; and that once mighty empire became a fallen kingdom, pierced by her crimes and dragged down by her transgressions."

"We did not," said Iola, "place the bounds of our habitation. And I believe we are to be fixtures in this country. But beyond the shadows I see the coruscation of a brighter day; and we can help usher it in, not by answering hate with hate, or giving scorn for scorn, but by striving to be more generous, noble, and just. It seems as if all creation travels to respond to the song of the Herald angels, 'Peace on earth, good-will toward men.'"

The next paper was on "Patriotism," by Rev. Cantnor. It was a paper in which the white man was extolled as the master race, and spoke as if it were a privilege for the colored man to be linked to his destiny and to live beneath the shadow of his power. He asserted that the white race of this country is the broadest, most Christian, and humane of that branch of the human family.

Dr. Latimer took exception to his position. "Law,"

he said, "is the pivot on which the whole universe turns; and obedience to law is the gauge by which a nation's strength or weakness is tried. We have had two evils by which our obedience to law has been tested—slavery and the liquor traffic. How have we dealt with them both? We have been weighed in the balance and found wanting. Millions of slaves and serfs have been liberated during this century, but not even in semi-barbaric Russia, heathen Japan, or Catholic Spain has slavery been abolished through such a fearful conflict as it was in the United States. The liquor traffic still sends its floods of ruin and shame to the habitations of men, and no political party has been found with enough moral power and numerical strength to stay the tide of death."

"I think," said Professor Gradnor, "that what our country needs is truth more than flattery. I do not think that our moral life keeps pace with our mental development and material progress. I know of no civilized country on the globe, Catholic, Protestant, or Mohammedan, where life is less secure than it is in the South. Nearly eighteen hundred years ago the life of a Roman citizen in Palestine was in danger from mob violence. That pagan government threw around him a wall of living clay, consisting of four hundred and seventy men, when more than forty Jews had bound themselves with an oath that they would neither eat nor drink until they had taken the life of the Apostle Paul. Does not true patriotism demand that citizenship should be as much protected in Christian America as it was in heathen Rome?"

"I would have our people," said Miss Delany, "more interested in politics. Instead of forgetting the past, I would have them hold in everlasting remembrance our great deliverance. Hitherto we have never had a country with tender, precious memories to fill our eyes with tears, or glad reminiscences to thrill our hearts with pride and joy. We have been aliens and outcasts in the land of our birth. But I want my pupils to do all in their power to make this country worthy of their deepest devotion and loftiest patriotism. I want them to feel that its glory is their glory, its dishonor their shame."

"Our esteemed friend, Mrs. Watson," said Iola, "sends regrets that she cannot come, but has kindly favored us with a poem, called the "Rallying Cry." In her letter she says that, although she is no longer young, she feels that in the conflict for the right there's room for young as well as old. She hopes that we will here unite the enthusiasm of youth with the experience of age, and that we will have a pleasant and profitable conference. Is it your pleasure that the poem be read at this stage of our proceedings, or later on?"

"Let us have it now," answered Harry, "and I move that Miss Delany be chosen to lend to the poem the charm of her voice."

"I second the motion," said Iola, smiling, and handing the poem to Miss Delany.

Miss Delany took the poem and read it with fine effect. The spirit of the poem had entered her soul.

A RALLYING CRY.

Oh, children of the tropics,
  Amid our pain and wrong
Have you no other mission
  Than music, dance, and song?

When through the weary ages
  Our dripping tears still fall,
Is this a time to dally
  With pleasure's silken thrall?

Go, muffle all your viols;
  As heroes learn to stand,
With faith in God's great justice
  Nerve every heart and hand.

Dream not of ease nor pleasure,
  Nor honor, wealth, nor fame,
Till from the dust you've lifted
  Our long-dishonored name;

And crowned that name with glory
  By deeds of holy worth,
To shine with light emblazoned,
  The noblest name on earth.

Count life a dismal failure,
  Unblessing and unblest,
That seeks 'mid ease inglorious
  For pleasure or for rest.

With courage, strength, and valor
  Your lives and actions brace;
Shrink not from toil or hardship,
  And dangers bravely face.

Engrave upon your banners,
  In words of golden light,
That honor, truth, and justice
  Are more than godless might.

Above earth's pain and sorrow
  Christ's dying face I see;
I hear the cry of anguish:—
  "Why hast thou forsaken me?"

In the pallor of that anguish
  I see the only light,
To flood with peace and gladness
  Earth's sorrow, pain, and night.

Arrayed in Christly armor
  'Gainst error, crime, and sin,
The victory can't be doubtful,
  For God is sure to win.

The next paper was by Miss Iola Leroy, on the "Education of Mothers."

"I agree," said Rev. Eustace, of St. Mary's parish, "with the paper. The great need of the race is enlightened mothers."

"And enlightened fathers, too," added Miss Delany, quickly. "If there is anything I chafe to see it is a strong, hearty man shirking his burdens, putting them on the shoulders of his wife, and taking life easy for himself."

"I always pity such mothers," interposed Iola, tenderly.

"I think," said Miss Delany, with a flash in her eye and a ring of decision in her voice, "that such men ought to be drummed out of town!" As she spoke, there was an expression which seemed to say, "And I would like to help do it!"

Harry smiled, and gave her a quick glance of admiration.

"I do not think," said Mrs. Stillman, "that we can begin too early to teach our boys to be manly and self-respecting, and our girls to be useful and self-reliant."

"You know," said Mrs. Leroy, "that after the war we were thrown upon the nation a homeless race to be gathered into homes, and a legally unmarried race to be taught the sacredness of the marriage relation. We must instill into our young people that the true strength of a race means purity in women and uprightness in men; who can say, with Sir Galahad :—

> 'My strength is the strength of ten,
> Because my heart is pure.'

And where this is wanting neither wealth nor culture can make up the deficiency."

"There is a field of Christian endeavor which lies between the school-house and the pulpit, which needs the hand of a woman more in private than in public," said Miss Delany.

"Yes, I have often felt the need of such work in my own parish. We need a union of women with the warmest hearts and clearest brains to help in the moral education of the race," said Rev. Eustace.

"Yes," said Iola, "if we would have the prisons empty we must make the homes more attractive."

"In civilized society," replied Dr. Latimer, "there must be restraint either within or without. If parents fail to teach restraint within, society has her check-reins without in the form of chain-gangs, prisons, and the gallows."

The closing paper was on the "Moral Progress of the Race," by Hon. Dugdale. He said: "The moral progress of the race was not all he could desire, yet he could not help feeling that, compared with other races, the outlook was not hopeless. I am so sorry to see, however, that in some States there is an undue proportion of colored people in prisons."

"I think," answered Professor Langhorne, of Georgia, "that this is owing to a partial administration of law in meting out punishment to colored offenders. I know red-handed murderers who walk in this Republic unwhipped of justice, and I have seen a colored woman sentenced to prison for weeks for stealing twenty-five cents. I knew a colored girl who was executed for murder when only a child in years. And it was through the intervention of a friend of mine, one of the bravest young men of the South, that a boy of fifteen was saved from the gallows."

"When I look," said Mr. Forest, "at the slow growth of modern civilization—the ages which have been consumed in reaching our present altitude, and see how we have outgrown slavery, feudalism, and religious persecutions, I cannot despair of the future of the race."

"Just now," said Dr. Latimer, "we have the fearful grinding and friction which comes in the course of an adjustment of the new machinery of freedom in the old ruts of slavery. But I am optimistic enough to believe that there will yet be a far higher and better Christian civilization than our country has ever known."

"And in that civilization I believe the negro is to be an important factor," said Rev. Cantnor.

"I believe it also," said Miss Delany, hopefully, "and this thought has been a blessed inspiration to my life. When I come in contact with Christless prejudices, I feel that my life is too much a part of the Divine plan, and invested with too much intrinsic worth, for me to be the least humiliated by indignities that beggarly souls can inflict. I feel more pitiful than resentful to those who do not know how much they miss by living mean, ignoble lives."

"My heart," said Iola, "is full of hope for the future. Pain and suffering are the crucibles out of which come gold more fine than the pavements of heaven, and gems more precious than the foundations of the Holy City."

"If," said Mrs. Leroy, "pain and suffering are factors in human development, surely we have not been counted too worthless to suffer."

"And is there," continued Iola, "a path which we have trodden in this country, unless it be the path of sin, into which Jesus Christ has not put His feet and left it luminous with the light of His steps? Has the negro been poor and homeless? The birds of the air had nests and the foxes had holes, but the Son of man had not where to lay His head. Has our name been a synonym for contempt? 'He shall be called a Nazarene.' Have we been despised and trodden under foot? Christ was despised and rejected of men. Have we been ignorant and unlearned? It was said of Jesus Christ, 'How knoweth this man letters, never having learned?' Have we been beaten and bruised in the prison-house of bondage? 'They took Jesus and scourged Him.' Have we been slaughtered, our bones scattered at the graves' mouth? He was spit upon by the mob, smitten and mocked by the rabble, and died as died Rome's meanest criminal slave. To-day that cross of shame is a throne of power. Those robes of scorn have changed to habiliments of light, and that crown of mockery to a diadem of glory. And never, while the agony of Gethsemane and the sufferings of Calvary have their hold upon my heart, will I recognize any religion as His which despises the least of His brethren."

As Iola finished, there was a ring of triumph in her voice, as if she were reviewing a path she had trodden with bleeding feet, and seen it change to lines of living light. Her soul seemed to be flashing through the rare loveliness of her face and etherealizing its beauty.

Every one was spell-bound. Dr. Latimer was entranced, and, turning to Hon. Dugdale, said, in a low voice and with deep-drawn breath, "She is angelic!"

Hon. Dugdale turned, gave a questioning look, then replied, "She is strangely beautiful! Do you know her?"

"Yes; I have met her several times. I accompanied her here to-night. The tones of her voice are like benedictions of peace; her words a call to higher service and nobler life."

Just then Rev. Carmicle was announced. He had been on a Southern tour, and had just returned.

"Oh, Doctor," exclaimed Mrs. Stillman, "I am delighted to see you. We were about to adjourn, but we will postpone action to hear from you."

"Thank you," replied Rev. Carmicle. "I have not the cue to the meeting, and will listen while I take breath."

"Pardon me," answered Mrs. Stillman. "I should have been more thoughtful than to press so welcome a guest into service before I had given him time for rest and refreshment; but if the courtesy failed on my lips it did not fail in my heart. I wanted our young folks to see one of our thinkers who had won distinction before the war."

"My dear friend," said Rev. Carmicle, smiling, "some of these young folks will look on me as a back number. You know the cry has already gone forth, 'Young men to the front.'"

"But we need old men for counsel," interposed Mr. Forest, of New York.

"Of course," said Rev. Carmicle, "we older men would rather retire gracefully than be relegated or hustled to a back seat. But I am pleased to see doors open to you which were closed to us, and opportunities which were denied us embraced by you."

"How," asked Hon. Dugdale, "do you feel in reference to our people's condition in the South?"

"Very hopeful, although at times I cannot help feeling anxious about their future. I was delighted with my visits to various institutions of learning, and surprised at the desire manifested among the young people to obtain an education. Where toil-worn mothers bent beneath their heavy burdens their more favored daughters are enjoying the privileges of education. Young people are making recitations in Greek and Latin where it was once a crime to teach their parents to read. I also became acquainted with colored professors and presidents of colleges. Saw young ladies who had graduated as doctors. Comfortable homes have succeeded old cabins of slavery. Vast crops have been raised by free labor. I read with interest and pleasure a number of papers edited by colored men. I saw it estimated that two millions of our people had learned to read, and I feel deeply grateful to the people who have supplied us with teachers who have stood their ground so nobly among our people."

"But," asked Mr. Forest, "you expressed fears about the future of our race. From whence do your fears arise?"

"From the unfortunate conditions which slavery has entailed upon that section of our country. I dread the results of that racial feeling which ever and anon breaks out into restlessness and crime. Also, I am concerned about the lack of home training for those for whom the discipline of the plantation has been exchanged for the penalties of prisons and chain-gangs. I am sorry to see numbers of our young men growing away from the influence of the church and drifting into prisons. I also fear that in some sections, as colored men increase in wealth and intelligence, there will be an increase of race rivalry and jealousy. It is said that savages, by putting their ears to the ground, can hear a far-off tread. So, to-day, I fear that there are savage elements in our civilization which hear the advancing tread of the negro and would retard his coming. It is the incarnation of these elements that I dread. It is their elimination I do so earnestly desire. Whether it be outgrown or not is our unsolved problem. Time alone will tell whether or not the virus of slavery and injustice has too fully permeated our Southern civilization for a complete recovery. Nations, honey-combed by vice, have fallen beneath the weight of their iniquities. Justice is always uncompromising in its claims and inexorable in its demands. The laws of the universe are never repealed to accommodate our follies."

"Surely," said Bishop Tunster, "the negro has a higher mission than that of aimlessly drifting through life and patiently waiting for death."

"We may not," answered Rev. Carmicle, "have the same dash, courage, and aggressiveness of other races, accustomed to struggle, achievement, and dominion, but surely the world needs something better than the results of arrogance, aggressiveness, and indomitable power. For the evils of society there are no solvents as potent as love and justice, and our greatest need is not more wealth and learning, but a religion replete with life and glowing with love. Let this be the impelling force in the race and it cannot fail to rise in the scale of character and condition."

"And," said Dr. Latimer," instead of narrowing our sympathies to mere racial questions, let us broaden them to humanity's wider issues."

"Let us," replied Rev. Carmicle, "pass it along the lines, that to be willfully ignorant is to be shamefully criminal. Let us teach our people not to love pleasure or to fear death, but to learn the true value of life, and to do their part to eliminate the paganism of caste from our holy religion and the lawlessness of savagery from our civilization."

"How did you enjoy the evening, Marie?" asked Robert, as they walked homeward.

"I was interested and deeply pleased," answered Marie.

"I," said Robert, "was thinking of the wonderful changes that have come to us since the war. When I sat in those well-lighted, beautifully-furnished rooms, I was thinking of the meetings we used to have in bygone days. How we used to go by stealth into lonely woods and gloomy swamps, to tell of our hopes and fears, sorrows and trials. I hope that we will have many more of these gatherings. Let us have the next one here."

"I am sure," said Marie, "I would gladly welcome such a conference at any time. I think such meetings would be so helpful to our young people."

CHAPTER XXXI.

DAWNING AFFECTIONS.

"DOCTOR," said Iola, as they walked home from the *conversazione*, "I wish I could do something more for our people than I am doing. I taught in the South till failing health compelled me to change my employment. But, now that I am well and strong, I would like to do something of lasting service for the race."

"Why not," asked Dr. Latimer, "write a good, strong book which would be helpful to them? I think there is an amount of dormant talent among us, and a large field from which to gather materials for such a book."

"I would do it, willingly, if I could; but one needs both leisure and money to make a successful book. There is material among us for the broadest comedies and the deepest tragedies, but, besides money and leisure, it needs patience, perseverance, courage, and the hand of an artist to weave it into the literature of the country."

"Miss Leroy, you have a large and rich experience; you possess a vivid imagination and glowing fancy. Write, out of the fullness of your heart, a book to inspire men and women with a deeper sense of justice and humanity."

"Doctor," replied Iola, "I would do it if I could, not for the money it might bring, but for the good it might do. But who believes any good can come out of the black Nazareth?"

"Miss Leroy, out of the race must come its own thinkers and writers. Authors belonging to the white race have written good racial books, for which I am deeply grateful, but it seems to be almost impossible for a white man to put himself completely in our place. No man can feel the iron which enters another man's soul."

"Well, Doctor, when I write a book I shall take you for the hero of my story."

"Why, what have I done," asked Dr. Latimer, in a surprised tone, "that you should impale me on your pen?"

"You have done nobly," answered Iola, "in refusing your grandmother's offer."

"I only did my duty," he modestly replied.

"But," said Iola, "when others are trying to slip out from the race and pass into the white basis, I cannot help admiring one who acts as if he felt that the weaker the race is the closer he would cling to it."

"My mother," replied Dr. Latimer, "faithful and true, belongs to that race. Where else should I be? But I know a young lady who could have cast her lot wlth the favored race, yet chose to take her place with the freed people, as their teacher, friend, and adviser. This young lady was alone in the world. She had been fearfully wronged, and to her stricken heart came a brilliant offer of love, home, and social position. But she bound her heart to the mast of duty, closed her ears to the syren song, and could not be lured from her purpose."

A startled look stole over Iola's face, and, lifting her eyes to his, she faltered:—

"Do you know her?"

"Yes, I know her and admire her; and she ought to be made the subject of a soul-inspiring story. Do you know of whom I speak?"

"How should I, Doctor? I am sure you have not made me your confidante," she responded, demurely; then she quickly turned and tripped up the steps of her home, which she had just reached.

After this conversation Dr. Latimer became a frequent visitor at Iola's home, and a firm friend of her brother. Harry was at that age when, for the young and inexperienced, vice puts on her fairest guise and most seductive smiles. Dr. Latimer's wider knowledge and larger experience made his friendship for Harry very valuable, and the service he rendered him made him a favorite and ever-welcome guest in the family.

"Are you all alone," asked Robert, one night, as he entered the cosy little parlor where Iola sat reading. "Where are the rest of the folks?"

"Mamma and grandma have gone to bed," answered Iola. "Harry and Lucille are at the concert. They are passionately fond of music, and find facilities here that they do not have in the South. They wouldn't go to hear a seraph where they must take a negro seat. I was too tired to go. Besides, 'two's company and three's a crowd,'" she added, significantly.

"I reckon you struck the nail on the head that time," said Robert, laughing. "But you have not been alone all the time. Just as I reached the corner I saw Dr. Latimer leaving the door. I see he still continues his visits. Who is his patient now?"

"Oh, Uncle Robert," said Iola, smiling and flushing,

"he is out with Harry and Lucille part of the time, and drops in now and then to see us all."

"Well," said Robert, "I suppose the case is now an affair of the heart. But I cannot blame him for it," he added, looking fondly on the beautiful face of his niece, which sorrow had touched only to chisel into more loveliness. "How do you like him?"

"I must have within me," answered Iola, with unaffected truthfulness, "a large amount of hero worship. The characters of the Old Testament I most admire are Moses and Nehemiah. They were willing to put aside their own advantages for their race and country. Dr. Latimer comes up to my ideal of a high, heroic manhood."

"I think," answered Robert, smiling archly, "he would be delighted to hear your opinion of him."

"I tell him," continued Iola, "that he belongs to the days of chivalry. But he smiles and says, 'he only belongs to the days of hard-pan service.'"

"Some one," said Robert, "was saying to-day that he stood in his own light when he refused his grandmother's offer to receive him as her son."

"I think," said Iola, "it was the grandest hour of his life when he made that decision. I have admired him ever since I heard his story."

"But, Iola, think of the advantages he set aside. It was no sacrifice for me to remain colored, with my lack of education and race sympathies, but Dr. Latimer had doors open to him as a white man which are forever closed to a colored man. To be born white in this country is to be born to an inheritance of privileges, to hold in your hands the keys that open before you the doors of every occupation, advantage, opportunity, and achievement."

"I know that, uncle," answered Iola; "but even these advantages are too dearly bought if they mean loss of honor, true manliness, and self respect. He could not have retained these had he ignored his mother and lived under a veil of concealment, constantly haunted by a dread of detection. The gain would not have been worth the cost. It were better that he should walk the ruggedest paths of life a true man than tread the softest carpets a moral cripple."

"I am afraid," said Robert, laying his hand caressingly upon her head, "that we are destined to lose the light of our home."

"Oh, uncle, how you talk! I never dreamed of what you are thinking," answered Iola, half reproachfully.

"And how," asked Robert, "do you know what I am thinking about?"

"My dear uncle, I'm not blind."

"Neither am I," replied Robert, significantly, as he left the room.

Iola's admiration for Dr. Latimer was not a one-sided affair. Day after day she was filling a larger place in his heart. The touch of her hand thrilled him with emotion. Her lightest words were an entrancing melody to his ear. Her noblest sentiments found a response in his heart. In their desire to help the race their hearts beat in loving unison. One grand and noble purpose was giving tone and color to their lives and strengthening the bonds of affection between them.

CHAPTER XXXII.

WOOING AND WEDDING.

HARRY'S vacation had been very pleasant. Miss Delany, with her fine conversational powers and ready wit, had added much to his enjoyment. Robert had given his mother the pleasantest room in the house, and in the evening the family would gather around her, tell her the news of the day, read to her from the Bible, join with her in thanksgiving for mercies received and in prayer for protection through the night. Harry was very grateful to Dr. Latimer for the kindly interest he had shown in accompanying Miss Delany and himself to places of interest and amusement. He was grateful, too, that in the city of P—— doors were open to them which were barred against them in the South.

The bright, beautiful days of summer were gliding into autumn, with its glorious wealth of foliage, and the time was approaching for the departure of Harry and Miss Delany to their respective schools, when Dr. Latimer received several letters from North Carolina, urging him to come South, as physicians were greatly needed there. Although his practice was lucrative in the city of P——, he resolved he would go where his services were most needed.

A few evenings before he started he called at the house, and made an engagement to drive Iola to the park.

At the time appointed he drove up to the door in his fine equipage. Iola stepped gracefully in and sat quietly by his side to enjoy the loveliness of the scenery and the gorgeous grandeur of the setting sun.

"I expect to go South," said Dr. Latimer, as he drove slowly along.

"Ah, indeed," said Iola, assuming an air of interest, while a shadow flitted over her face. "Where do you expect to pitch your tent?"

"In the city of C——, North Carolina," he answered.

"Oh, I wish," she exclaimed, "that you were going to Georgia, where you could take care of that high-spirited brother of mine."

"I suppose if he were to hear you he would laugh, and say that he could take care of himself. But I know a better plan than that."

"What is it?" asked Iola, innocently.

"That you will commit yourself, instead of your brother, to my care."

"Oh, dear," replied Iola, drawing a long breath. "What would mamma say?"

"That she would willingly resign you, I hope."

"And what would grandma and Uncle Robert say?" again asked Iola.

"That they would cheerfully acquiesce. Now, what would I say if they all consent?"

"I don't know," modestly responded Iola.

"Well," replied Dr. Latimer, "I would say:—

"Could deeds my love discover,
Could valor gain thy charms,
To prove myself thy lover
I'd face a world in arms."

"And prove a good soldier," added Iola, smiling, "when there is no battle to fight."

"Iola, I am in earnest," said Dr. Latimer, passionately. "In the work to which I am devoted every burden will be lighter, every path smoother, if brightened and blessed with your companionship."

A sober expression swept over Iola's face, and, dropping her eyes, she said: "I must have time to think."

Quietly they rode along the river bank until Dr. Latimer broke the silence by saying:—

"Miss Iola, I think that you brood too much over the condition of our people."

"Perhaps I do," she replied, "but they never burn a man in the South that they do not kindle a fire around my soul."

"I am afraid," replied Dr. Latimer, "that you will grow morbid and nervous. Most of our people take life easily—why shouldn't you?"

"Because," she answered, "I can see breakers ahead which they do not."

"Oh, give yourself no uneasiness. They will catch the fret and fever of the nineteenth century soon enough. I have heard several of our ministers say that it is chiefly men of disreputable characters who are made the subjects of violence and lynch-law."

"Suppose it is so," responded Iola, feelingly. "If these men believe in eternal punishment they ought to feel a greater concern for the wretched sinner who is hurried out of time with all his sins upon his head, than for the godly man who passes through violence to endless rest."

"That is true; and I am not counseling you to be selfish; but, Miss Iola, had you not better look out for yourself?"

"Thank you, Doctor, I am feeling quite well."

"I know it, but your devotion to study and work is too intense," he replied.

"I am preparing to teach, and must spend my leisure time in study. Mr. Cloten is an excellent employer, and treats his employés as if they had hearts as well as hands. But to be an expert accountant is not the best use to which I can put my life."

"As a teacher you will need strong health and calm nerves. You had better let me prescribe for you. You need," he added, with a merry twinkle in his eyes, "change of air, change of scene, and change of name."

"Well, Doctor," said Iola, laughing, "that is the newest nostrum out. Had you not better apply for a patent?"

"Oh," replied Dr. Latimer, with affected gravity, "you know you must have unlimited faith in your physician."

"So you wish me to try the faith cure?" asked Iola, laughing.

"Yes, faith in me," responded Dr. Latimer, seriously.

"Oh, here we are at home!" exclaimed Iola. "This has been a glorious evening, Doctor. I am indebted to you for a great pleasure. I am extremely grateful."

"You are perfectly welcome," replied Dr. Latimer. "The pleasure has been mutual, I assure you."

"Will you not come in?" asked Iola.

Tying his horse, he accompanied Iola into the parlor. Seating himself near her, he poured into her ears words eloquent with love and tenderness.

"Iola," he said, "I am not an adept in courtly phrases. I am a plain man, who believes in love and truth. In asking you to share my lot, I am not inviting you to a life of ease and luxury, for year after year I may have to struggle to keep the wolf from the door, but your presence would make my home one of the brightest spots on earth, and one of the fairest types of heaven. Am I presumptuous in hoping that your love will become the crowning joy of my life?"

His words were more than a tender strain wooing her to love and happiness, they were a clarion call to a life of high and holy worth, a call which found a response in her heart. Her hand lay limp in his. She did not withdraw it, but, raising her lustrous eyes to his, she softly answered: "Frank, I love you."

After he had gone, Iola sat by the window, gazing at the splendid stars, her heart quietly throbbing with a delicious sense of joy and love. She had admired Dr. Gresham and, had there been no barrier in her way, she might have learned to love him; but Dr. Latimer had grown irresistibly upon her heart. There were depths in her nature that Dr. Gresham had never fathomed; aspirations in her soul with which he had never mingled. But as the waves leap up to the strand, so her soul went out to Dr. Latimer. Between their lives were no impeding barriers, no inclination impelling one way and duty compelling another. Kindred hopes and tastes had knit their hearts; grand and noble purposes were lighting up their lives; and they esteemed it a blessed privilege to stand on the threshold of a new era and labor for those who had passed from the old oligarchy of slavery into the new commonwealth of freedom.

On the next evening, Dr. Latimer rang the bell and was answered by Harry, who ushered him into the parlor, and then came back to the sitting-room, saying, "Iola, Dr. Latimer has called to see you."

"Has he?" answered Iola, a glad light coming into her eyes. "Come, Lucille, let us go into the parlor."

"Oh, no," interposed Harry, shrugging his shoulders and catching Lucille's hand. "He didn't ask for you. When we went to the concert we were told three's a crowd. And I say one good turn deserves another."

"Oh, Harry, you are so full of nonsense. Let Lucille go!" said Iola.

"Indeed I will not. I want to have a good time as well as you," said Harry.

"Oh, you're the most nonsensical man I know," interposed Miss Delany. Yet she stayed with Harry.

"You're looking very bright and happy," said Dr. Latimer to Iola, as she entered.

"My ride in the park was so refreshing! I enjoyed it so much! The day was so lovely, the air delicious, the birds sang so sweetly, and the sunset was so magnificent."

"I am glad of it. Why, Iola, your home is so happy your heart should be as light as a school-girl's."

"Doctor," she replied, "I must be prematurely old. I have scarcely known what it is to be light-hearted since my father's death."

"I know it, darling," he answered, seating himself beside her, and drawing her to him. "You have been tried in the fire, but are you not better for the crucial test?"

"Doctor," she replied, "as we rode along yesterday,

mingling with the sunshine of the present came the shadows of the past. I was thinking of the bright, joyous days of my girlhood, when I defended slavery, and of how the cup that I would have pressed to the lips of others was forced to my own. Yet, in looking over the mournful past, I would not change the Iola of then for the Iola of now."

"Yes," responded Dr. Latimer, musingly,

"'Darkness shows us worlds of light
We never saw by day.'"

"Oh, Doctor, you cannot conceive what it must have been to be hurled from a home of love and light into the dark abyss of slavery; to be compelled to take your place among a people you have learned to look upon as inferiors and social outcasts; to be in the power of men whose presence would fill you with horror and loathing, and to know that there is no earthly power to protect you from the highest insults which brutal cowardice could shower upon you. I am so glad that no other woman of my race will suffer as I have done."

The flush deepened on her face, a mournful splendor beamed from her beautiful eyes, into which the tears had slowly gathered.

"Darling," he said, his voice vibrating with mingled feelings of tenderness and resentment, "you must forget the sad past. You are like a tender lamb snatched from the jaws of a hungry wolf, but who still needs protecting, loving care. But it must have been terrible," he added, in a painful tone.

"It was indeed! For awhile I was like one dazed. I tried to pray, but the heavens seemed brass over my head. I was wild with agony, and had I not been placed under conditions which roused all the resistance of my soul, I would have lost my reason."

"Was it not a mistake to have kept you ignorant of your colored blood?"

"It was the great mistake of my father's life, but dear papa knew something of the cruel, crushing power of caste; and he tried to shield us from it."

"Yes, yes," replied Dr. Latimer, thoughtfully, "in trying to shield you from pain he plunged you into deeper suffering."

"I never blame him, because I know he did it for the best. Had he lived he would have taken us to France, where I should have had a life of careless ease and pleasure. But now my life has a much grander significance than it would have had under such conditions. Fearful as the awakening was, it was better than to have slept through life."

"Best for you and best for me," said Dr. Latimer. "There are souls that never awaken; but if they miss the deepest pain they also lose the highest joy."

Dr. Latimer went South, after his engagement, and through his medical skill and agreeable manners became very successful in his practice. In the following summer, he built a cosy home for the reception of his bride, and came North, where, with Harry and Miss Delany as attendants, he was married to Iola, amid a pleasant gathering of friends, by Rev. Carmicle.

CHAPTER XXXIII.

CONCLUSION.

IT was late in the summer when Dr. Latimer and his bride reached their home in North Carolina. Over the cottage porch were morning-glories to greet the first flushes of the rising day, and roses and jasmines to distill their fragrance on the evening air. Aunt Linda, who had been apprised of their coming, was patiently awaiting their arrival, and Uncle Daniel was pleased to know that "dat sweet young lady who had sich putty manners war comin' to lib wid dem."

As soon as they arrived, Aunt Linda rushed up to Iola, folded her in her arms, and joyfully exclaimed: "How'dy, honey! Ise so glad you's come. I seed it in a vision dat somebody fair war comin' to help us. An' wen I yered it war you, I larffed and jist rolled ober, and larffed and jist gib up."

"But, Aunt Linda, I am not very fair," replied Mrs. Latimer.

"Well, chile, you's fair to me. How's all yore folks in de up kentry?"

"All well. I expect them down soon to live here."

"What, Har'yet, and Robby, an' yer ma? Oh, dat is too good. I allers said Robby had san' in his craw, and war born for good luck. He war a mighty nice boy. Har'yet's in clover now. Well, ebery dorg has its day, and de cat has Sunday. I allers tole Har'yet ter keep a stiff upper lip; dat it war a long road dat had no turn."

Dr. Latimer was much gratified by the tender care Aunt Linda bestowed on Iola.

"I ain't goin' to let her do nuffin till she gits seasoned. She looks as sweet as a peach. I allers wanted some nice lady to come down yere and larn our gals some sense. I can't read myself, but I likes ter yere dem dat can."

"Well, Aunt Linda, I am going to teach in the Sunday-school, help in the church, hold mothers' meetings to help these boys and girls to grow up to be good men and women. Won't you get a pair of spectacles and learn to read?"

"Oh, yer can't git dat book froo my head, no way you fix it. I knows nuff to git to hebben, and dats all I wants to know." Aunt Linda was kind and obliging, but there was one place where she drew the line, and that was at learning to read.

Harry and Miss Delany accompanied Iola as far as her new home, and remained several days. The evening before their departure, Harry took Miss Delany a drive of several miles through the pine barrens.

"This thing is getting very monotonous," Harry broke out, when they had gone some distance.

"Oh, I enjoy it!" replied Miss Delany. "These stately pines look so grand and solemn, they remind me of a procession of hooded monks."

"What in the world are you talking about, Lucille?" asked Harry, looking puzzled.

"About those pine-trees," replied Miss Delany, in a tone of surprise.

"Pshaw, I wasn't thinking about them. I'm thinking about Iola and Frank."

"What about them?" asked Lucille.

"Why, when I was in P——, Dr. Latimer used to be first-rate company, but now it is nothing but what Iola wants, and what Iola says, and what Iola likes. I don't believe that there is a subject I could name to him, from spinning a top to circumnavigating the globe, that he wouldn't somehow contrive to bring Iola in. And I don't believe you could talk ten minutes to Iola on any subject, from dressing a doll to the latest discovery in science, that she wouldn't manage to lug in Frank."

"Oh, you absurd creature!" responded Lucille, "this is their honeymoon, and they are deeply in love with each other. Wait till you get in love with some one."

"I am in love now," replied Harry, with a serious air.

"With whom?" asked Lucille, archly.

"With you," answered Harry, trying to take her hand.

"Oh, Harry!" she exclaimed, playfully resisting. "Don't be so nonsensical! Don't you think the bride looked lovely, with that dress of spotless white and with those orange blossoms in her hair?"

"Yes, she did; that's a fact," responded Harry. "But, Lucille, I think there is a great deal of misplaced sentiment at weddings," he added, more seriously.

"How so?"

"Oh, here are a couple just married, and who are as happy as happy can be; and people will crowd around them wishing much joy; but who thinks of wishing joy to the forlorn old bachelors and restless old maids?"

"Well, Harry, if you want people to wish you much happiness, why don't you do as the doctor has done, get yourself a wife?"

"I will," he replied, soberly, "when you say so."

"Oh, Harry, don't be so absurd."

"Indeed there isn't a bit of absurdity about what I say. I am in earnest." There was something in the expression of Harry's face and the tone of his voice which arrested the banter on Lucille's lips.

"I think it was Charles Lamb," replied Lucille, "who once said that school-teachers are uncomfortable people, and, Harry, I would not like to make you uncomfortable by marrying you."

"You will make me uncomfortable by not marrying me."

"But," replied Lucille, "your mother may not prefer me for a daughter. You know, Harry, complexional prejudices are not confined to white people."

"My mother," replied Harry, with an air of confidence, "is too noble to indulge in such sentiments."

"And Iola, would she be satisfied?"

"Why, it would add to her satisfaction. She is not one who can't be white and won't be black."

"Well, then," replied Lucille, "I will take the question of your comfort into consideration."

The above promise was thoughtfully remembered by Lucille till a bridal ring and happy marriage were the result.

Soon after Iola had settled in C—— she quietly took her place in the Sunday-school as a teacher, and in the church as a helper. She was welcomed by the young pastor, who found in her a strong and faithful ally. Together they planned meetings for the especial benefit of mothers and children. When the dens of vice are spreading their snares for the feet of the tempted and inexperienced her doors are freely opened for the instruction of the children before their feet have wandered and gone far astray. She has no carpets too fine for the tread of their little feet. She thinks it is better to have stains on her carpet than stains on their souls through any neglect of hers. In lowly homes and windowless cabins her visits are always welcome. Little children love her. Old age turns to her for comfort, young girls for guidance, and mothers for counsel. Her life is full of blessedness.

Doctor Latimer by his kindness and skill has won the name of the "Good Doctor." But he is more than a successful doctor; he is a true patriot and a good citizen. Honest, just, and discriminating, he endeavors by precept and example to instill into the minds of others sentiments of good citizenship. He is a leader in every reform movement for the benefit of the community; but his patriotism is not confined to race lines. "The world is his country, and mankind his countrymen." While he abhors their deeds of violence, he pities the short-sighted and besotted men who seem madly intent upon laying magazines of powder under the cradles of unborn generations. He has great faith in the possibilities of the negro, and believes that, enlightened and Christianized, he will sink the old animosities of slavery into the new community of interests arising from freedom; and that his influence upon the South will be as the influence of the sun upon the earth. As when the sun passes from Capricorn to Cancer, beauty, greenness, and harmony spring up in his path, so he hopes that the future career of the negro will be a greater influence for freedom and social advancement than it was in the days of yore for slavery and its inferior civilization.

Harry and Lucille are at the head of a large and flourishing school. Lucille gives her ripening experience to her chosen work, to which she was too devoted to resign. And through the school they are lifting up the homes of the people. Some have pitied, others blamed, Harry for casting his lot with the colored people, but he knows that life's highest and best advantages do not depend on the color of the skin or texture of the hair. He has his reward in the improved condition of his pupils and the superb manhood and noble life which he has developed in his much needed work.

Uncle Daniel still lingers on the shores of time, a cheery, lovable old man, loved and respected by all; a welcome guest in every home. Soon after Iola's marriage, Robert sold out his business and moved with his mother and sister to North Carolina. He bought a large plantation near C——, which he divided into small homesteads, and sold to poor but thrifty laborers, and his heart has been gladdened by their increased prosperity and progress. He has seen the one-roomed cabins change to comfortable cottages, in which cleanliness and order have supplanted the prolific causes of disease and death. Kind and generous, he often remembers Mrs. Johnson and sends her timely aid.

Marie's pale, spiritual face still bears traces of the beauty which was her youthful dower, but its bloom has been succeeded by an air of sweetness and dignity. Though frail in health, she is always ready to lend a helping hand wherever and whenever she can.

Grandmother Johnson was glad to return South and spend the remnant of her days with the remaining friends of her early life. Although feeble, she is in full sympathy with her children for the uplifting of the race. Marie and her mother are enjoying their aftermath of life, one by rendering to others all the service in her power, while the other, with her face turned toward the celestial city, is

> "Only waiting till the angels
> Open wide the mystic gate."

The shadows have been lifted from all their lives; and peace, like bright dew, has descended upon their paths. Blessed themselves, their lives are a blessing to others.

NOTE.

FROM threads of fact and fiction I have woven a story whose mission will not be in vain if it awaken in the hearts of our countrymen a stronger sense of justice and a more Christlike humanity in behalf of those whom the fortunes of war threw, homeless, ignorant and poor, upon the threshold of a new era. Nor will it be in vain if it inspire the children of those upon whose brows God has poured the chrism of that new era to determine that they will embrace every opportunity, develop every faculty, and use every power God has given them to rise in the scale of character and condition, and to add their quota of good citizenship to the best welfare of the nation. There are scattered among us materials for mournful tragedies and mirth-provoking comedies, which some hand may yet bring into the literature of the country, glowing with the fervor of the tropics and enriched by the luxuriance of the Orient, and thus add to the solution of our unsolved American problem.

The race has not had very long to straighten its hands from the hoe, to grasp the pen and wield it as a power for good, and to erect above the ruined auction-block and slave-pen institutions of learning, but

> There is light beyond the darkness,
> Joy beyond the present pain ;
> There is hope in God's great justice
> And the negro's rising brain.
> Though the morning seems to linger
> O'er the hill-tops far away,
> Yet the shadows bear the promise
> Of a brighter coming day.